'Beneath Golden Holden's charm and warmth lurks the brain of a rattlesnake . . . Holden is a marvellous reporter, and as gutsy as Red Rum . . .'

Michael Thompson-Noel, *Financial Times*

'Rollickingly enjoyable . . . It has a remarkable kid-in-a-candy-store momentum.'

Andrew Martin, *The Listener*

'A fascinating, funny, firsthand book about the great characters of the greatest of card games – not least my friend London Tony himself, a man who knows America better than most Americans.'

Cleveland Amory

'The best book about poker I've ever read.'

Walter Matthau

'Precise, provocative and enlightening. A "must" for every poker player's library.'

Telly Savalas

'Tony is toney . . . When the pot gets high, the hour late, and you need to see what he has in the hole, then the lounge lizard melds into a loan shark . . .'

Martin Amis

BIG DEAL

Anthony Holden

An *Abacus* Book

First published in Great Britain
by Bantam Press
A division of Transworld Ltd

This edition published by Abacus in 2002
Reprinted 2002, 2003, 2004, 2005

A CIP catalogue record for this book
is available from the British Library.

ISBN 0 349 11519 2

Typeset by Palimpsest Book Production Limited,
Polmont, Stirlingshire
Printed and bound in Great Britain by
Bookmarque Ltd, Croydon, Surrey

Abacus
An imprint of
Time Warner Book Group UK
Brettenham House
Lancaster Place
London WC2E 7EN

www.twbg.co.uk

For
AL ALVAREZ
(a.k.a. The Crony)

who won't mind splitting this pot with
Anne and Cindy, his moll and mine.

Son, you are now going out into the wide, wide world to make your own way, and it is a very good thing to do, as there are no more opportunities for you in this burg. I am only sorry that I am not able to bank-roll you to a very large start, but not having any potatoes to give you, I am now going to stake you to some very valuable advice, which I personally collect in my years of experience around and about, and I hope and trust you will always bear this advice in mind.

Son, no matter how far you travel, or how smart you get, always remember this: Some day, somewhere, a guy is going to come to you and show you a nice brand-new deck of cards on which the seal is never broken, and this guy is going to offer to bet you that the jack of spades will jump out of this deck and squirt cider in your ear. But, son, do not bet him, for as sure as you do you are going to get an ear full of cider.

Damon Runyon, 'The Idyll of Miss Sarah Brown'

CONTENTS

Preface to the Fourth Edition

One Saturday evening in the mid-1990s, a few years after this book was first published, a genial young American approached me in the bar of London's Victoria Casino, introduced himself, and asked if I was the guy who had written *Big Deal*. Indeed I was, I replied with a modest smile, and looked over to my wife (the sometime 'Moll' of the ensuing pages) for the gently mocking smile which usually greets these occasional little boosts to my ego.

'That was a wonderful book,' continued the American. 'It altered my life.' As compliments go it was not entirely without precedent, especially in a casino about to start a poker tournament, but none the less welcome for that. Inviting our new friend to sit down and join us for a drink, I asked him what he did. 'I work for IBM in Mississippi,' came the reply. 'At least I did until I read your book. Then I quit my job and became a professional poker player. Just like you.'

Not seeming to notice that he had struck me dumb, he continued: 'And you see my friend over there, the guy at the craps table – he's a lawyer. Works in the office of the Governor of Mississippi. Or he did until I lent him your book. Then he decided to quit his job too, and now we travel the world together as poker partners.

'The point is, we're off to Austria on Monday. I was just wondering if you had any tips about the Hold 'em scene in Vienna . . .?'

I was still a sentence or two behind him. It was not just

that I knew nothing at all about the poker scene in Vienna. Never before, despite the friendly remarks about their work to which writers become relatively accustomed, had I met someone who had actually given up his job – and a pretty damn good job, too – because of me.

Over the few years since *Big Deal* was first published, I had grown uneasily aware that I had inadvertently altered a few lives. There were several regulars here at the 'Vic', and indeed elsewhere, who had told me they'd taken up poker because of the book. But they hadn't, so far as I knew, given up their jobs, or left their wives and children, or wound up in jail. Or worse.

'My God,' I finally managed to gasp. 'And how are you doing?'

'Well, Mr Holden . . .' – 'Call me Tony, please . . .' – 'Well, Tony, I don't want to be rude . . . That was, as I said, one wonderful book. Beautifully written, very funny, really captured life out there on the circuit . . .' Anxious purrhs. 'But the truth is: we're doing rather better than you did. We're in our second year as pros now, and we're making a lot more money than we ever did back in Mississippi.'

Both Americans proceeded, as that Saturday evening wore on, to reach the final table of the tournament, and then to get in the money. The following day they duly flew off to Vienna. Six months later, at the World Series of Poker in Binion's Horseshoe Casino, Las Vegas, I met them again. Both were leading contenders for that year's world title.

I have since become less fazed by such encounters. On my frequent forays to Las Vegas, even more than in Britain, people come up to me all the time and tell me that they're there because of me. They read the book and they took up poker. They took up poker and they started to win. They won so much that now, look, here they are in Vegas. If they'd known I was going to be here, they'd have brought their copies along for me to sign. Maybe I'd like to sit down and play with them awhile? It would really be an honour . . .

There are limits even to my vanity. I'm well aware that the poker played in these pages is far from world standard. Whether or not these guys have even opened the book – if they haven't, it's a stylish scam – I know they're better players than me.

But, the hell, who cares? *Big Deal* is my own favourite among the twenty-plus books I've published – the only one, for sure, that was as much fun to write as to research – and who am I to mind being taken for a ride by people who have actually enjoyed it? Within the wildly fluctuating parameters of my passing bankroll, I've won and lost money with the best of them, and had a great time in the process.

Over the dozen years since *Big Deal* first appeared, the most unlikely people have approached me in bars or restaurants, on trains and planes or merely on the street, and told me *Yes*, this was what they had always wanted to do: to give up their jobs and turn poker pro. A few were celebrities; most were not. I could drop famous names from both sides of the Atlantic who quoted my own words back to me without knowing who I was. But the true satisfaction comes from meeting people who've actually gone out there and achieved what I attempted so ineffectively – and chronicled, if truth be told, to cover my losses. The book's readers are my real gain.

On countless occasions, I'll have been playing at a particular table a few hours, among total strangers, whether in London or Vegas, when something quirky happens and Stetson Hat in Seat Four will drawl: 'Put *that* in your next book.' Usually, of course, Stetson will be the victim of a bad beat, perhaps inflicted by me. What I love is the way he's sat there all that time, knowing who I was but saying nothing, while I've been relishing my assumed anonymity. Playing his advantage, then blowing it to psyche me in a moment of stress. Very pokeresque.

Among the many letters I have received from readers – outnumbering even the complaints I receive these days from British royalists – was one from Cellblock C of an American state penitentiary. 'Joe Ingargiola' (a.k.a. Joe Thomas) had found a copy of *Big Deal* on the shelves of the Bayside State Prison in Leesburg, N.J. Seeing me as an egghead-turned-gambler, Joe declared himself a kindred spirit: 'As one who has also made the transmogrification from academia to Glitter Gulch, I can attest that you have captured the essence and the spirit of the journey with impeccable accuracy and panache . . . The Oxford-bred literacy adds some legitimacy to a profession often thought of as dubious.' There were more compliments in this vein, and many great poker stories, even details about his doctoral thesis on Kierkegaard, before Joe got around to the point. He was doing eighteen months for his role in bilking Donald Trump out of £250,000 in an Atlantic City casino scam. By the time his letter reached me, however, he would have paid his debt to society and returned to Vegas, where he hoped to meet me across a seven-card-stud table.

The following May, during the 1994 World Series, I did indeed meet the newly liberated Joe, who was all ready to shuffle up and deal. It was an emotional moment for both of us, not least because stud is more his game than mine. At the time, however, I had the misfortune to be 'stuck' (*see* Glossary) in a dangerous pot limit Hold 'em game, in which I would lose my seat if I stayed away much longer. Gentleman Joe quite understood. When a man's stuck, his priority has gotta be getting himself unstuck. By the time I had managed this unexpected feat, alas, Joe had vanished into the infinite Vegas night. Ah well, maybe next year.

The same wishful thinking still applies to the world title. Readers returning to the book will not be surprised to know that, for all my annual efforts at Binion's, I have still not managed to win the coveted bracelet – if I had, you'd sure have heard about it – or indeed to be recognized for my services to sport by Her Majesty's fount of honours. Back in London, however, I have managed to score some successes in the regular tournaments at the 'Vic' and other London clubs whose names (and indeed card rooms) keep changing. More radical change is due soon with the long overdue reform of the gambling legislation I bemoan on pages 109–10.

Which brings me to the only section of the book I now regret. Very little has been said publicly – even about my calling their patrons 'anal-retentive vultures' – but British casino staff have good reason to feel aggrieved by my brutal dismissal of the London club scene in these pages. So I am glad of this chance to report that it has since improved immeasurably – not least because of the introduction of lively tournaments which generate usually decent, occasionally excellent side action. I myself have become a much more regular club player – primarily, however, as relaxation from the rigours of the Tuesday Night Game, which still proceeds as compulsively and dangerously as ever.

A few unfortunates have fallen by the wayside; a few new faces have come and gone; some, including David Spanier, have alas died; but the hard core of us who have been playing together for quarter of a century look like carrying on as long again, should we be spared – all the way into the Twilight Home for Broken-Down Cardsharps, where the furious arguments over who is £1 light (the dealer, always) will still be drowning out the more gentlemanly disagreements over much larger sums. The separate bank account these days has to cope with a new and worrying enthusiasm for sports spread betting, an overdue innovation in the UK; but it is, at the time of writing, in pretty healthy shape.

People tell me *Big Deal* has made poker almost respectable in Britain, where the game had hitherto been regarded almost exclusively as a seedy offshoot of East End gangsterdom. The book earned me the world's first regular poker column in a mainstream publication, *Esquire*, and the first-ever poker documentary on, of all places, BBC Television. It has even been hawked around Hollywood (as yet, alas, to no avail) as a potential vehicle for some of the more rugged stars. In 2000 I was even lucky enough to win £7,000 on TV in a 'celebrity' version of Channel 4's cult series *Late Night Poker*, eliminating such hardened opposition as Martin Amis, Stephen Fry and Patrick Marber, before a tense head-to-head with this book's dedicatee.

But nothing has given me as much satisfaction – or worry – as the response it has wrung from my sons. It's the only book of mine they've all read, certainly the only one they're prepared to show off to their friends. All three have turned their apprenticeships in club tournaments into (generally) winning ways in their own private games – also frequented by the offspring of other Tuesday Night regulars, so that game seems likely to continue long after its founders are meeting at the great green baize beyond the clouds. In family games, one of them always seems to fill his flush or full house when I finally manage to hit a straight. May the poker gods be with them – and all of you.

See you at the final table.

ANTHONY HOLDEN
London, 2002

1

Living Right

♥ ♣ ♦ ♠

Not until I heard my name called, and turned to see a uniformed heavy of prehistoric proportions, a pair of handcuffs on his belt and a gun on his hip, did I know that I could at last relax.

Struggling through the crowd to the sanctuary he offered, and mustering a throaty gasp of 'I'm Holden', I gratefully surrendered myself to his protection. With a beam belying his menacing mien, this mammoth grabbed my hand luggage and declared, 'Welcome to Las Vegas, Mr Holden. You look tired.'

Hank, as a label on his lapel identified him, was one of the security team from Binion's Horseshoe Casino, whose golden horseshoe logo adorned his chest and upper arms, and whose regulation khaki safari gear, scarcely able to contain the sheer bulk of muscle within, made him look like an urban mercenary out for blood. When not guarding the million dollars in cash displayed in a giant perspex horseshoe in Binion's lobby, or patrolling the many more millions wagered each day on the casino floor, the Horseshoe heavies double in an unlikely way as mere limousine chauffeurs, catering to the few mobile whims of otherwise sedentary high rollers.

Over there, indeed, beyond the silver palm fronds and neon hoardings which distinguish McCarran Airport from all others, through the giant glass walls which keep the 105°F heat at bay, stood my transport of delight, a sleek black limo a block long. After plucking my leaden suitcases off the carousel as if they were paper bags, Hank gestured me towards it. This was the moment I had been savouring for fifteen long, dreary hours – and, come to think of it, twelve long, dreary months.

You know you've arrived in Las Vegas while your insides are still on the plane. Even as you stumble up the chute from aircraft to terra firma, dazed by the throbbing, stateless tedium of long-haul flight halfway round the world, the shrill electronic wails of the slot machines are already assailing the ears, the clangs and shrieks of jackpots heralding your arrival in Dreamland. To reach the baggage carousels you thread your way through a maze of what used to be one-armed bandits, now replaced by sophisticated video slots, surrounded by bars, cocktail waitresses and all the seductive trappings of a downtown casino. The first-time visitor could be forgiven for thinking that this was it, that he had already checked in to a second honeymoon with his Muse.

All around are suitably garish stores where personalized everything is on offer, from playing cards and gambling chips to lighters and licence plates, so long as your name is Randy or Tex, Cindy or Donna. The disembodied voice of Frank Sinatra or Wayne Newton then escorts you down the mobile walk-way, urging you to come pay homage at Bally's or Caesar's Palace, reminding you that demi-gods are freely available for worship in Las Vegas amid the exotic desert shrines otherwise dedicated exclusively to Mammon and the making and losing of fortunes.

From the air, your first sight of the place has already been other-worldly, whether you approach it from Los Angeles and the West across Death Valley, or from London, New York and the East over the Grand Canyon, the Hoover Dam and Lake Mead. Either way, there's an hour or so of infinite desert to savour from a safe seat above, with misty imaginings of the wagon trains of the old frontiersmen, and of the certain death facing anyone wandering about down there right now, before you catch your first extraordinary, breathtaking glimpse of this clutch of fantastical towers and glass palaces slapped down at random in the middle of this moonscape, this vast and utter nowhere. By night, Las Vegas from the air looks like a convention of ocean liners huddled in the midst of a dark and limitless sea.

Touch-down and disembarkation are your last, brief contacts with reality before entering a world like no other on earth, where all normal values swiftly evaporate, all lifelong interests and enthusiasms erode, and all curiosity about the outside world is absently abandoned – overmastered by the Siren song of life in the fast lane, of limos, gold bath-taps and heart-shaped beds, of craps tables, roulette wheels and baccarat banks, of the chance around every corner to spend the rest of your days a millionaire. There is the prospect, if you really go under, of never having to leave, never having to face the grim realities of life again.

Vegas doesn't waste time. The place begins to weave its spell at once, half into the limo, as Hank holds open the door and ushers me into a deep-piled, air-conditioned cocoon of cocktail bars, ice machines, stereo music and remote-control television, with room enough for a football team reserved for my lone delectation. The leg room alone makes me feel seven feet tall. As he climbs into the driver's seat, already a mile or two ahead of me, Hank silently, electronically, raises the glass panel dividing my world from his. He will not speak unless he is spoken to. The man whose mere appearance would have me babbling polite inanities, as if buying time by tossing fish to a surly shark, is now at my disposal, his only duty to cater to my every whim. We are all high rollers now.

The immediate problem is a built-in obligation to behave like one. There is no charge, of course, for this courtesy, a limo being the least that Binion's will offer a regular visitor like myself. But by the time Hank has glided us silently and smoothly past the Tropicana, on to the freeway parallel to the tacky tourist attractions of the Strip, and finally downtown to Glitter Gulch, where the real gamblers go, a $50 tip – twice as much as it would have cost to *rent* a limo, let alone hail a taxi – seems the least he deserves. By the time he takes me back to the airport, a week later if I'm lucky, $100 will seem insultingly cheap.

'That wasn't necessary, sir,' he drawls, trousering the fifty, and lugging my ridiculously heavy bags (full of books, though I daren't whisper that in Vegas) through the slots to the reception desk of the Golden Nugget, overflow annexe to the Horseshoe at this time of year. Hank and I now have a silent compact. He will muster a grin for me around the casino floor this coming week – as now does Jerry, the bell-boy, who astonishingly remembers me from last year. There goes another $50, and I haven't even made it to the elevator.

The receptionist's smile widens suddenly as my entry comes up on the computer. 'Complimentary suite, Mr Holden. You are Mr Binion's guest for the week, so there'll be no need for your credit card. I believe you requested the same suite as on your last visit?' Did I? Could I? It seemed the kind of thing a high roller would do, so I decide on a knowing smile. 'No problem, sir. Please just wait here a moment, as the casino shift manager would like to formally greet you.'

The split infinitive evaporates with the arrival of the shift manager, who turns out to be young, female and attractive, which for some reason comes as a shock. I find myself kissing her, on the mistaken assumption that we met here the last time, a year ago, and that this ritual somehow takes account of the fact. 'Oh no, sir,' blushes Karen, as her lapel proclaims her, 'I've only been here six months.'

Jerry whisks me up to my room, reminiscing about the last time, remembering more of my casino adventures than I do, and speculating on my prospects for the week. 'One of our best suites, Mr Holden. You were smart to re-request it. Always nice to see you back, sir. Anything I can do to make your stay more enjoyable, you just let me know.' That in itself is worth a fifty.

The room is huge, and smells of new carpet. The bed alone would accommodate an extended family. The bathroom contains every aquatic luxury known to man, plus a person-alized bathrobe. There is, of course, an enormous television, and a battery of telephones. But the vast acreage is otherwise curiously empty. No mini-bar. No sofa. No in-house televi-sion movies. In Vegas, the management wants you to feel like a millionaire, but it wants you to do so downstairs in the casino. The inducements to stay up in your room are minimal.

Not that I need any. But somehow it seems wrong to head straight back downstairs with Jerry. My instinct is to give him three minutes to get clear, then plunge back down without even changing my transatlantic shirt. I have, after all, waited so long for this moment.

The reluctant Englishman in me tangles briefly with my Yankee *alter ego* before my tediously tidy mind prevails. I thus enjoy the ritual of unpacking, hanging my clothes, sort-ing my books and creating a little living-and-working area – if not actually changing my shirt – before I pour myself a glass of complimentary champagne, light a duty-free cigarette and savour the thrilling fact of rearrival in Utopia. Besides, it builds more time to relish the prospect of heading back down to that bewitching clatter of activity which never ceases by night or day, to the mad babble of the slots, the deranged shrieks of the crapshooters, and above all that Music of the Vegan Spheres which spells every poker player's dream come true: the eternal, ubiquitous riffle of chips, like the chatter of cicadas who never sleep, drawing him ineluctably towards the wonderful certainty of immediate, open-ended action.

I was tired, a little the worse for drink, jet-lagged and light-headed – four out of four conditions in which one should certainly not play poker in Las Vegas, where the sharks gather in well-disciplined schools. They have a tried and tested saying hereabouts for moments like this: 'If you can't spot the sucker in your first half-hour at the table, it's you.'

But, hey, what the heck, the card room awaited. I hadn't come all this way to go to sleep.

It is time, perhaps, to put my cards on the table. Over the years I may have been something of a gambler, dabbling in everything from dice to the gee-gees. But not any more. No, now I am a poker player – an amateur one, alas, but as dedicated and determined as anyone who has played in a high-stakes weekly game for half his lifetime.

The difference between a gambler and a poker player is a crucially simple one. A gambler, be he one who bets on horses or sports events, on casino games or raindrops running down window-panes, is someone who wagers unfavourable odds. A poker player, if he knows what he is doing, is someone who wagers favourable odds. The one is a romantic, the other a realist. It is a distinction, a truth worthy of inscription upon a Grecian urn. It was certainly all I knew at that moment, and all I needed to know, as I zipped $1,000 into a secret pocket deep inside my favourite blue jeans.

This was my tenth visit to Las Vegas in as many years, since I had first come here in May 1978 to report the World Series of Poker held each year in Binion's Horseshoe, right across the road from the Nugget. By the following summer I was living and working in America as the Washington Correspondent of a London Sunday newspaper, whose foreign editor proved remarkably open to persuasion that the prospects for the Nevada primary were a crucial early test of the 1980 election campaign. As gas lines grew and President Carter's fortunes began to nosedive, I spent the early summer watching Stu 'The Kid' Ungar carry off the world crown, and learning my trade in modest side-games until my plane left without me. I was hooked.

Ten years on, I had covered the World Series for virtually every colour magazine in British Sunday journalism, and watched it grow from a clubbish gathering of a dozen leading players into a truly international event involving some two hundred card-sharps from all over the world – all prepared to pay $10,000 to enter the final, climactic four-day game which sees one of them crowned World Champion.

From a privileged seat on the rails I had watched many historic showdowns, involving pots approaching a million dollars, while nipping back and forth across Fremont Street to the card room of the Nugget, to be sure of keeping my seat in the $3–$6 game. With the first two rounds of betting and raising limited to three bucks, and all subsequent rounds to six, the nursery slopes of Glitter Gulch offered a cut-price foundation course. After a few years of, shall we say, containable losses, I began to hold my own with the small-time professionals of Vegas, who eke out a living of a few hundred bucks a week by fleecing 'tourists' – the word is poker code for patsies – like me.

I had, like everyone, made my rookie mistakes. You bet I had. In the first few years I always started as nervous as a schoolboy, shaking enough to show everyone the kind of hand I held. There was the year I was dealt a straight flush, and promptly spilt my Bloody Mary right across the green baize – not merely the worst possible breach of poker etiquette, but crass enough to make everyone fold at once. Lesson Number One: it's not enough in poker to hold good cards; you have to disguise them sufficiently to make money out of them. The player who watches everyone fold each time he bets a good hand is playing a seriously transparent game.

The Golden Nugget's low-stakes regulars are the world's tightest players – 'rocks' who bluff very little, risking everything only when they have the best available hand, known in the trade as the 'nuts'. To hold your own against them requires large quantities of patience – the one quality which, in life, has never been my strong suit. The solution, I discovered after a few years, was to sit there wearing a Walkman. Some Mozart in my ears (*perdono*, Amadeus, *perdono*) seemed to give me the patience I needed to lie in wait for a strong hand. It shut out the casino clatter – 'Seat open on Table Five', 'Cocktails, Table Three', 'Jake Finkelstein, telephone call for Mr Finkelstein' – which can lay on a cumulative earthquake of a headache. The trouble was that it also shut out the table talk, which is very much part of the cut and thrust of a developing poker hand. Every time some interesting cards came my way, I found myself fumbling under the table for the volume control – again revealing to the world and his moll to watch out for the guy in Seat Five.

The apprenticeship years were expensive. While I lived in Washington I developed an understanding with my bank manager – it became, I confess, a written understanding – that, no matter how pleading or authoritative my demands down the telephone, he was under no circumstances to wire me more funds. The few grand I took with me for my birthday treat – the World Series each May tends to coincide with this annual milestone – were more than enough to risk. When I blew them, it was time to blow town.

In time, I graduated to the dizzier limits of the Nugget's $10–$20 table, where I soon felt quite at home. The game we were playing, Texas Hold 'em, was the same game played by the leading pros across the street in the $10,000 world title event. But ten grand – a year's profit, if I was lucky, in my weekly game back home – had always seemed an awful lot to hand over to the pros in the first five minutes of their four-day marathon. So a railbird, and a small-time player, I had always remained.

Which did nothing to diminish my perennial thrill of antic-ipation as now I summoned the elevator, swapped hard-luck stories with my fellow-travellers, and sauntered towards the bustling card room with all the studied nonchalance, I devoutly hoped, of a local. That afternoon there was time for a little cheap practice with some perennially familiar faces before the Horseshoe's media tournament, traditionally held on the day before the Main Event to familiarize mere reporters with the game they are here to watch. In the Nugget's card room I tried to seek out a table where no-one would know me. Playing the tyro in a low-limit game, and making the act last as long as possible, was always the way in which I liked to begin a stay in Vegas. With a bit of luck you could make enough money to sit down in a heavier game, where the players were more likely to remember you from the year before.

Fortunately, there was an immediate vacancy in a low-limit game: Seat Six on Table Eight, $3–$6 Texas Hold 'em, with a quiet, pensive-looking group whose average age I must have reduced to barely sixty. Self-confidence, for a while, would now be a matter of making mistakes – and not minding being thought a klutz – in the interests of mopping up later on. First, I had to pretend I had never played Hold 'em before.

Texas Hold 'em is a variant of seven-card stud, regarded by the top professionals for more than a decade as the most refined and testing of poker's many and varied disciplines. It is one of the simplest of poker games to follow, and one of the most complex to play.

Each player is dealt two cards, with which he must improve on five communal cards – 'the board' – gradually revealed in the centre of the table. There are four rounds of betting. The first comes after the deal, testing the strength of the two cards you hold in the hole (or 'in the pocket'); the second follows the unveiling of the first three communal cards ('the flop'); another after the fourth centre card ('the turn', or 'Fourth Street'); and a final and decisive round after the fifth ('the river', or 'Fifth Street').

'Do you have to use *both* concealed cards?' I asked the dealer as I settled into my seat, arranging $200 in chips in front of me as if it were all I had in the world. 'No, sir,' he explained with surprising patience. 'Either or both will do. And of course the board can win.'

'The board can win?' I repeated, in a tone of voice designed to suggest that he might have been speaking a foreign language.

'Say the board shows a straight or a flush, and none of the showdown players can improve on it, then the pot is split.'

'Ah, I *see*,' said I, with an Oscar-winning hint of doubt. Knowing looks were exchanged around the table. Now they were ripe for the final trick: to lay on the English accent really thick, rub my hands together like a tourist with more money than sense, and declare like a true son of Colonel Blimp: 'Then let battle commence!'

All around me people were riffling their chips – splitting them into piles of six or more, then melding the two stacks into one with a graceful arc of the fingers. It's one way of telling the people who know what they're doing. Riffling is the sign of a true pro, or at least of someone who's spent too much of his or her life at the poker table, where it eventually becomes an unconscious habit – an absent way to pass the time while making tough decisions, or merely waiting out a hand. If you muck it up, it can be very embarrassing. Just when you're trying to look cool, your chips splay out all over the table, exposing your stumblebum amateur status. So in case anyone was watching, as I knew they all were, I now looked idly at the dealer and essayed a relaxed riffle. The two piles, as always, refused to unite, wheeling around each other like an angry rugby scrum before spilling all over my newly arrived cards. Despite lessons from experts, I have never managed to master the art of riffling. At moments like this, however, my incompetence could be turned to advantage.

Misplaying hands deliberately can at times be a higher art form than playing to win. It takes luck as well as judgement to stay in cheaply with a low pair, or four to an inside straight, when the betting clearly shows that someone down the other end has already made a higher pair, perhaps two pairs or even three of a kind ('trips'). If you want to be thought an idiot, you don't want it to cost you too much money.

This is a weird kind of investment, I thought to myself, as I misriffled awhile, then paid eighteen dollars in the certain knowledge that I was a loser. As the little old lady in Seat Three – a poker killer if ever I saw one – slapped down her concealed pair of queens with some glee, smiling over at the third queen on the board, I looked long and hard at my hand before rolling over a 4-3. There was one four in the flop, as well as 5-7, giving me astronomical odds against the worst available inside straight. The other players could scarcely believe it. I'd gone all that way with a pair of fours, and I had even been naïve enough to show them so. They began to shuffle excitedly in their seats, to lean forward, light cigarettes, and generally show signs that they smelt a sucker. One even rolled up his sleeves and recounted his ammunition. A couple more plays like that from me, and they would all be staying in hands much longer than they should, chasing rainbows for a rare crock of gold. To them, I was a licence to print money.

The truth, as the trick began to work, was the other way round. Within an hour or so, they were thoroughly conned. A couple of edgy but calculated wins all too easily looked like lucky ones, of the kind you must get if you are dumb enough to play almost every hand. Then I folded a few, to look like I was sitting on my modest winnings, and waited patiently for the killer punch. It came when I fluked the 'boss' trips, the best available three of a kind, as the flop brought a pair of jacks to match the A-J in my hand. I raised the maximum, and now none of them knew quite *what* to do. After much thought three of them – more than enough – decided that it had all gone to my head, that I still didn't know what I was doing. I was the kind of player against whom it was worth playing 'on the come', with 'pulling hands' – staying in after the flop with four to a straight or a flush, despite the odds against either materializing on Fourth or Fifth Streets.

Now I had them where I wanted them, defying the odds despite their better instincts. My three jacks held up, and were good for $75, a huge pot by local standards. My stack was continuing to climb steadily when I had an outrageous stroke of luck. Not merely did I again hold the top trips on the flop; after some lively betting they turned into an unbeatable four-of-a-kind on Fifth Street. With (as it proved) a straight and a full house against me – even better luck – I was able to raise twice and get callers. I had them cold. When I showed my hand, the old lady threw in her house good-humouredly, and smilingly offered me one of Las Vegas's perennial poker greetings: 'What have you gotta do to get a hand like that?'

I could not resist giving her the equally time-honoured reply: 'Live right!'

She looked at me suspiciously as I hauled in the chips. 'Ah well,' I crowed, 'it's a tough way to make an easy living.'

Thanks to that exchange, the game was up, my cover blown, and suddenly they all knew they had been suckered. If I'd been able to riffle right, I would now have indulged in a triumphant twirl. Three hundred bucks ahead – a fortune in the $3–$6 game – I instead bid them a polite farewell and moved up to the $10–$20 table, for which I had left a secret application with the floorman. Another little rush of cards, combined with my comparative anonymity, helped me run my stack up to six hundred, just as time before the media tournament was running out. Exhilarated and jet-lagged, my impatience for action now made me break one of my golden rules. My sense of money already sliding awry, I decided to play blackjack for five minutes in $100 units. The dealer hit a bad streak, and my $600 had soon become $1,000. That, too – a round figure – is usually my time to stop. But I allowed myself three more hands before losing one, another superstitious reason to quit, and heading over to the Horseshoe with $1,200 in my pocket, a handsome 500 per cent profit on my original $200.

Through the seething Nugget mob, out into the pulverizing heat, past the sign declaring Fremont Street 'World Series of Poker Avenue' for the duration of the tournament, I struggled across the road into the even greater crush of the Horseshoe. In the cramped, cordoned-off poker-area at the back, an all-day world championship stud tournament was nearing its evening dinner break. Players who had blown their stack stood around commiserating with each other, looking for consolation action in the side-games, perennially played for much higher amounts than the tournaments. Bulging wads of $100 bills, casually secured by rubber bands, were in play at the real high rollers' table, where they take over when the chips can no longer cope with the stakes. It is an eternally hypnotic sight, to watch these guys count out five or ten thousand dollars in cash as casually as if buying a bus ticket. This is a world in which a bet or raise of 'a nickel' can mean five hundred dollars, 'a dime' a thousand. The greenhorn who sits down here and calls a 'big dime' can find himself in the pot to the tune of ten grand.

At the time, these were the only three weeks of the year in which poker was played at the Horseshoe. The other forty-nine saw the tournament area vanish beneath a sea of slot machines, which offer the management a much better return on its square-footage. But for these three weeks, Binion's is the world headquarters of poker, and the place buzzes like no other on earth. It may not be as glitzy as the casinos on the Strip, or even the Golden Nugget across the road, where a mosaic of flashing lights and silver mirrors can dazzle you into rash decisions. But that is quite deliberate. The Horseshoe offers a more down-home, old-Western style, designed to combine with its loose percentages and higher limits to build faster, more furious action. It eschews the fancy floor shows, gift shops and cosmopolitan restaurants which symbolize the tourist's Vegas. Nor does it need the seedier attractions of Glitter Gulch, home of the legalized red light district, where 'Nudes on Ice' is on permanent offer within sight of the Horseshoe at the Union-Plaza. No, this place is about gambling – serious, twenty-four-hour, no-frills gambling. It's no wonder there are more pawn shops within this square mile than in the whole of Greater London.

As the stud tournament neared its climax in one corner of the room, the authorities were now wearily making way for the amateurs of the media to slow things up in the other. Wary greetings were exchanged, business cards swapped like baseball cards, as the ladies and gentlemen of the press geared up for their annual re-creation of the *New Yorker* magazine's Algonquin round table, every one of us wanting to win with the style of a Damon Runyon, or lose with the wit of a James Thurber.

The debonair Mr Henri Bollinger of Los Angeles, thrice president of the Publicists Guild of America, is the ringmaster in charge of this annual circus, who makes every journalist's dreams come true by securing them free rooms and meals for the duration of their stay in Las Vegas. Right now Henri was handing out press releases which proudly declared that 'the World Series of Poker is today an international event important enough for the results to be reported in *The Times* of London'. That I could vouch for, being the reporter in question, who had long enjoyed the raising of Vegas eyebrows at the sight of such smart accreditation on my press badge. But now there were some sixty journalists jostling to enter this media tournament – the only one in the World Series with no entry fee, a $1,000 first prize and a cup I have always coveted: a many-tiered silver wedding cake of a trophy loudly inscribed, FOR EXCELLENCE AT POKER IN LAS VEGAS.

Some contestants were indeed rookies, from regional American newspapers, still scarcely believing their luck at netting this plum assignment. Too many others, however, were the Hold 'em correspondents of newspapers like *Poker Player* and columnists of magazines like *Gambling Times*. Always it was one of these who carried off the trophy which should surely by now have been mine, if only as a long-service award. Could tonight, at last, be the night?

Already I was running into week-a-year local buddies and chums over from London, all of them with their eyes on that absurdly tantalizing trophy. Everywhere I heard my name being paged, only to realize it was not a constant refrain of 'Tony Holden', but the public address system summoning players to 'Ten-'n-twenny Hold 'em'. Coming from London, where casino games are played in funereal silence, I can take an hour or so to adjust to the rackety clatter of Vegas life, where the hubbub is pierced only by the regular shrieks of slot-machine jackpot winners. In the Horseshoe they were three deep around the craps tables; every blackjack seat was occupied; the roulette and baccarat tables were in full swing; yet still a huge, amorphous tide of humanity, among them most of the world's largest behinds, ebbed and flowed this way and that – everywhere but towards the exit.

Through the babble there came an authentic greeting from one of my poker brethren from London, David Spanier, himself the author of learned treatises on poker and gambling, here to cover the proceedings for an English daily paper. Because of the crush of players, it transpired, the media tournament had been put back an hour. The notion was that I joined him and the Reuters man for a quick meal before the off. This, I knew, was another bad idea; poker pros of my acquaintance have long since persuaded me that eating before a game dulls the brain. Spanier, besides, had already been in town a week, and to my jet-bagged eyes looked disturbingly spry. But, hell, I was already too far gone for my fifth meal today to make a whole lot of difference. Over cheap chicken and cheaper wine, none too warmly welcomed down below by my vintage in-flight Château Talbot, David and I agreed on a side-bet: a bottle of champagne to whoever lasted longer in the media tournament.

Four hours later, having mustered my twelfth lease of life, I was by some miracle one of just ten players left out of sixty starters. Every tournament player's ambition is to get to the final table – the last nine players, all of whom finish 'in the money' with a cash prize and a commemorative satin jacket. Until one more was eliminated, therefore, we played at two tables of five. A sly glance at the other revealed, to my dismay, that Spanier was still there too.

From the corner of my eye I could see him watching me, and it was clear that we had entered some absurd English twilight zone, where we were competing with each other rather than our real opponents across the table. Neither of us had many chips left; the only way to have any chance of winning this thing was to risk them all urgently on a halfway-decent hand, in a do-or-die attempt to double them and live to fight another hour. Instead, both of us were folding every hand, in a pathetic attempt to outlast the other and win that bottle of ersatz champagne. At moments like this, in competitive people like these two Brits a long way from home, the male ego has an irritating habit of suspending natural poker instincts.

Having laboriously worked all this out, I found myself in possession of a concealed pair of jacks, and so made the logical decision to sock it to Spanier by doubling my stack. I was called by a chump in search of a diamond flush which did not materialize. As I piled my winnings into a tall single column, just to upset Spanier, I looked over to see if he had registered my coup. He had indeed. His own pile of chips was now too small to last beyond the next hand, in which he was required to wager it all as his ante.

Spanier, so he told me later, played as slowly as he dared in the hope that I would do something rash. He was in luck. A glance at my hole cards revealed the A-K of diamonds – a very powerful hand, but occasionally accident prone. Among the Texans, who after all invented the game, A-K is nicknamed 'Walking Back to Houston', because the card-sharps of Dallas play it so well that many a Houstonian has indeed hitch-hiked home broke. A-K of the same suit ('suited') is even better. Aflush with dreams of victory, I bet my entire pile, only to find myself called by some idiot with a pair of jacks – the very hand which had just come good for me. Imagine my horror as the flop came 3-4-J – none of them diamonds – giving my opponent three-of-a-kind and leaving me in need of Q-10 or 2-5 as the last two cards. Some hope. Exit Holden, with the result that Spanier's slow play was enough to ensure him a ninth-place prize of $75 when he was, inevitably, eliminated only seconds later.

Over hideously cheap champagne, which I hoped would choke him, Spanier was in expansive mood. He now proposed that we join a one-and-three-dollar stud game about to be played by the 'inner circle' of professional poker journalists, led by Len Miller, editor of *Gambling Times*. Others at the table included Tex Sheehan and Bill 'Bulldog' Sykes, veteran columnists for *Poker Player* magazine, and long-standing Vegas professionals. With a groan, I protested that I had better things to do – though right now, I had to confess, I couldn't think of any apart from sleep, for which there would be time later. I was too tired to play poker for serious money; and to join in this game, an annual tradition in the immediate wake of the media tournament, was an elementary courtesy to people who had shown me much kindness over the years. Still smarting from Spanier's wily triumph, therefore, I took a $20 bill out of my pocket, and prepared to make it last several hours.

An hour later I had worked it up to $45 – an immense achievement in a game so tight and rinkydink. Despite an amazing run of cards, my heart was scarcely in it. Was it jet-lag or boredom which had me on the verge of sleep? That was the only question on which to walk my wits as the public address system announced a $1,000 'satellite' for the 'Big One'. A satellite is like a heat for the main event; ten players sit down with $1,000 each and play until one of them has won the lot – thus securing a seat in the $10,000 world championship Hold 'em event for a mere thou.

Satellites are mini-tournaments in themselves, giving the amateur the extra edge he enjoys in tournament play, which amounts to limited liability. In a real poker game, in other words, if you lose all your money, you have to dig in your pocket for more; in a tournament, losing the lot merely means losing your seat, or being eliminated. All you have lost is the entry fee. Tournaments can thus be a cheap way of buying invaluable experience, playing alongside the big boys without risking too much money. As can satellites, though this one wasn't so cheap. There was still, persisted the disembodied voice, just one seat left. The other players were waiting. 'Come on, fellas, isn't there one more player prepared to put up a grand?'

My thoughts went to the grand in my pocket, won by dint of luck and judgement across the road at the Nugget. Before I knew it, my arm was in the air, and I was shouting my name across the room to 'Satellite Betty', the lady in charge of these things, whose amplified voice was now the siren song beckoning me to retire that first night minus my thousand profit. The guys in the $1–$3 game looked at me gobsmacked. I gave them a despairing glance, not wishing to offend any feelings by confessing that it was sheer boredom which had precipitated this act of overweening ambition. The players in these $1,000 satellites are among the best in the world; a Daniel in the lion's den I could certainly call myself, though a David among Goliaths might be overstating the case.

I wish I could tell you what happened. Drunk, jet-lagged and so tired that I would have been pushed to say where I was, I seem to have played on automatic pilot – perhaps the best way when a player is so far out of his depth with so much at stake. But I must have been doing something right, for I was one of only three players left when the inspiration I so sorely needed arrived – in the shape of a sudden, pungent wave of *Fracas*, a powerful and to me very familiar fragrance, heralding the arrival at my side of my moll, who had finally caught up from a side-trip to friends in San Francisco. The effect appears to have been electrifying. From that moment on I could do no wrong, and another half-hour saw me return to the $1 game in triumph – a winner, and a theoretical $9,000 to the good, as an officially paid-up, signed-on entrant for the world championships themselves.

For a few more hours, I destroyed them. After ten years watching from the rails, an impossible dream had come true. I was going to play in The Big One.

2

The Big One

'Tough times make tough people,' Benny Binion would say if you asked about the jail sentence for non-payment of taxes lurking deep in his eighty-three-year past. By the end of his long life Binion was a figure of such power and venerability in Las Vegas that they had immortalized him with an equestrian statue outside the casino which bears his name, and mounted a loyal campaign to win a presidential pardon for his youthful sins.

With Benny's health long in decline, his friends and admirers wanted him to depart this world with the slate wiped clean. At a time when he was otherwise dishing out pardons like confetti, however, President Reagan remained unmoved. 'I'll see him out,' said Benny when he heard of the presidential thumbs-down, 'and I'll dance on his grave.'

For once, Benny called it wrong. When Binion died on Christmas Day 1989, Reagan was barely a year into the tenth of his nine lives. Maybe he was the one who had lived right.

It was in 1946 – 'the year,' he used to say, 'that my sheriff got beat in the election' – that Benny Binion felt obliged to leave his native Dallas, where his police record included theft, possession of illegal weapons, bootlegging and gambling. He had also killed two men, but successfully pleaded self-defence. The son of a dirt-poor stockman, Benny had made his first pile as a 'hip-pocket' bootlegger, selling illicit liquor pint by pint. In the mid-1930s, after the repeal of prohibition, he went on to become 'kinda the king of gambling down there'. But gambling was also kinda illegal in Dallas, then as now. When 1946 saw Binion leave town in a hurry, he naturally headed for Nevada, then the only state where gambling had been legalized. He bought the run-down Eldorado Hotel and Casino, renamed it Binion's Horseshoe, and put up a sign offering THE WORLD'S HIGHEST LIMITS. The punters headed straight downtown in droves, and have stayed there ever since.

Three years later, in 1949, a legendary gambler by the name of Nick 'the Greek' Dandalos wandered into town in search of a game of poker. Not just any old game. As befitted his reputation, the Greek wanted to play 'heads-up', with just one opponent; he wanted to play 'freeze-out', or winner-take-all; and he wanted to play no-limit. In short, he told Binion, he wanted 'the biggest game that this world can offer'. It was a time when most poker played in Vegas – in public, anyway – was strictly 'limit', with fixed levels of betting, the highest being some sixty dollars a round. So it was hardly surprising that the Greek found no-one prepared to sit down with him on his terms.

Benny Binion, however, knew just the man. He offered to stage the game, and to lay on an opponent worthy of the Greek – if he would agree to play in public, at the Horseshoe. Nick nodded, and Binion hit the phone to Dallas, to his friend since childhood, Johnny Moss. Though he had then never been to Vegas, and was already weary from a non-stop four-day game, Moss agreed to set off right away. On arriving at the Horseshoe, after the long, slow drive from Dallas, he shook hands with the Greek and sat straight down to business.

They played, so legend has it, for five months. As Benny

Binion had hoped, the crowd stood six deep around the table, marvelling at the nerve and stamina of these two poker titans, and at the vast amounts of money passing back and forth between them. Binion's subsequent fortune was founded on the dollars these same spectators then poured into his casino's coffers. Other players came and went in the Big Game, tolerated only if prepared to risk a minimum of $10,000, a considerable sum in the aftermath of war; but these mere mortals would tire after a day or two, and Moss and the Greek would smile at each other as one by one they broke them.

Each of the protagonists could manage four or five days' play at a stretch before agreeing to pause for some rest. Though the younger man – he was then forty-two, the Greek in his late fifties – Moss tended to sleep longer during these intervals. He would usually return to the card room after ten or more hours to find Dandalos killing the time by playing craps. 'Whaddaya gonna do?' Nick the Greek would greet his opponent. 'Sleep your life away?'

The banter may have masked each man's ruthless will to win. But it also betokened the mutual respect and unfailing courtesy which characterizes the game of poker at its best and highest level. This was evident to the last, in the classic line which finally signalled that the game was over, as Dandalos took one beat too many, rose from his seat and said simply: 'Mr Moss, I have to let you go.'

No-one knows for sure – and Mr Moss, to this day, ain't telling – but the Greek is said to have lost at least two million dollars. Forty years on, Moss still loves to talk about one famous hand of five-card stud which he regarded as the turning-point. With each player anteing $100, there was $200 in the pot when he was dealt a concealed nine and an exposed six. The Greek's exposed (or 'up') card was an eight. At stud, the low hand makes the first bet, the high hand thereafter. Moss's treacle-thick Texas drawl takes up the story: 'Low man brings it in. I bet two hunnerd with a six. He raises fifteen hunnerd or two thousan', I call him. Next card comes, I catch a nine, he catches a six. I got two nines now, and I'm the high man. I make a good bet, five thousan' maybe, and he plays right back at me, twenny-five thousan'. I jus' call him. I'm figurin' to take all that money o' his, and I don' wanna scare him none.

'The next card comes, and he catches a trey, I catch a deuce. Ain't nothin' he got can beat my two nines. I check then to trap him, an' he bets, jus' like I wanted. So I raise him *wa-a-ay* up there, an' he calls. I got him in there, all right. There's a hunnerd thousand dollars in that pot – maybe more, I don't know exactly – an' I'm a-winnin' it.'

Johnny's last card was a three, Nick's a jack. So Moss was showing 6-9-2-3, the Greek 8-6-3-J. With Moss's concealed pair of nines, the only hole card with which the Greek could beat him was another jack. But he might have figured that Moss had no pair, and that his jack-high hand was enough to win the pot. 'He's high now on the jack, and he bets fifty thousan'. I can't put him on no jack in the hole, you know. He ain't gonna pay all that money jus' to outdraw me. I don't care what he catches, he's gotta beat those two nines of mine. So I move in with the rest of my money.'

If the Greek were to call, the pot would total half a million dollars. Dandalos sat quiet for a while, apparently pondering the enormity of Moss's bet, and the clear implication that Johnny had a pair – any pair – to beat his own jack-high hand. Eventually he said: 'Mr Moss, I think I have a jack in the hole.'

'Greek,' replied Moss, 'if you've got a jack down there, you're liable to win yourself one helluva pot.'

There was another long, tortuous silence before the Greek pushed all his money to the centre of the table and turned over his hole card – the jack of diamonds. 'He outdrawed me,' Moss remembers. 'We had about two hunnerd fifty thou apiece in that pot, and he won it. But that's all right. That's better than all right. If he's gonna go chasin' dreams like that, I know I'm gonna break him in the en'.'

And break him he duly did. Still talked about far beyond the Horseshoe, the Dandalos–Moss marathon has gone down in poker history as the biggest and best game of all time. Nothing like it has been seen since. Nothing like it had certainly been seen for twenty years when Benny Binion, in 1970, decided to try and re-create the occasion by inviting the world's leading poker players to compete in public, at the Horseshoe, the winner to be accorded the title of world champion. They would play several different types of poker, at high stakes of their own choosing, and the title would go to the most consistent player in all events – the best all-rounder. After a grimly contested week of play, the six other professionals threw in their hands and unanimously elected Johnny Moss – hereinafter nicknamed 'The Grand Old Man' – poker's first official world champion.

Thus was the World Series of Poker born. Moss won it again the following year – this time by right rather than acclamation – and again in 1974, after briefly lending the title to two of his most colourful contemporaries, Amarillo 'Slim' Preston and Walter Clyde 'Puggy' Pearson. Another old-timer, Brian 'Sailor' Roberts, filched it in 1975 before the torch passed for two years running to the greatest player of the next generation, Doyle 'Texas Dolly' Brunson. The subsequent decade saw the World Series grow wildly in fame and stature, with the supreme title going year by year to a range of top

professionals. By the 1988 world championships only one, Stu
'the Kid' Ungar, had equalled Brunson's feat of successfully
defending his title, in 1980–81. As the 1988 World Series got
under way the reigning champion, Johnny Chan, was given a
good chance of equalling Ungar. But no-one, as yet, had
matched Johnny Moss by winning the world crown three times.

The octogenarian Moss is still a great all-round player,
unnerving his opponents above all with an uncanny ability to
read what cards they are holding – as much through the expressions on their faces, plus a little body language, as by the
patterns of their betting. This is why he is a supreme player
of 'no limit' poker, where raw psychology outranks strategy
in dictating betting patterns, with the actual cards on display
coming a distant third. It is a foolish player who assumes that
Moss's advanced age has led him to fall asleep at the table;
even as a young man his almost imperceptible eyes, as hooded
as a lizard's, could give the impression that he had nodded off
during a hand. Over the years many a sucker has lived to rue
this rash assumption. A bet to test an apparently unwary Moss
has all too often led to a terrifyingly effective raise.

To this day Moss competes every year at the Horseshoe,
and regularly wins one of the World Series titles, making more
than one appearance at a final table and a remarkably consistent showing in the world crown event itself. This particular
year he had already carried off the ace-to-five (lowball) draw
competition – celebrating his sixty-second wedding anniversary with his wife Virgie, as ever, loyally at his side, by beating 193 younger entrants to a record first prize of $116,400.

Sixty-two years before to the day, so Virgie once told me,
Moss had inevitably got involved in a poker game on their
wedding night. So confident was he of winning one pot that,
after running out of money, he reached behind him to his bride,

felt for her left index finger without taking his eyes off the table, and started tugging at her engagement ring. Virgie disentangled herself from his grasp, removed the ring herself, and handed it over. 'If'n ah hadn't,' she said, 'Johnny would've ripped mah whole finger off.'

And had Johnny, I asked her, won the pot? 'Sure he did,' said Virgie, holding up her left hand for my inspection – the ring still in place, sixty years and millions of dollars later.

Moss's presence at any card table is still feared. His remarkable capacity for reading the opposition, and acting on his hunches with brutal aggression, rarely lets him down – though now, in his mid-eighties, he confesses that his stamina may. Highly capable of turning crotchety, he can be dismissive of *arrivistes* players from around the world, who occasionally strike it lucky in Vegas without having worked out their apprenticeship there, let alone on a Texas circuit known only by word of mouth to its veterans.

Long gone are the days when the likes of Moss would be out on the road, perpetually hustling, literally riding shot-gun on illegal winnings in ever-present danger of violent hijack. Poker is now an almost respectable activity, formally legalized in the state of Nevada, scrutinized by the Internal Revenue, the subject of academic studies and learned treatises – so securely part of the fabric of American life that it may even be visited by tourists. For all his world-weary air, his quietly elegant clothes, and his millions come and gone, the elderly Moss still radiates the impression that he hankers for the romantic, pioneer days when poker really was about the survival of the fittest – and excellence at cards a mere symbol of a man's all-round ability to look after himself in any situation, violent if need be, which might arise.

So this pugnacious eighty-year-old had this year won one

event, and come a moody second in another to a first-time tournament player from Atlantic City. By taking the $158,000 first prize in the seven-card stud championship, a Norwegian, Thor Hansen, had become the first non-American ever to win a World Series title. Maybe there was hope for me, after all? And the first prize in this year's world championship event was climbing to well over half a million dollars.

The World Series of Poker lasts three weeks every May, and now consists of fifteen events ranging from draw to stud, razz (or lowball) to Omaha (Hold 'em with four hole cards). Some events are 'limit', with fixed betting intervals; some are 'pot limit', in which the maximum bet is the total pot at any given moment; and some are 'no limit', which means exactly what it says. The climactic event, which carries with it the world title, is No Limit Texas Hold 'em, with a $10,000 buy-in.

Even more than most other forms of poker, No Limit Hold 'em is a game which sorts sheep from goats, men from boys, locals from tourists and pros from amateurs, as the prime requisite of a good Hold 'em player is aggressiveness. If you hold a strong hand in the pocket, or after the flop, you should bet heavily, to drive out the players holding four cards to a straight or a flush, either of which can materialize on 'the turn' or 'the river', the fourth and fifth communal cards to be exposed. Players who make their straight or flush at the end – without the cushion of a concealed pair, or four to a straight, which would give them other 'outs' (or routes to winning hands) – are often weak players who have defied the odds against them to stay in the pot that long. They may score the occasional win this way, but they will lose in the long run. They may last longer than they should in a championship, but they are never going to win it.

The other major factor in the game is 'position' – or the seat you occupy in relation to the dealer, which determines your position in the betting sequence. The way Hold 'em is played in Vegas, the player on the dealer's left will put up a mandatory 'small blind' (of, say, $10 in a $20–$40 game) and the next player the 'big blind' ($20, or the opening bet, in a $20–$40 game). These 'blind' bets give these two players the right to raise or re-raise when the betting has circulated the table and returned to them.

When the game is played with a house dealer, a 'button' or 'buck' is passed clockwise round the table to indicate which player is notionally dealing the hand. (Hence the phrase 'passing the buck'; few laymen realize that President Harry Truman was immortalizing a poker term when he declared, 'The buck stops here'.) In the toughest position is the first to bet, who is said to be 'under the gun'; the later your position, the more free information you will have by the time it is your turn to 'speak'. If in early position – within three or four of the button – you should generally have a very strong hand to call the big blind, as there is a high chance of a raise behind you. If you cannot call it, you are going to risk a cardinal poker error: throwing 'good' money after 'bad'. It is essential, in other words, to remember that money you have already paid into the pot is no longer yours; to defend it with more, in defiance of the odds, is an act of supreme folly.

In 'middle' or 'late' positions, the Hold 'em player can 'creep in' with a weaker hand, given the higher chance of not being raised. These guidelines vary, of course, depending on the number of players in action, and whether the table is unusually 'tight' or 'loose'. And so it goes on. Understanding the endless subtleties of 'position' is regarded by most leading players as the key to success at Texas Hold 'em.

Today there are countless textbooks and manuals about Hold 'em, some of them chatty, staccato hints from former world champions, some of them costly computer analyses by statistical scientists, calculating the odds on all available hands at each stage of the game. None of them was in my possession, or ever had been, as I tentatively took the elevator from the fourteenth floor of the Golden Nugget to what I saw as certain doom across the road in the world championship arena at the Horseshoe.

The previous evening, gratifyingly excited by my satellite victory, the Moll had switched into her remarkably selfless mode and effortlessly waxed supportive. Now the Moll is no mean poker player herself, and no slouch about life either. It had needed no drawn-out dialogue, when first we set up shop together, for us to agree on a relationship conducted on utterly equal terms. I did not see her as a housewife or laundress any more than she saw me (or wanted to see me) as a nine-to-five, piped-and-slippered breadwinner. Fifty-fifty was the basic contract, its only sub-clause being an agreement to give each other the right and freedom, whenever and wherever possible, to be ourselves. So it was with gratitude as well as awe that I had let her pamper me the night before the Main Event, offering to go along with my every passing whim, withdrawing for the nonce her standing request to head for the nearest disco, and putting the prospect of Sinatra at Bally's on hold. This was a night to get some sleep. The only trouble was that there wasn't much of it left.

It was five-ish before we had tottered up to our spacious suite, just eight hours before I was due to sit down in an event for which my every mental faculty needed to be at its sharpest. I had not slept for some thirty-six hours; I had drunk more than I normally do in seventy-two; and I was so exhausted by twelve solid hours of poker, including two concentration-draining tournaments, that I was ready to sleep for a week. No Nick the Greek I. Tony the Brit was out for the count, according to the Moll's subsequent report, before his head had hit the doorpost, let alone the pillow.

Vegas being Vegas, however, none of this much mattered. This is a town where night and day become indistinguishable. During open-ended sessions at the poker table, it is quite possible to look at your watch and be stupendously innocent about the a.m. or p.m. dimension to the hour on display. The time to go upstairs and sleep is simply when you feel like it. Should you order an alarm call, the taped message on the phone by your bed blandly chants, 'Good evening, this is your wake-up call', whatever the time of day or night. The curtains in your room remain permanently drawn, on the assumption that its only use is for acts of darkness.

Just as the air-conditioning renders you immune to the absurd summer temperatures outside, which hit you like a cosh when you are required to cross the street, so the absorptions of casino life make mock of the futile cycles of sun and moon. Daylight, in Vegas, is the pushy, intrusive irritant delaying the beauties of neon-clad night – brighter, more beautiful and far more exciting. There are no clocks in view on any Las Vegas casino floor, another deliberate ploy by the management to speed your passage further and further from reality. The only time you keep in Glitter Gulch is that set by your body clock, whose alarm bell you ignore at your peril.

Mine, this momentous morning, felt in need of a new quartz battery. Breakfast, the Moll gently suggested, might prove a good investment. But up in the room, or down in the coffee shop? Decisions, decisions. I let her take command, and a cornucopia of fruit and yoghurt, muesli and oatmeal, eggs and bacon, pancakes and waffles soon escorted a giant vat of steaming coffee through our door. If I were to stay alive in the tournament for any length of time, this might be the last I would eat for the foreseeable future. Chased down by a timeless Scotch, perhaps, to steady my nerves?

No way. It is a movie myth that poker players drink at the table. The game does tend to be played in smoke-filled rooms; even those players with portable fans, an increasingly tetchy minority these days, must passively smoke the equivalent of a pack during the course of most Vegas tournaments. But the refreshments constantly supplied by the cocktail girls range, at their most daring, from mineral water (Mountain Valley, not Perrier) to coffee. Even 'regular' (as opposed to diet) Coca-Cola draws dark looks from the other players, as if one were downing a purée of anabolic steroids. Only one sometime world champion, the genial Bill Smith of 1985, doggedly drank his way to victory. Bill still drinks at the table – mostly beer, with Scotch chasers – and still manages to win tournaments, a double-act at which he is unique among the ranks of professional players.

Well-fed and sober, therefore, ill-slept but Moll-massaged, clad in the T-shirt and blue jeans which befitted his incipient middle age, Britain's only representative in these particular world championships blinked his way across Fremont Street into the legendary, arc-lit tournament arena of the Horseshoe. Awed by the company he was about to keep, he pondered everything he didn't know about odds, outs and position. It was already 12.50 p.m., ten minutes before the tournament's scheduled starting time, but there were more spectators than players milling around. Like transatlantic flights and Spanish meals, poker tournaments in Las Vegas rarely start within sixty minutes of the advertised hour.

As the only Englishman taking part in the world championships, I was just resenting the lack of press attention when the *Daily Telegraph*, in the shape of the aforementioned David Spanier, generously swallowed its pride and requested an interview. David knew that it was only by persuading my English publishers that I had an important literary conference to attend on the West Coast, and that publication of my new book must therefore be postponed by at least a week, that I had managed to be here at all this year. My first objective, I told Spanier, was to avoid being the first player to be knocked out. My second was to last out the first hour. I would be delighted to last as long as the first break, due to be taken after two hours. Would I survive as far as Day Two? It was impossible to think that far ahead.

Was I sure, Spanier gently enquired, that I was going into this thing with the right attitude? To give him his due, David was behaving, in the rather awkward circumstances, like a proper gent. Like all my poker pals from England, he would have given his right earlobe to take part in the World Series, but he was treating me with generous concern, as well as the modicum of respect that he knew I felt I deserved. His question was a gentle encouragement to stop feeling so pessimistic, to think of England; and he was absolutely right. But it was hard to feel confident when all one's poker heroes were milling around in relaxed mood, reminiscing about great pots of the past, flashing all the ornate, trademark jewellery they had won or earned over the green baize. A dozen or so, of course, were wearing poker's most coveted accessory: the solid gold bracelet, with their name engraved in diamonds, which denotes a sometime world champion; and they seemed to find plenty of excuses to shoot their cuffs and let this awe-inspiring bauble glint in the television lights.

Professional poker players measure each other by their jewellery. Gold Rolex watches are virtually standard issue; it is the dead-weight of 23-carat, diamond-studded bracelets, rings, even necklaces which are the medals of their trade, conspicuously worn to denote status and achievement. Back in England, going about what passes for normal life, such baubles would look unspeakably vulgar; after a few days in Vegas, however, the hypnotic powers of the place always have me thinking them rather stylish, even beginning to covet the stuff glinting from the displays laid out by itinerant card-room jewellers. So it was very much in the spirit of the moment that the Moll now presented me with the most wonderfully kitsch timepiece either of us had ever beheld: a gold-banded wrist-watch whose face showed the king of diamonds, the diamonds themselves represented by glittering *diamanté* studs. It was *spectacularly* vulgar – just the thing I needed to help me pretend I knew what I was doing.

This year's world title event boasted a record 167 entrants, whose ten thousand bucks apiece added up to prize money of $1.67 million, not to mention the bracelet. In the old days, it was literally winner-take-all, though a little private negotiation might go on between the last two or three players left out of a hundred or so. These days, because it seemed so tough to last four days, reach the final table, and win nothing, the distribution of the prize money has been revised at the players' request. Everyone who survives to the fourth day will be 'in the money' – though positions 19 through 27 will get only their $10,000 entry fee back, and 28 through 36 will actually lose money by recouping merely $7,500. So by general consent the worst position to come – much worse than being the first out on Day One – is thirty-seventh, for you will have played at least three whole days, seen off many tough competitors, and then find yourself going home with nothing to show for it except the loss of your $10,000 entry fee. For players like myself, who risked only *one* thousand dollars to win a seat in the ten-thousand-dollar event, positions 19 through 36 would of course represent a substantial profit.

Eleventh through eighteenth receive $12,500 each – still a modest 25 per cent profit on outlay, very much beneath the expectations of a professional poker player for four days' hard work. The top ten, as they should, receive the *real* money, the balance being divided between them in growing increments until the eventual winner takes 50 per cent of the pot – this year a not unsatisfying $835,000. With the runner-up on only 20 per cent, the difference between first and second is a staggering half-million.

To me, as I spotted Moss and Brunson, Pearson and Preston, Ungar and Chan among my relaxed, well-slept opponents, these figures were no more than mirages. As my interview with Spanier progressed, however, I expressed new-found confidence that a win at my first attempt would not alter my life . . . well, not beyond retiring from writing, emigrating to the United States and starting a *vita nuova* as a full-time professional poker player.

As the public address system finally crackled into life, it was time at last for action. First, as every year, there was the long-drawn-out, crowd-pleasing ritual of introducing all the players individually as they took their pre-assigned seats. The microphone was handed over to Jack Binion, son of Benny, president of the Horseshoe, and himself no mean poker player, to whom most of the participants were old buddies and highly valued customers. A reluctant public speaker, Jack nevertheless had a wisecrack ready for almost everyone.

Twelve of the fourteen former world champions were

among this year's entrants, including the reigning champ, Chan, nicknamed the Oriental Express, and rated by the bookies as one of the hot favourites. Born in the People's Republic of China, Chan arrived in the United States at the age of nine when his parents fled the Cultural Revolution. It did not take long for this son of Mao to sniff out Vegas. From the family's Chinese restaurant in Houston, he soon graduated to the kitchens of the Fremont Hotel in Glitter Gulch, where he worked as a fry cook. People remember him heading straight from his shift to the poker tables in the card room, his white apron still round his waist. Now, barely a decade later, here he was next door at the Horseshoe, the most feared poker player in the world.

Chan still calls Houston home. 'I phone my wife and kids there nearly every day,' he says, as if it were a matter of pride. Like most leading pros, his life is a peripatetic treasure-hunt, lived out of suitcases, where the card room is his office and a 'comped' hotel room his home. But if he lives anywhere, it is in the southern Los Angeles suburb of Cerritos, close to the rash of Californian card clubs, where the action is fast and loose, and the opposition softer than in Vegas. He has few friends in the social sense; the one regular face in the Chan roadshow is that of John Formica, a heavily-built, grey-haired watchdog known as 'the Italian stallion'. Formica used to play poker with Chan, but got out of his depth; now he gives him neck-rubs during long spells at the table. 'I guess you could call me his best friend in the gambling world,' says Formica. 'But Johnny doesn't really open up to anybody. Not even his wife and kids.'

He certainly wasn't going to open up to anyone between him and his second world title. Chan's eyes were hidden, as always, behind Yves St Laurent shades. Like many of the younger pros, he was dressed in tracksuit and sneakers, the difference being that Chan actually *had* been out jogging that morning. His hair was still slicked back from his post-workout shower. He doesn't smoke; he doesn't drink; the only night life he samples is at the card tables. If superstition is a vice, it is his only one – and even that is double-edged, designed to unnerve the other players. The 'lucky' orange he now placed in front of him, and would sometimes stroke during play, is designed to convince Chan's opponents – not himself – that he's a lucky player. But the crowd remembered it from last year, and loved it. It's a sign that he might even be human. As Chan waved half-heartedly in acknowledgement of their roar, his thoughts were visibly elsewhere, as if silently repeating stern instructions to himself about the long-drawn-out trials ahead.

Further roars greeted the 1973 champ, Walter Clyde Pearson, universally known as 'Puggy', a feisty little barrel of a man sporting pince-nez spectacles, a clutch of torpedo-scale cigars protruding from his shirt pocket. Then the throng pressed forward at the name of perhaps the most celebrated poker player alive, Amarillo 'Slim' Preston, his stetson wound round with the remains of a surly rattlesnake, its jaws perpetually snarling at any player rash enough to call his bets. A broad path then had to be cleared for poker's other current immortal, Doyle 'Texas Dolly' Brunson, all 320 pounds of him, who rolled towards his seat like a stately galleon wholly indifferent to the armada out to get him.

'And at Table Three, Seat Nine, the grand old man of poker, the only three-time winner in the history of the world championships, the indestructible Mr Johnny Moss.' The room erupted. The other competitors all stood to applaud the only living founder-member of poker's Hall of Fame, who turned eighty-one two days previously. The hint of a rare smile playing around his lips, Moss nodded his scant acknowledgement with the physical economy of a monarch. He was already saving his energy for the long and pensive hours ahead.

Unexpectedly, it was suddenly time for '"London Tony", "Golden Holden", biographer of poker players and princes, here at the Horseshoe by royal appointment' to take his seat at Table Six. There was the odd ironic whoop from friendly players, and a gratifying, if lonely, cheer from Spanier and the Moll, while the crowd subsided into baffled silence and the other players continued their heedless chatter. As the interminable introductions continued, I stole a glance around our half-filled table, relieved to see not a single face I recognized. They would all be good, by definition, but not yet good enough to be known around town. Morale began, against all logic, to rise. Well, why shouldn't I win this thing? Then Jack Binion greeted the only remaining contestant to arouse the cheerleaders: another of this year's favourites, two-time champion Stu 'the Kid' Ungar, a diminutive stick-insect of thirty-four-going-on-twelve, who bounced with crackling nervous energy towards – horror of horrors – Table Six. I was up against the Kid.

Eight years before, in 1980, I had been celebrating my thirty-third birthday with some stern $3–$6 stud in the card room of the Golden Nugget, when word arrived from across the road that the world championships had been won by a player scarce out of diapers. The news fell upon my ageing companions like lava from Mount St Helens, which was at the time making its presence felt in those parts. Winners joined losers in an exchange of glances which might plausibly have signalled cardiac arrest; their faces had then sagged into drop-jawed aspects of ineffable gloom. Though myself no chicken, and a year older than I had been the day before, I calculated that I was still the youngest player at the table by some three decades, and proceeded to mop up all night. 'You kids,' a crew-cut Army veteran known as 'Silent Harry' had sneered at me. 'You kids oughta go find a job, not sit here all day playing poker. It's no life for a youngster. Get a lifetime's work behind you before you sit down here again.' I chose instead to get what seemed like a lifetime's sleep, quitting while ahead, and humbly thanking the Kid for psyching old-timers all over town for a good week or so.

The following year, Ungar had done it again – and again the wrinklies had gone on tilt. My thirty-fourth birthday was spent drowning in an avalanche of chips, as the Vegas vets felt obliged to attempt some grim, inevitably doomed, assault upon Father Time. Now here we were about to join in the climactic battle of my poker life so far, and I was in the last week of my life as a forty-year-old. Having felt forty for at least five years already, the age itself did not bother me at all. But the presence of the Kid, whose rampant years at the top had left their mark upon his sallow complexion, certainly did. His frame was still as thin as a shadow, his wrists so emaciated that his championship bracelets all but pinned them to the table. But behind those dead eyes the mind was seething – and it was a far more finely-tuned instrument than mine.

My reverie was barely interrupted by the gushy excitement which greeted the arrival of the final player at our table, Telly Savalas: he of the Kojak dome, the gravel-pit voice, and a nose left by Michelangelo on the chipping-room floor. Among fellow poker players, this sometimes surly fellow is at his most genial. We were collectively greeted as 'Pussy-cats', and the crowd on the rail inexorably surged our way.

I was still adjusting to this unwonted stardom when Jack

Binion cried 'Good luck players. OK, ante up and deal.' The first hand arrived before I'd had time to absorb the devastating fact that I had $10,000 in plastic in front of me, mine for the losing. Trying not to let my new watch distract me, I peeped down in the hope of an unsuited 7-2, the worst Hold 'em hand the deck can deal. Oh, for the freedom to fold, mop my brow, gather my wits about me, and work out a strategy! In the hole, alas, I beheld the A-10 of spades, a hand well worth playing. I was in an uncomfortably early position, only four to the dealer's left, and merely called Ungar's big blind of $50 – which he now proceeded to raise by $300.

Although I knew this was a standard tactic among the pros – both to protect their forced investment, and to intimidate the faint-hearted – I doubted that his hand was as good as mine. Impulsively, I raised him back $500. The entire table, round to Ungar, folded. The Kid looked at me sulkily, rolled his eyes towards Savalas, and re-raised me $1,000. It was the first hand of the tournament, and I was heading towards extinction at the hands of the Kid. My calculations were thrown by the absurd appearance in my head of a line from Shakespeare's *Macbeth*: 'Of all men else I have avoided thee!' Remembering that Macduff, unlike Macbeth, had lived right, I decided to call.

A biggish confrontation on the very first hand, between a two-time champ and a complete unknown, had the crowd leaning far enough over the rail for the sky to seem to darken. I vaguely took in a muttered, 'Isn't he the guy from England? Do they *play* poker over there?' as the dealer took for ever over the ritual drama of burning the top card – setting it aside, face down, among the discards – before rolling the three of spades, the seven of spades . . . and a beautiful shiny red ace.

Having put Ungar on a highish pair, probably jacks or queens, I was none too surprised when he checked to me, and as confident as I ever would be that he wouldn't raise a fat bet. If I had read him wrong, and he was slow-playing a pair of sevens in the hole, or an ace with a higher kicker than mine (an A-K?), or even the last *two* aces, then I was doomed unless my flush came up. But at least I would have gone out in style. *Not* to bet now would be unforgivably wimpish; I would probably lose sleep over it for the rest of my life. With as little hesitation as possible – but with great alarm at seeing my hands, as if someone else's, begin to shake uncontrollably – I bet three thousand dollars.

This move seemed to have an almost physical impact on Ungar, who hit the back of his chair as if invisibly socked on the jaw, and stared moodily at the flop. It was now as clear as Mountain Valley water, of which I was taking a supposedly nonchalant sip, that not one little bit did he like the sight of that ace on the board. Maybe he was even holding a pair of kings – in which case he was quite justified in the oath that followed, as he ill-humouredly picked up his cards and threw them into the discards (locally known as 'the muck'), in the standard Vegas gesture of silent surrender.

The dealer pushed $6,825 my way, of which $4,850 was mine, $1,850 Ungar's and the rest sundry contributions from others before the flop. The Kid was off to a dispiriting start, losing almost a fifth of his stack on the first hand, and I was in serious danger of thinking there was nothing to all this. As I stacked the chips blankly, trying to control the perceptible tremor still in my fingers, I repeatedly told myself not to let it go to my head.

Sit quiet and watch for a while. Play ridiculously tight. Get in cheap if you can, and wait for the nuts. You might well have lost that hand. One win on a lucky flop does not make you a world-class player.

The drilling-in of these excellent precepts was ruffled only by a cry of 'Tournament leader!' from the rails, in an incongrously English accent. I looked up to see a grinning Spanier trying to help me enjoy the moment. The cautious smile he received back from me was nothing to the venomous scowl he earned from Ungar. Then there was a shout of 'Table Fourteen, Seat Eight' from a distant dealer, signalling the departure of one hapless player on the very first hand. Whoever had won it, by definition, had already doubled his stack. My moment as tournament leader had been an all-too-brief, if shining, one. Ungar's eyes still seemed intent on conveying this truth to Spanier. Visibly chastened, the *Daily Telegraph* touched the peak of its baseball cap and beat a hasty retreat towards the bar. I was happier, as its Las Vegas correspondent well knew, to be left to my own devices, to be free to make my own mistakes.

For the next two hours I played very cautiously, perhaps over-cautiously, tenderly nourishing my early profit rather than using it to beat up the others. To be fair to myself, I didn't really see many cards worth playing. This became doubly annoying when Ungar, apparently irritated beyond belief by that first hand, seemed bent on self-destruction. A wily cove in a pony tail and dark glasses, whom I had never seen before (or since), was using a remarkable run of hands to destroy the Kid systematically. After some seventy minutes of play, when a dozen or so players had been eliminated, Ungar became the first former world champ to go broke.

Like most other competitive sports, poker demands a particular hunger for success from aspirants for its world crown. Maybe because he had won it twice already; maybe because of his reputation for wild impulse betting on sports events; maybe because of his supposedly turbulent private life – for whatever reason, the Kid had not sat down today with that hunger. I was quite sorry to see him go.

After eighty minutes eighteen players – or two whole table-fuls – had been eliminated. This literally meant that Binion's armed guards were removing tables from the arena – a grim, symbolic business akin to some kind of gambler's funeral rite in which Hank and his pals played pallbearer. As ours was the table next to the exit, with the crowd still leaning in on a pensive Savalas, these heavy objects were being lifted bodily over my head, something of a distraction as I tried to calculate the true values of my hands. Was I playing too tight? Should I take more risks? This was the first major tournament in which I had ever played, and I knew there were guidelines about these things. To last four days, it seemed to me, you had to be pretty cautious about going 'all-in' – risking every penny you have left in an attempt to build your stack. Yet people were doing it all over the room, the successful ones earning themselves a useful early lead. To last to the first break, however, I merely had to sit tight. With the blinds at $25 and $50, and a round taking some twenty minutes, it was costing me only $225 an hour just to sit and watch.

Playing this way, I was naturally marked down as a tight-wad by the other players, who now tended to fold if I ever came into a pot. This is the classic fate of the over-cautious player, but it can also be turned occasionally to advantage. There are hands when very little action before the flop seems to suggest that no-one is holding very interesting cards. In the right position – preferably as late as possible – an early raise can frighten all the others out, even if you are holding 'rags', or rubbish. I tried it once or twice, and it worked. Then, from Dark Glasses, there was a murmur of 'Stealing again, London?' Though genial enough, it was more of an enquiry than a statement. He wanted to see how I would respond, whether I would blush like the amateur I was, thus giving my game away. The Moll, who was keeping an eye on me at the time, later testified that I maintained a commendably blank expression while giving him the most politely inscrutable of European smiles.

With little further incident, we reached the first break. I was still alive, and very proud of myself. Twenty-three players had been eliminated, including another former title-holder, Jack 'Treetop' Straus. I grabbed the Moll and headed for the bar, where I suddenly felt utterly drained. Two hours of total concentration now felt like ten; the thought of four more hours of play today seemed impossibly daunting. Breaking all the rules, I permitted myself a gin and tonic, and raised it in a grinning toast down the bar to Bill Smith, who was ordering up a beer and whisky. A subscriber to the Denis Thatcher school of gin-swiggers, who find that it can occasionally act upon the system like a much-needed shot of adrenalin, I felt the stuff course through me like an electric shock. It was just what I needed. Another, however, would have proved disastrous.

A sound judge of my own metabolism, I survived to the second break both alert and cautious. Hours three and four passed far more quickly than the first two. Initial nerves had settled down all round; hyperactive players had nearly all committed hara-kiri; now we were playing a finely tuned, mutually respectful waiting game. With the arrival of 'rolling' antes, every player now had to pay $25 a hand, with the blinds still at $25 and $50, so each round was costing a minimum of $300. But there were, after all, three more days to go. There was no need to chase unnecessary drama; nor could one be excused for missing chances to mop up. My main concern during this period was to vary my play: to be thought neither tight nor loose, merely unpredictable and mysterious. This, of course, is every poker player's prime objective. To be feared, however: that is the consummation most devoutly to be wished. Try as I might, I could not yet see a face around the table which was actually in awe of me.

The fact that no-one knew who I was, beyond a hazy notion that I was some English amateur with ideas above his station, certainly helped. So did the reflected glory as the tournament director, Eric Drache, a good friend these ten years, occasionally stopped by to see how I was doing. It occurred to me, nevertheless, to wonder how many of my opponents knew that I had fluked my way this far via a satellite, and that $10,000 seemed to me an awful lot of money. The fact that after four hours, back at the bar with the Moll, I had advanced my stack to $14,500 was concentrating my mind in totally the wrong direction. If only we could cash it in and leave, I was saying to her. I started this time yesterday with $200, and now I'm showing a paper profit of more than 7,000 per cent. Think how many months' rent that is. It's a car, goddamnit. Hang in there, she pointed out, and it could be a house.

For another three hours, I hung in there. By the last hour of play the ante per hand per player had risen to $50, and the blinds to $100 and $200. At $750 a round, the weaker brethren were getting desperate, and facing rapid extinction unless a risk or two paid off. To see how you stand, you must keep dividing the remaining number of players into the $1.67 million in play, and compare the result with your stack. Mental arithmetic never having been my strong point, I figured there would be around a hundred players left at the end of the day, meaning I would need $16,700 in front of me to be holding my own. I had around $13,000 when, with twenty minutes to go, the right opportunity came.

The true professionals among poker players remember hands they have played twenty years before; I can barely remember hands I have played twenty minutes before. The true amateurs will tell you in great detail about the hands they won; my problem is that I remember only the hands I lost. This turned out to be one such, a painful one, as I watched my two pairs beaten on the river by three kings – belonging, of all people, to Savalas, who had been quietly tagging along all evening.

I had played my 10-J cautiously, because the flop had brought a king as well as J-3. But Kojak was betting too little – little enough, anyway, to let me stay in. Then maybe I didn't bet enough when a ten appeared on fourth street, giving me two pairs. Savalas and his singleton king stayed in, and pulled the third king on the final card. Now his huge bet drove me out, clinging to the assumption that I had read him right. Could he even have a full house? It was too late to worry. By this time of day people were thinking only about surviving till the morrow, and Savalas was decent enough to flash me his king after I had folded. In the process he gave my wrist-watch a scornful look; it was scarcely up to high-roller standards. But I couldn't let that psyche me. I felt a little better about the way I had played my hand, but wretched about the $4,500 his good fortune – and my weakness – had cost me.

As the day's proceedings were declared closed, however, such details melted away. I permitted myself to feel pretty good. I had survived the first day – far beyond my expectations, and indeed those of my thin line of English supporters, who gathered round with more cheap champagne. I had $8,000 left, and was lying overnight in eighty-third place. Only 104 players were left out of the 167 starters. Among those to have been eliminated before me, apart from Ungar and Straus, were such well-fancied former champions as Doyle Brunson and Tom McEvoy. Behind me lay two former champs: Bobby Baldwin, in ninety-second place, with $6,425, and sixteen behind me, lying ninety-ninth with $4,125, the Man himself, Johnny Moss.

The overnight returns showed that the tournament leader, with $52,700, was a Californian pro called Mike Cox. In twenty-second place, with $22,325, Johnny Chan was already looking ominous. Thanks largely to me, Telly Savalas had doubled his stack to $20,000, which placed him thirty-third. Most of the big names were still in there pitching, and the guys at the bottom would need a lot of luck to hang in there much longer.

Eight thousand dollars was not going to last me long. When play resumed next morning, after a pill had consigned me to twelve hours of deep and dreamless sleep, the rolling antes had risen to $100 and the blinds to $200 and $400. At $1,500 a round, or some $4,500 an hour, I was soon going to be 'anted away' unless I made some early advances. I can offer only the poker player's feeble, perennial excuse: that the cards went dead on me. I saw so few court cards in my hole, not even a low pair, that crisis was looming soon after the first break.

A few increasingly desperate risks had failed to pay off, and I was down to my last $3,000. The antes were now $200, the blinds $300 and $600, so I had barely enough to survive one round. There was no point now in sitting and waiting for extinction. Besides, there is a fine romantic tradition in the event of getting down this low, going all-in a few times, hitting a couple of lucky flops, and fighting back into contention. That's how Jack Straus won it in 1982. When I saw a king of spades in the hole, with a suited seven, I decided to go for broke.

The way to do this is to raise before the flop, to build a pot worth winning. Maybe you can *more* than double your stack. So it was with mixed feelings that I watched two players with huge piles call my raise; the $3,000 they needed to match my all-in bet scarcely trimmed the tops of their towers of chips. With $9,000 in the middle, I watched with disbelief as the flop brought a king of diamonds, to pair the one I held in the hole as well as the one I wore on my wrist. It had to be a lucky omen. With no money left, I could not bet; but Seats Three and Four were still in contention, and Three bet $5,000. Four folded. With only two of us left, and no more betting possible, Three enquired politely, 'You gotta pair?' I rolled over my K-7. 'I gotta better kicker,' he muttered, and revealed an A-K.

I was familiar with the drill. What you do now, with the odds so heavily stacked against you, is rise ritualistically from your seat, and prepare to make a graceful exit as the rest of the flop is rolled. The fourth card was a black eight, making no difference to either of us. I was in the course of picking up my assembled detritus – cigarettes, lighter, half-drunk Coke – when the dealer burnt the final card and turned a seven. I had fluked two pairs, and was back in business. To a gratifying roar from the crowd, who love a lucky underdog, I sat right down again and started stacking my surprise $9,000. Seat Three grunted in dismay, but otherwise remained expressionless.

At this stage, however, even $9,000 wasn't going to get me too far. I had to repeat my little trick, pull off another private miracle, to be back in this thing with any chance of survival. And my chance came almost immediately. For the first time in the tournament, a peep at my hole cards revealed every Hold 'em player's dream hand: a pair of aces. The fact that both happened to be black somehow made them look even stronger. My position was not too good, only four to the dealer's left, so I made a tactical decision. Don't give your hand away by raising the maximum; build the pot with a modest raise, by their standards, if not mine; and if any other player thinks you're fishing and raises back, as the strong often do to the weak at this stage, put the boot in with a maximum re-raise.

So I called the big blind of $600, raised it by a mere $1,000, and waited to see what happened. Sure enough, everyone folded round to the dealer's left, who was already in the pot for his enforced 'small blind' of $300. He called the extra $1,300, looked at my stack, and raised another two. The 'big blind' and the man on my right folded. It seemed almost obligatory, given the style of play, to sit and pretend to think for a moment. I fingered my chips, publicly recounted them and sighed, hoping to feign weakness. Then I pushed the whole lot into the middle. I had called the small blind's raise, and bumped him $5,400.

Now it was his turn to think. He began to count his stack, and I began to speculate on his hand. Thus far, I guiltily confess, I hadn't really bothered, knowing that as yet I held a better one. Were he to call, however, the flop could change all that. Also to his advantage was the fact that there could be no more betting, as I was again all-in. Five-four, he decided, was worth the small dent it would make in the twenty-some thousand in front of him. He called, and showed me an A-Q of diamonds. When I replied with my two black aces, the buzz around the table seemed to indicate, with some displeasure, that they were going to be stuck with me for some time yet. Slow-playing aces is the height of either cheek or idiocy.

The flop brought a black queen, giving my opponent a

useless pair, and the last thing I wanted to see: two small diamonds, giving him four to a flush. This time I did not rise to my feet – I was, after all, still winning the hand – as an irrelevant seven of spades came up. The fifth and final card, on which my future would be determined, was . . . the ten of diamonds. He had defied odds of 4–1 and made his flush. My bid for the world title was over.

As gracefully as I could, but utterly crushed within, I gathered my belongings and quit the scene. There was a smattering of applause from the crowd; but the other players merely got on with the business, quite unmoved to see the amateur get his just deserts. The Moll, my personal cheer-leader, greeted me with the news that Bobby Baldwin and, yes, Johnny Moss, had gone out before me. That was a start on the road to spiritual recovery. Had I beaten my personal overnight target of coming higher than a hundredth? I'd been too absorbed to keep track. A check at the tournament desk, in the company of the *Daily Telegraph*, revealed that I had been eliminated in ninetieth place.

'Ninetieth in the world,' said a friendly stranger from the homeland. 'Well, that's a higher world ranking than any British tennis player.'

I hadn't quite thought of it that way. This stranger had cheered me up wildly, more than enough to be bought a drink. David Spanier duly noted the comparison, while doubting its accuracy; with no means at hand of checking it for publication, I urged him to swallow his better judgement and go for it. What else I said I quite forget, as I slumped into an exhausted, drunken meal, during which my disappointment perceptibly turned into elation as people persuaded me that this had been a more than decent performance for a novice. At some point I must, I suppose, have wondered aloud: 'Does this make me the best poker player in Britain?', for that is what I was quoted as asking in the next day's *Daily Telegraph*. It prompted no less an organ than *The Times* itself, heedless of international time zones, to telephone me in the middle of the night and request a personal account of my 'triumph'. I could have done without the interruption to my slumbers, but the word 'triumph' made amends.

Financially, I was back to square one. Even my initial $200 had gone down the chute with that flukey flush. But I could recall few past excitements in my life, private or professional, to compare with the thrills I had just been through. Astute as ever, the Moll pointed out how tough it would be for me, in future years, to visit Vegas in May without playing in the World Series. It was another thought which had not yet occurred to me – still fretting about those ten thousand dollars – but I knew immediately that she was right.

Just *how* right neither of us would know for another month or so – by which time we had stayed in Vegas long enough to see Johnny Chan retain his world title, then headed back through the darkling gloom of the Heathrow flight path to the even darker gloom of literary London. Until next year's World Series of Poker, which seemed a very long way off, I would have only the Tuesday Night Game to sustain me.

3

Shut Up And Deal

♥ ♣ ♦ ♠

Throughout our childhood, my brother and I were repeatedly told a cautionary tale from the youth of our otherwise unimpeachable father. On the troopship back from the war, the end of which he had spent in East Africa, twenty-seven-year-old Major John Holden of the Lancashire Regiment lost £50 playing poker – *fifty pounds*, virtually everything he had managed to save throughout his long years away. Our mother, whom he had married in 1940, would still turn pale at the memory.

Though ours was a family which enjoyed weekend card games, poker was thus strictly discouraged. We played all the usual English childhood games, some of them involving modest wagers: Hearts, Racing demon, Newmarket, Canasta, and many different types of patience. But above all my parents were dedicated amateur bridge players, who pored over the Sunday bridge columns and played in weekly penny games to the ends of their lives.

One weekend in the mid-1970s, when I was visiting them in Lancashire, my mother grew very impatient with my ineptitude as her bridge partner. I was always overbidding, flouting what few conventions I understood, and generally letting the side down. 'I don't understand it,' I remember her saying. 'You have such good card sense.'

Thus did my secret leak out: I had got involved in a weekly poker school in London, and it had ruined me for all other card games. Bridge especially. I overbid all the time simply because I didn't want to be dummy. What was the point of a game where you didn't get to play? And, I had to confess, I didn't much enjoy games where I had a partner. Poker players like to be their own man, in charge of their own destiny, unreliant on partners, conventions and other bourgeois refinements of good, honest, gambling games. Poker is the ultimate monument to the anti-Musketeer code: Every Man For Himself (and be sure, while you're at it, to kick the other guy when he's down). For all these reasons, poker players tend to make weak bridge players, and vice versa.

It was little use quoting Somerset Maugham, though he was the unlikely *locus classicus* on this issue. In a short story entitled 'Cosmopolitans', Maugham has one of his world-weary old clubland codgers splutter: 'You talk of your cricket and baseball, your golf and tennis and football. You can have them. They're all very well – for boys. Is it a reasonable thing, I ask you, for a grown man to run about and hit a ball?

'Poker's the only game fit for a grown man. Then, your hand is against every man's, and every man's is against yours. Teamwork? Who ever made a fortune by teamwork? There's only one way to make a fortune, and that's to down the fellow who's up against you.'

At the time, this wasn't quite the point, as my father's youthful transgression was trotted out yet again. But I could see a wistful gleam in his eye as he asked me what kind of stakes we played for. Was I sure I could afford it? Who were the other players? Was I good enough to avoid total ruin? For the ten remaining years of his life, not a parental visit would go by without my father asking me how the poker was going. I got the distinct impression that, had he not feared my mother's wrath, he would have asked to be dealt in.

The poker game about which I told my dad that night, and in which I still play every week twenty years later, is known to its *habitués* as the Tuesday Night Game, under which name it has something of a reputation around the poker clubs of London. Over the years, the stakes seem to have grown even faster than inflation. But they have always been, as they should be, enough to hurt – enough to make you fret about your mortgage, your car payments, the school fees, the tax man. In 1970, fresh out of university, newly embarked on a career as a trainee journalist, and newly shacked up with a young lady (later my first wife) called Amanda, I got hurt all right. The first time I played in the Tuesday Night Game, I did *not* tell my father, I lost £100.

It was an action replay of his dread return from the war. *A hundred pounds!* To the deputy Watford correspondent of the *Hemel Hempstead Evening Echo*, it was more than a month's pay, before tax – a sum of such enormity that I had to write a post-dated cheque and leave at once, causing only marginally more embarrassment to myself than to the man who had brought me along.

And who was he, this corrupter of British youth, this shuffling Svengali, this finessing Fagin, ever on the lookout for a new Artful Dodger? He was my literary hero, one of Britain's sharpest post-war poetry critics, a poet and novelist himself, a man I thought I was proud to call my friend. I had met him in 1968, as his self-appointed campaign manager for the Professorship of Poetry at Oxford University, where I was then editor of *Isis*, the student magazine. We lost the election comprehensively, but remained pals. As our friendship grew, however, A. Alvarez and I soon discovered that we would rather talk poker than poetry. And we would much rather play poker than talk about it.

Al had been playing in the Tuesday Game for a decade when he suggested that I come along one evening. The prospect, frankly, terrified me. I hadn't played poker since Oxford, where I had never had enough money to graduate to the major league. I was still penniless, newly married, and a poker rookie. But this was a man's world, and I was too green to admit to being a boy. The game rotated around players' houses, and this week was due to be held in Hampstead Garden Suburb, at the home of a man called Bernie. It was duly agreed that Al would pick me up at 7.30 p.m.

I spent the day exploring the minutes of the last meeting of Watford Council's public health committee with mounting trepidation. When the *Echo*'s news editor came on the line to ask where my story was, I had to confess that I had been unable to locate one. Nonsense, he said, there were a dozen to every page if I knew what to look for. In my heart I knew it was true: I was as bad a Watford correspondent as I was a poker player. At knocking-off time I drove slowly back to London praying for divine intervention.

At seven o'clock it seemed to materialize. I answered the phone to hear Al saying, with some irritation: 'Bernie's just slipped on his front door step and broken his collar-bone.'

'Oh, dear,' said I, with a huge internal sigh of relief. 'So the game's off, then?'

'Hell, no. We're looking for somewhere else to play . . . How about your place?'

And so it came to pass, an hour or so later, that this motley crew of rogues and vagabonds began to arrive at my front door. One particularly large American terrified me so much that I heard myself asking him the ultimately daft question of someone who has just sat down at your kitchen table: 'Did you, er, find your way here all right?'

'Sure,' he replied genially, 'I used to visit Reg and Ron in this street.' Thus did I discover that the Kray twins, the most notorious villains of Britain's supposedly Swinging Sixties, were my ex-neighbours. Or, to be more precise, their molls were.

The evening passed in a blur, my one memory being the moment Amanda popped her head round the door, only to withdraw it smartly when the Krays' pal grunted: 'Who's the dame?' Suffice it to say that I survived. But don't ask me how. I suspect the boys took pity on me, an arrant amateur whose humble home they had hijacked, and who was now pathetically stammering yes, please, do finish up the few scraps left for the household breakfast. I have thus never reckoned this my real début in the Tuesday Game. It was the following week at Bernie's house, our host's head safely propped up by a neckbrace, that I lost the hundred quid. That was the beginning and end, for a while, of me and the Tuesday Night Game, though it did prompt a memorable exchange between myself and my supposed friend Alvarez. Feeling a need to absolve him from embarrassment, I sent the great critic a little verse:

> *I lost, but I learnt how not to bid;*
> *I say that, Al, with perfect candour.*
> *But don't forget it was thirty quid*
> *Next time you see the fair Amanda.*

Back, by return post, came the reply:

> *Thirty quid is far too much,*
> *Beyond the little woman's ken,*
> *Her mind intent on meat and such.*
> *Take my advice: divide by ten.*

Through the early 1970s I paid infrequent, heart-in-mouth visits to the Tuesday Game, preferring a less daunting apprenticeship in another London poker school. It was comprised, as every weekly game should be, of the most disparate collection of people – largely, in this case, media folk like myself, gathered together by an unlikely pair of music critics.

Readers of upmarket arts pages might be surprised to hear that Stephen Walsh and Dominic Gill, though very different in character, were both card-sharps of the highest order. It was from these two, and their friends in publishing, journalism and television, that I really began to learn about odds, bluff, nerve and sharp practice generally. We played all kinds of weird and whacky poker variants, many involving wild cards – anathema, I now know, to purists. Twenty years later, Gill can still remember the details of a particular hand of 'Prostitute', a game whose very name I had forgotten.

The entrepreneurial streak which made Dominic a good poker player has since held good in the mainstream of his life; the author of several musical tomes, such as the definitive *Book of the Piano*, he is also the publisher of *Loot*, a hugely successful newspaper composed entirely of classified adverts. The more academic Stephen, meanwhile, has long been a lecturer in the music department of University College, Cardiff; as an overworked and underpaid father of four, he has had to put his poker days behind him. Like my father, however, he still develops a wistful glint in his eye when I talk about my Tuesday evenings.

The group eventually broke up as people's lives moved on. When Stephen got married, Dominic suddenly became the owner of his Notting Hill flat, venue for most of our games; upon discreet enquiry, I was disappointed to find that this was a regular financial transaction rather than a poker debt. By now, however, I had started my own Friday game, of which the musical diaspora formed the core. Through them, and word of mouth, another unlikely *mélange* of human flotsam began to gather around my North London kitchen table each week. One of them, so I was told, worked in a betting shop. An untidy-looking youth with lank, greasy hair, he was the only one who pulled grubby bunches of tenners out of his pocket, rather than a cheque book, when required to settle his debts. One Friday he happened to be the first to arrive, and I actually had to engage him in conversation for the first time in the two years or so I thought I had known him. I lost a lot of money that night, stunned by the revelation that he had never even set foot in a betting shop. He worked as a statistician in the Cabinet Office.

At the time I was writing the diary column of the *Sunday Times*, then a rather grand spread occupying the entire back page of the paper's front section. Although my week's real work was done by Friday night, I was obliged to appear in the office early next morning, to see my page 'off the stone' – or through the wonderfully tactile ink-and-metal printing process which has now, alas, given way to newer technology. This required me to be more or less awake on Saturday mornings, though not necessarily in sharply creative mode. Given any host's perennial difficulty in ending a poker game, as the winners count their chips and the losers open-endedly plead for 'just one more hour', it rather suited me to play all night Friday and go straight to work from the game. If I looked a bit baggy-eyed, the horny-handed printers would chuckle knowingly; as a reason for substandard performance in the chain gangs of real life, poker has a high masculine approval rate.

Even my editor, Harold Evans, took a surprisingly indulgent attitude, not least because he, too, fancied himself as a bit of a poker player: 'I've won money off Art Buchwald, you know.' This tacit complicity continued five years later, despite somewhat higher stakes, when I became Evans's assistant editor, in charge of features, at *The Times* – and by now a committed Tuesday Night regular. The Wednesday morning version of the editor's daily conference, which expected me to be bubbling with ideas, took on a particular charm from Week One, when I nodded off during a discussion of the European Monetary Fund. Gradually the entire (and all-male) editorial board would know to refer their enquiries to my assistants on Wednesday mornings, leaving me to doze quietly in the corner, contributing only occasional cries of 'Fold!' or 'Raise!' – a Features Editor with all the authority of Alice in Wonderland's dormouse.

After years of avoiding the dread Tuesday Night Game, it was in 1978, with a ninth-place finish in the British Open Poker Championships, that I had achieved the breakthrough in self-confidence I needed to become a regular. The first British Poker Championships were held in a casino called Cromwell's, in Birmingham (and also turned out to be the last, as the place was closed down the following year). I travelled up from London by train – playing seven-card stud, naturally, all the way – with the nucleus of the Tuesday Night Mob as then constituted: a poet, a painter, a philosopher and a playwright. The jeweller, estate agent and, er, financier were arriving separately by car.

We foregathered in a numinous underground cell, a designer Hades of deep pile and green baize, all stone-cold sober at Saturday lunchtime. The London pros hugged the walls and crept into corners to avoid recognition; the amateurs were easily recognizable as the simple, affable souls who came up to introduce themselves, offered to buy you drinks, even wished you luck – and, of course, as the only participants who actually put on the green eyeshades handed out by the management. The event was preceded by an auction, in which players could buy each other, or indeed themselves, with the prospect of a fat percentage if they purchased a winner. The pot had passed £2,000 by the time the auctioneer introduced one potential champion as 'Babyface'; this intriguing character had been purchased by some fool for £105 before I realized it was me.

For two days and nights we fought it out, though the overnight side-games in the Grand Hotel made the tournament prize money look like peanuts. In the Vegas manner, the Grand had cut room rates for poker players that weekend – a decent but foolish gesture, in view of the fact that most of the pots contested in my palatial Buckingham Suite could have bought the entire joint. That weekend saw a Cabinet reshuffle and the Prince of Wales's thirtieth birthday, but neither was exactly a matter of heated debate. Everywhere you went – in the bars, the elevators, the smoke-filled cloakrooms – all you heard was poker talk, usually from losers.

It was the first time I learnt another perennial poker truth: that memorable hands, no matter how long ago they were played, are always recalled in the present tense. 'So I have trips on the flop. Naturally, I raise. This idiot calls, stays with me on Fourth Street and flukes his straight. I mean, what can you do against luck like that?' I also learnt to see through two amateur truisms which a spell as a professional will quickly disprove: that losing is always the fault of the cards, never the player; and that the person who beats you is either lucky or a fool, usually both. These broken braggarts will swear off the game for life, then within hours will be asking you where the action is. They are all life members of the Obsessive School of Poker Players, who live by Nick the Greek's memorable motto: 'The next best thing to playing and winning is playing and losing.' It would not be long before I joined their ranks.

Much Tuesday Night machismo was at stake in Birmingham. By winning our side bets on who came highest, I also won a tad of the respect I needed to hold my own back in London. Since the British championships, apart from my three-year spell in America, I have been a pillar of the Tuesday Night Game, watching many another come and go. In my head, and those of five or six others, the word Tuesday is now synonymous with poker. Nothing, but nothing is allowed to get in the way of the game. Invitations to Buckingham Palace have been turned down because they fell on a Tuesday night. Even my more distant friends know never to invite me over on a Tuesday evening, or indeed to telephone too early on a Wednesday morning. Tuesday night, for veterans of the game, is the still point of our turning world.

Members unavoidably absent have been known to calculate time differences and ring in from all corners of the globe, around midnight UK time, to find out who is winning and losing. I once called in from the Falkland Islands, but that was just showing off. So was the guy who kept the line open from Zimbabwe because he wanted to play a hand blind.

Perhaps the most celebrated example of the Tuesday Night syndrome was the day Al Alvarez was mooching around in a Hampstead bookshop, surreptitiously moving copies of his new novel to the front of the display shelves (and Norman Mailer to the back), when a voice behind him interrupted with, 'Aren't you A. Alvarez? I'm a great admirer of your work.' Al, who does not number height among his leading characteristics, spun round guiltily to find himself confronted by a spindly giant whose face he immediately recognized as that of one of his great heroes, the pianist Alfred Brendel. It transpired that they were neighbours. Al's joy could scarce be confined when the great Brendel proceeded to announce that he and his wife would be delighted, nay honoured, if the Alvarezes would join them for dinner on . . . let's see, it's a busy month . . . the *Tuesday* after next? It was the sternest of tests, but Al passed it, declining this most coveted of invitations with all the grace he could muster.

It would make a better story if the dinner had not then been switched to the Saturday, and the two couples become firm friends. But to Al, perhaps more than to any other player, Tuesday nights were sacred. He would spend the day quietly at home, clocking up a few hundred words on his current *oeuvre*, before taking a swim in Hampstead Pond and then sneaking a couple of hours' sleep to ensure that he arrived at the game daisy-fresh. Not a whiff of alcohol would pass his lips for a good twenty-four hours before the proceedings, let alone during them. A much less self-disciplined person, I became so irritated by Al's Olympian approach to Tuesday nights that I would usually find some excuse to call him between 6.30 p.m. and 7 p.m. – 'Where's the game tonight?' 'Could you bring that copy of *Lolita*?' – just to ensure that I interrupted his nap. This, I believe, was the sole reason that the Alvarez family finally joined the twentieth century and invested in an answering machine.

There was an awkward moment in 1982–3 when Al was offered a job hosting a weekly television programme and I was approached about a weekly chat show on BBC Radio, both to go out live on *Tuesday* nights. This presented a stern dilemma. Dinner parties were one thing; but the chance of some easy regular income – merely thinking and talking rather than the dread task of writing, akin in both our minds to breaking rocks – was a tough one to spurn. After lengthy joint deliberations, we begged leave before the following week's game to raise a procedural point of some importance. Amid cries of 'Shut up and deal', we asked if the game could possibly be held on *Wednesday* evenings for a trial period of six months or so (which, of course, happened to be the trial periods of both our programmes). After an appalled silence, a lone voice said simply: 'But, Al, it's the *Tuesday* Game.'

For a while that seemed to settle the matter. But Al and I had a pre-arranged ace up our sleeves. Both of us managed to lose a containable amount that night – not, I have to say, the most difficult of tasks – and were able to plead at the end that the game now risked losing its two plumpest pigeons. That made them think. Amid much huffing and puffing, a show of hands narrowly and reluctantly voted to try Wednesday for a while. It would in fact make no difference at all to the lives of the other players, all total layabouts who might as well stay in bed all day Thursday for a change. Knowing, however, that to us it was life or death, they made us sweat for the privilege. On the second week of the new game, as the players took their seats, Al thoughtfully announced: 'You know, it seems a lot longer from Wednesday to Wednesday than it did from Tuesday to Tuesday.'

When, inevitably, both shows (or, to be precise, their presenters) were duly killed off six months later, the Tuesday Game immediately reverted to its sacred night – with one blissfully short changeover week, when Al had to wait for his weekly fix only from Wednesday to Tuesday.

Meanwhile, I had made an accounting breakthrough of lasting significance. In the early 1980s, along with many others lucky enough to lead expense-account lives, I was the proud recipient of junk mail offering me an American Express Gold Card. With it came a compulsory bank account carrying an overdraft with no questions asked up to £10,000. Now, a Gold Card was at the time something of a status symbol; but I had no particular need of another bank account, especially one bound to drag me yet further into debt. Unless . . .

AmEx, though until now they did not know it, were to prove the secret of several years of sustained success in the Tuesday Night Game for their new Gold Card holder. After a brief and evasive visit to the relevant bank manager, in which I stressed only my lofty status in society as an assistant editor of *The Times*, I secretly dedicated this new and otherwise useless account entirely to my poker fortunes. By removing the amounts of money involved from the arena of real financial life, they suddenly became – as they should be – entirely theoretical. If, when contemplating a terrifying raise, your thought processes entangle it with the parlous state of your current account, equating it to the imminent payments on the house or the car, you are going to make an incorrect decision. Similarly, a pot won should not be regarded as a new Savile Row suit, or the down payment on a Cadillac. Poker may be a branch of psychological warfare, an art form, or indeed a way of life – but it is also merely a game, in which money is simply the means of keeping score.

This was another early lesson which I had to learn the hard way, with or without the magic bank account. I made the big mistake once, and once only. One Wednesday, after a satisfying win of some £800 or so, I took the day off to go shopping. Suddenly my study at home sported a handsome new Chesterfield sofa, from which I could behold a sleek new television and video (then very much a luxury item). The material satisfaction they provided was doubled when I could point at them and say, to myself or anyone else, that I had won them at poker. I could even tell you, to this day, which player had generously 'paid for' them. It may be gratifying, to the poker rookie, to go around pointing at things and saying, 'John Mudd paid for that by check-raising into my full house aces'; but it is an extremely bad habit, even for the un-superstitious. I had less than a week to enjoy my new video-watching zone before losing even more the following Tuesday night, and finding myself embarrassed about payment.

This, however, is a world in which there are no excuses, especially if you were a big winner the week before. Poker players, with good reason, expect winnings to be ploughed back into the poker economy – preferably, what's more, back into the school in which they were won, rather than down the road at some other mug's game. No mercy was shown, quite rightly, and the shining new bank account plunged into the red – which, for a high-rolling Gold Card account, was of course a punitively high-interest zone. Far from being given the sofa, the television and the video, I now realized I had paid for them myself, and I had paid over the odds.

That lesson learnt, the separate bank account began to pay its way. If I won, it was other people's money with which I was playing the following week, which gave me the freedom to take a few calculated risks, and a psychological advantage over the players from whom I had won it. If I lost, I would punish myself by suffering the interest rates rather than paying off the debt with real money from my real account. The ploy worked so well that, after a while, the poker account boasted more money than I could possibly lose in one game, or even two. So the odd self-indulgence was then permitted. An impromptu vacation takes on several extra dimensions of pleasure when you can sit beneath the Caribbean sun and raise your banana daiquiri in a toast to the mugs who have paid for it all.

It was not always thus. A dose of good luck will generally be followed by a stronger dose of bad, and there are naturally some nights on which one plays better than others. It is a statistical and fiscal truth – it has to be – that the same seven or eight people cannot play poker together every week for twenty years unless the money runs back and forth in fairly equal proportions. Sure, over the years a few stalwarts have fallen by the wayside; but that is a matter of regret to the survivors, who miss their company as much as their cheques. Ours is essentially a social game, where people are there to enjoy themselves, to escape from the mundane realities of the rest of their lives.

Spouses and/or girlfriends are generally – well, they have to be – most understanding, even to the point of being grouped among life's mundane realities. Alvarez once made this very point on the radio, with predictably disastrous consequences. Plugging his poker book on a radio chat show, he began to explain how Tuesday Nights had taken on such a landmark role in his life. 'Well, at my age,' he said, 'there are few thrills left. I climb mountains, but reading, writing, even sex . . .' Listening on my car radio, I grew so anxious that I had to pull over. As is so often the case when a friend appears on radio or television, my anxiety about every nuance had me physically cringing with concern, even though alone, and incapable of concentrating on anything else. Despite desperate cries from behind my distant steering-wheel of 'No, Al, NO!', my buddy was reaching the disastrous coda I had feared. 'But on Tuesday Nights . . . well, I *know* I am going to enjoy myself, win or lose. What I'm trying to say is that Tuesday Night is the only *guaranteed* enjoyment left in my life.' When he got home, needless to say, Mrs Alvarez was not amused.

It was in fact the same, almost *too* shrewd Mrs Alvarez who once made a mathematical point which has since resonated through the lives of all Tuesday Nighters and their partners. 'What I don't understand,' she said meditatively, when yet another Hampstead dinner conversation had been irretrievably hijacked by the subject of poker, 'is how, when you crawl into bed at 5 a.m. on Wednesday mornings, you have either won £500 or lost £50. How come it's never the other way round?' It was the only time I have ever known Al swiftly change the subject back to the current state of Polish cinema.

Only the players involved will ever know the amounts which exchange hands. It is bad form to discuss them with any outsider, let alone reveal individual wins and losses. Sometimes people *do* get into financial difficulties, and the ultimate proof that ours is a social game is that one of the current winners will most likely help them out for a while. With some exceptions, such as my friendship with Alvarez, we do not much socialize outside the game, but nor are we total monsters within it. For me, the Tuesday Game is a form of psychological warfare which gives my wits some enjoyable and much-needed exercise well away from the rockface at which they must otherwise toil. Beyond ingenuity with the cards, and the eternal joys of deception, much of the fun lies in the elegant, often literary barbs which fuel the backchat.

The Bard, who popped up so aptly during the World Series, provides a host of useful taunts. When confronted by an awkward Alvarez raise, for instance, which I know must force me into a reluctant fold, I can make him sweat a bit first by intoning: 'Thou wretched, rash, intruding fool . . .' (pick up huge pile of chips, as if re-raising) '. . . farewell!' (put chips down again and surrender cards to the discard pile). Something too much of this, however, let alone a discussion of the new *Hamlet* at the National Theatre, and you can be sure that a losers' chorus will soon be yelling 'Shut up and deal!'

We may not be angels, but nor are we in the business of fleecing suckers. To sit down with a group who know each other inside out is a tough proposition indeed. Winning money off strangers is not what a game like ours is about, with the result that would-be players are heavily warned off, and only the most persistent allowed to take us on, at their pre-advised peril. Then, of course, we destroy them.

As Walter Matthau put it: 'The game exemplifies the worst aspects of capitalism which have made our country so great.'

It was in much this spirit, in the summer of 1988, that I reported back from Las Vegas to the Tuesday Game brimming with confidence – a quality so important at the poker table that for a few weeks I won effortlessly. The boys, only two of whom had ever tried their hand in Vegas, were genuinely impressed. I was ranked, after all, ninetieth in the world. Being the only Briton in the world championships, moreover, I insisted that I must – if only by default – be regarded as the British Number One. Any day now would surely bring my MBE for services to sport.

Everyone who came to the house was told of my achievement; fashionable dinner tables were forced to sit and listen to my heroic traveller's tales; like some Ancient Mariner of the green baize, I had to be restrained from bearding strangers in the street and burbling in the present tense about flops and finagles. Poker had become obsessive, and London's literary life seemed by comparison inordinately dull. Even though, for the first time in years, I was at a crossroads I should have enjoyed thoroughly, with one book newly published and the next already written, I was hopelessly downcast. As I set off on a round-Britain promotion tour, an ego trip of the order I would normally have relished, all I really wanted to do was head straight back to Vegas.

At the time, the Moll and I were renting a handsome but expensive house on the Thames in Chiswick. For two years I had managed to pay my share of the rent out of poker winnings. However, after half a lifetime on the UK property ladder, a much sounder investment than any stocks or bonds, unit trusts or privatization issues, I was sorely missing my footing. I had a large lump sum in the bank, earning paltry, taxable interest, from my half-share of the proceeds of the sale of my marital home. We were being endlessly frustrated in our attempts to buy the house we were renting, and faced the open-ended prospect of haemorrhaging money in rent. While discussing it all one evening, after yet another setback, I came up with an impulsive proposition to concentrate both our minds. Why didn't I just go down to Curzon Street, London's Glitter Gulch, and invest all my worldly goods on red at roulette? That way, we would either be able to pay over the odds for the house we wanted, or I'd be broke. At least we would know where we stood. The idea had an attractive, and terrifying, simplicity to it.

Now, the Moll is far from averse to a flutter. What's more, she understands the undulations of the gambler's mind – and is even prepared to live with them – far more level-headedly than any female I have ever encountered. But this fundamentalist approach quickly had her urging caution. She was not sure that either of our hearts was strong enough to survive the experience of that little silver ball bouncing in and out of red holes with my entire standing in the financial community at stake. OK, so she'd always had a soft spot for hoboes. But this was a sucker bet. It went against all my principles, which she had heard until she knew them by rote. Even if I won, she continued with some force, I would only want to double it again – and go on doubling until I lost. Why not practise, instead, what I preached: take the money – well, some of it – and set out on the road, for an experimental year, as a professional poker player?

It was an inspirational moment, much as if the road to Damascus had been rerouted through our kitchen. I would set out along it at once; and, like St Paul, I would write an account of the journey, complete with epistles home.

Bristol, Manchester, Birmingham, Norwich . . . as the book tour got under way, there were months of other inescapable commitments to get in the way of my new ambitions. Although I had already completed my next book, I had just begun five months' intermittent work on a television documentary to be screened that autumn. Luckily, the poker season itself goes somewhat dormant during the summer months – with the exception of the Diamond Jim Brady Tournament at the Bicycle Club, Los Angeles, during most of August. That one, alas, I would have to miss. The first major event of my professional poker career would have to be the European Championships, scheduled to be held in Malta in November. Until then I would have to accumulate myself a bank-roll by rather more conventional means.

So for the first time in three years I took a regular job, in the shape of a weekly newspaper column, just to remind myself how hideous the real world is. Meanwhile, I edited four extracts from my forthcoming book for serialization in a Sunday paper. Some occasional journalism, combined with a regular broadcasting contract with breakfast television, had my system signalling 'overload' as the Moll and I worked out the ground rules.

The capital on deposit I declared *hors de combat*. I was prepared to risk my own future, but not my children's. All royalties from my books and opera translations – two were soon due back in the English National Opera's repertoire at the London Coliseum – would be placed in trust to pay my alimony, life insurances, school fees, rent and other fixed outgoings. Any surplus would swell the joint fund set up to buy that house. These sums, at least, would be sacrosanct. But I had to have something with which to hit the road.

My final fling as a jobbing journalist earned me a little over £20,000, $20,000 of which was now officially declared my bank-roll. Out of what I could make of it, in the twelve-month period ending with the next World Series, it was formally decreed that I must now pay all travelling expenses and other incidentals in pursuit of my new career; any perks such as vacations; and, of course, I must earn my $10,000 entry fee for my next crack at the world crown. The global challenge would be twofold: to finish the year in profit, and to improve on my world ranking.

During the book tour I wore my King of Diamonds wrist-watch as a declaration of intent, immune to the appalled grimaces it provoked among literati. Then I set aside my journalist's green eyeshade, donned my poker player's, and got down to work.

4

Read 'Em And Weep

♥ ♣ ♦ ♠

The good news is that in every deck of fifty-two cards there are 2,598,960 possible five-card poker hands. The bad news is that you are going to be dealt only one of them.

The best news, however, is that you don't have to hold the best hand to win. The one dimension unique to poker, which sets it above and apart from any other game ever invented, is the element of bluff. By betting *as if* you are holding the best hand, by 'representing' strength, you can frighten every other player out of the pot and take their money without even having to show your cards.

This is true of no other game except life, with which poker has a great deal in common. Most human beings conduct their lives as a series of risks, some more calculated than others. They may not like to admit it, especially to themselves, but they bluff their way through life's complexities, both professional and personal, every day.

At least fifty, perhaps sixty million Americans play poker regularly, and as many as eight million Britons. Those are remarkably high percentages of each country's respective populations – many more adventurous spirits, to be sure, than go to some lengths to meet up once a week to play Monopoly or Trivial Pursuit, even bridge or chess. These teeming hordes, by definition, will be the kind of human beings nursing a *penchant* for risk, at work as much as at play, at home as much as outside it. Compulsive risk-takers tend to believe that they are more interesting, and often more successful, than their brethren who prefer to play life safe. Their passion for poker, often strong enough to outweigh their domestic or professional responsibilities, is a direct reflection of the way they tend to conduct their other relationships, and of the values by which they choose to live their lives. It is not a question of *whether* they bluff, but when, how often, and how well.

You could say that there are 2,598,960 possible permutations of each of us, which we marshal according to current demands or needs. There is nothing too reprehensible about this. Humankind, as the poet said, cannot bear very much reality. Men and women do not have to be overtly competitive to regard life as a complex adult game, whose rules are there to be bent or even broken. So why do so few of them care to admit that deceit and chicanery are part of their everyday stock-in-trade – at work, at home, even when alone?

Like weak poker players, they fight shy of self-knowledge. They fail to see, for instance, that some of the people they bluff most consistently, and effectively, are themselves. In life as in poker, there are 'tells'. At the table a player may tend to scratch his ear, or fiddle nervously with his ring, if he is bluffing; or, more subtly, a hollow note in his betting pattern – a raise too aggressive or a call too timid – may betray him. He probably will be the last person to recognize this: it is axiomatic that no poker player, unless of course he is double-bluffing, is aware of his own 'tells'. Once his opponents have isolated them, however, such giveaway habits are worth a great deal – at least as much as they are to the husband or wife who can say, 'You were never a very good liar'.

Whether he likes it or not, a man's character is stripped bare at the poker table; if the other players read him better than he does, he has only himself to blame. Unless he is both able and prepared to see himself as others do, flaws and all, he will be a loser in cards as in life.

These mysteries are one reason why the game of poker has always appealed so strongly to literary and artistic types, who see in it many makeshift metaphors for the human condition. At first, as in countless Westerns, poker was used merely as an index of male virility; in art as in life, it was no surprise that cheating was rife, with most games ending in confrontation and violence. Already poker was being used as a measure of character, but usually to flesh out or glamorize the brutish side of human nature. The Marshal would occasionally sit down with the boys – poker was too quintessentially American to be *all* bad – but even Wyatt Earp's presence could not guarantee a straight game.

Since the early twentieth century, however, writers have used poker less as a *macho* motif – James Bond, after all, played bridge and baccarat – than as an analogue of life's vicissitudes, to be accepted and borne with good humour. In the eternal struggle of the little man, the loser, against unforgiving odds, there was a rich seam to be mined by Damon Runyon, James Thurber and their inheritors. The 'Broadway' school of poker writers, commuting between the offices of the *New Yorker* magazine and the Algonquin round table, found its true voice in the gallows humour of the doggedly pessimistic poker player, not so much self-deprecating as cheerfully masochistic. 'Read 'em and weep', still one of the great poker incantations, amounted to their manifesto. Built into the genre was a resigned expectation of failure, a wry acceptance that the odds are stacked against you – that life, like the fall of the cards at poker, is basically out to get you, though that will never stop you attempting to take it on.

All this really means is that these fine writers were lousy poker players. They may have been right about life, but they were wrong about poker. The eternal poker pessimist, like the compulsive gambler, *wants* to lose. Losing makes him happy, confirming as it does a wide range of his most deeply-held beliefs: that life is a bum rap, that his true qualities will never be appreciated by a cruelly misguided world, that he is generally undervalued and misunderstood. He will go on cheerfully defying the odds under the endearing delusion that there is more to himself than meets the eye.

The poker optimist, by contrast, is either a cheat or a liar; but his sheer self-confidence will give him a much better chance of winning. If he tells you that he *always* wins, he is certainly a liar; the odds cannot work for all of the people all of the time. The poker *braggart*, therefore, is a surefire loser. Listen to him, humour him, gasp at his tales of derring-do, and you can be certain to win money off him next time you sit down together.

The player who admits to losing will usually halve the true amount, for a variety of reasons. If he is relaying the news to his wife, or to any other non-poker playing dependant, it is because they are unlikely to agree that the money was lost in a good cause, namely the pursuit of more; that it was bad luck, rather than his own ineptitude, which wreaked the damage; that the attempt was worth its consequences, namely a severe and immediate cut-back in the domestic budget; that there is no inconsistency between his freedom with money at the poker table and his meanness about it in every other department of his life; and, above all, that he has a good chance of winning it back next week. If he is recounting his ill fortune to fellow-players, however, he will have lost just enough to moan about the fickleness of fate without the embarrassment of admitting incompetence.

The player to watch out for is the one who is honest about the scale of a big loss. Though he will say he has been on a losing streak for months, he will usually have won more yesterday than he lost today. If he compounds his confession by telling you that he is a lousy player, out of his league – that he is thinking about giving it all up to become a hermit, perhaps take holy orders – you can be sure that he is an excellent player who will be flush again before long, probably at your expense.

But beware, above all, of the man who simply tells you he broke even. *He* is the big winner.

Which one was I? In my time, usually without realizing, I had been all of them. If my odyssey were to have any chance of success, it was clear, this must be as much a voyage of self-discovery as a mere quest for a crock of gold. The road from amateur to professional status would involve frequent pit-stops for self-examination and overhaul.

Amateurs tend to play with chums, to enjoy the acerbic backchat as much as the flow of the cards, to find all sorts of reasons for playing poker other than the mere prospect of profit. This is social poker, once-a-week poker, where the boys use various excuses to get away from their wives, their homes, their offices, the real responsibilities of their everyday lives, and act *irresponsible* for a while. It adds to their sense of excitement to be playing not with Monopoly money but with real money, the commodity which otherwise makes their lives such misery. This means that they will play hands they shouldn't, cheerfully defy the odds and attempt impossibly stylish bluffs, because they are there to enjoy themselves.

To the pros, this is kids' stuff. Unless trying to sucker them into a game, they will laugh these home-towners to scorn. One of the leading professionals once told me: 'I can be anywhere in the world; and if I don't know your face, I know I can beat you.' Profit is their only motive, their only criterion when making decisions. Poker may be a more congenial business than most, but to professionals it remains precisely that – a business. A forceful reminder of this is the briefcase and legal pad some of them bring to the table, to keep detailed notes on profits and losses for subsequent inspection by the Internal Revenue.

Though their inhabitants have much in common, the modern game of poker thus encompasses two very different worlds, with sharply different attitudes to the game, and wholly different styles of play. It can be either a relaxed social activity, an escape from the mundane routines of the workaday world, or a way of making a living. The jump from one to the other – the leap of faith I was about to make – looked wider and more frightening than anything attempted by Evel Knievel. One week, poker is an escape from work; the next, it *is* work. This was a metamorphosis of such proportions that, before attempting to survive it, I had to talk the whole thing through with someone who would understand. Beyond the Moll, who had already done her stuff, there remained only the Crony.

Alvarez was only too happy to be prised away from his work-in-progress to a free lunch at his local trattoria. It was, after all, a Wednesday, the day which all Tuesday Night regulars abandon to mundane chores like clearing their desks, borrowing money, writing their wills, being bought lunch – anything which might help them adjust to whatever happened the night before. It was thus in our poker-lagged Wednesday mode – still, despite a few hours' sleep, in a turmoil of withdrawal from last night's game – that I told the Crony of my plans. In the same breath he responded that I was mad ('They'll eat you alive'); that it was a great idea ('I wish I'd thought of it myself'); and that he was unspeakably jealous. Most of his subsequent sentences began: 'The real point about poker is . . .'

Over the hors-d'oeuvres: 'The real point about poker is that it's serious. If you make a mistake as a writer, you can catch it next day on the word processor, or later when correcting the proofs. If you still miss it, no-one's going to notice, anyway . . . But if you make a mistake when playing poker, you're going to get hurt. Poker is fun, but it's also a serious business. Writing ought to be serious, but it is never fun.'

Over the main course: 'The real point about poker is that it's company . . .' Over the dessert: 'The real point about poker is the art of calculated risk . . .' And so to coffee and liqueurs: 'Ah, fuck it. Shut up and deal!'

Though himself the author of one of the best descriptive books ever written about poker, *The Biggest Game in Town*, Al's valedictory advice was to re-read 'the Bible' – alias Herbert O. Yardley's indispensable classic, *The Education of a Poker Player*. This, more than any other, is the book which has altered poker players' lives, the Crony's among them. 'When I first picked it up,' Al recalled, 'I was ignorant not only in the ways of poker. I also had the deep ignorance which goes with excessive education. I had been through the most high-minded academic mill: a monastic public school, Oxford, Princeton, Harvard. I had read a vast number of books and written a couple of my own. Yet in practice I was naïve to a degree which still, nearly thirty years later, makes me blush . . .'

He broke off in mid-paragraph to remind me that I, too, by remarkable coincidence, had attended the very same monastic public school, and the same university. I had also written a few books, though I probably hadn't read anything like as many. Alvarez was a professional literary critic, and an amateur poker player, when first someone lent him a copy of Yardley in the late 1950s. As soon as he had read it, the pendulum began to swing, as he later confessed in the introduction to a British edition:

> *I had a marriage I could not handle, a childish desire to be loved by the whole world, and an equally childish conviction that everything would turn out all right in the end. When it didn't I was – simply and profoundly – outraged. I had lived my life as I had played poker, recklessly and optimistically, all my cards open on the table and nothing in reserve. I had also assumed that everybody else was doing the same.*
>
> *I was wrong, of course, and it was about the time I began to realize this that I first read Yardley . . . What applied so cogently to money in a poker pot applied equally to the feelings I had invested in my disastrous personal affairs: 'Do the odds favour my playing regardless of what I have already contributed?' I knew the answer. The only puzzle was why I should have discovered it not in Shakespeare or Donne or Eliot or Lawrence or any of my other literary heroes, but in a funny, vivid, utterly unliterary book by an American cryptographer and intelligence agent. It seemed absurd, disproportionate to the efforts I had made. But it was the beginning of my real education and I sometimes wonder if that was what Yardley, too, was implying in his title. In the end, what he is describing is not so much a game of cards as a style of life.*

Herbert Yardley was a proto-James Bond. A First World War State Department maverick, the man who cracked the Japanese diplomatic cipher, he was subsequently hired by the Chinese as their foreign adviser on codes and counter-espionage. The latter part of the book tells of his adventures while under threat of assassination by the Japanese; smuggled incognito around

China, he teaches his interpreter seven-card stud with one hand while trapping a Nazi secret agent with the other. But the book's real delights, and its essential wisdom, lie in his account of his early days as the protégé of James 'Monty' Montgomery, who ran the only clean saloon in the Indiana frontier town where Yardley was born in 1889.

> *I saw the big Swede, Bones Alverson, a poor weather-beaten corn farmer, bet the last of his farm against a tent-show, only to die three minutes later, his cards clutched in his hand – a winner. I saw Jake Moses, a travelling shoe salesman, lose ten trunks of shoes. I saw a bank teller trapped with marked money he had stolen from the bank; a postmaster go to jail for shortages at the post office. Horses, cattle, hogs, wagons, buggies, farming implements, grain, sawmills – all sold to play poker . . .*

Yardley alternates these tales of doom with ruthless analyses of the hands which wrought them – evolving, under Monty's stern instruction, a set of exceptionally rigorous rules for winning. 'I do not,' he growls, 'believe in luck, only in the immutable law of averages.' In Alvarez' gloomy summary, which he now commended to me as a creed for the trials ahead, Yardley's Law amounts to: 'Assume the worst, believe no-one, and make your move only when you are certain that you are unbeatable or have, at worst, exceptionally good odds in your favour.'

But the Crony added a dispiriting footnote:

> *This is an ironclad system when playing against weak players who do not understand the odds or the endless finesses possible. Against strong players who know the book and have the necessary discipline it may be less immediately effective,*

since they will recognize your tactics and simply fold when
you bet. That, however, is not Yardley's business. He was a
purist writing for embryo purists, concerned only with the rules
and values of classical poker.

Classical poker was not exactly what I had in mind, intent as
I was on developing my skills at Texas Hold 'em and its immediate family. Like any aspirant artist, however, I needed to
brush up on my classical background before attempting some
contemporary improvisation. Poker may be about character,
self-knowledge, even the psychopathology of interpersonal
relationships, but it is also about odds. Before embarking on
my journey, I had to drum the figures into my subconscious.
The reader intending to come along for the ride would also
do well to ponder the following immutable laws.

In each thousand deals of regular five-card draw poker, the
ranking hands will appear with the following frequency:

No pair	*503 times*
One pair	*422 times*
Two pairs	*47 times*
Three of a kind	*21 times*
Straight	*3.9 times*
Flush	*1.9 times*

So how likely are you to pull a straight flush? Try looking at
the figures another way.

In a full deck of fifty-two cards there are ten possible straight
flushes in each suit, making forty in all four suits. Divide that
into the 2,598,960 hands available in the deck, and you will
figure that you have one chance in 64,974 deals of receiving
a straight flush, whether a high one or a low one. The odds

against your being dealt a straight flush are therefore 64,973:1.

The odds against holding all the other combinations after being dealt five cards can be reached by the same method. For the uninitiated, this table is a mathematical affirmation of the ranking of poker hands – a visual aid as to why a full house beats a flush, a flush a straight, and so on.

QUANTITY IN DECK		ODDS AGAINST
4	Royal flush	649,739:1
40	Straight flush	64,973:1
624	Four of a kind	4,164:1
3,744	Full house	693:1
5,108	Flush	508:1
10,200	Straight	254:1
54,912	Three of a kind	46:1
123,552	Two pairs	20:1
1,098,240	One pair	1.25:1
1,302,540	No pair	EVENS

Five-card draw is the original, to many the 'pure' poker game, the one you saw the heavy mob playing in all those Westerns. It is still favoured in many home-town games, though less played by professionals because it provokes less action. There are only two betting rounds: one after the deal, and another after players have changed as many cards as they choose. The odds against improving on the draw are also highly instructive:

CARDS KEPT	CARDS DRAWN	IMPROVED HAND	ODDS AGAINST
Ace on its own	4	One pair	4:1
	4	Three aces	63:1

Ace with king	*3*	*Pair of Ks or As*	*3:1*
One pair	*3*	*Two pairs*	*5.25:1*
	3	*Three of a kind*	*8:1*
	3	*Full house*	*97:1*
	3	*Four of a kind*	*359:1*
	3	*Any improvement*	*2.5:1*
Pair with ace	*2*	*Two pairs*	*8:1*
	2	*Trips*	*12:1*
Two pairs	*1*	*Full house*	*11:1*
Triplets	*2*	*Full house*	*15.5:1*
	2	*Four of a kind*	*22.5:1*
Four-straight (open-ended)	*1*	*Straight*	*5:1*
Four-straight (inside)	*1*	*Straight*	*11:1*
Four-flush	*1*	*Flush*	*4.5:1*
Three-flush	*2*	*Flush*	*23:1*
Two-flush	*3*	*Flush*	*96:1*

The strongest play, of course, is to 'stand pat' – to change no cards, while your opponents pull to their pairs, their straight and flush draws. As they look gloomily at hands which haven't improved, or see their pair of tens turn into trips, they have to consider whether you were really dealt a five-card hand – a straight, a flush or a full house. Or have you merely decided that this is the moment to run a bluff?

You bet the maximum, to put the pressure on them. Most, if not all, will fold. If someone raises, then the pressure is back on you. Did you merely keep two pairs, in the hope of bluffing a pat hand? If so, you probably have to fold. Were you really dealt a natural straight? If so, how many cards did the raiser change? Just the one? Can he really have pulled his 4.5:1 shot – the flush? When he called your original bet, was the pot offering him the right odds to take that chance? If so, is it now offering you a profit proportionate to the investment he is forcing you to make?

Luckily you are spared these agonies. The player who has pulled trips is the only one hesitating over his move. There is little incentive for him to raise, as you would then be sure to re-raise. As he wonders whether to call your bet, he is past pondering the odds, and deep into other important considerations. Has he ever seen you caught in a bluff before? Have you been behaving cheerfully or gloomily, noisily or quietly, during the game so far? What is your current financial state, both on and off the table? What does he know of your character: your courage, your vanity, your fears? What kind of state is he in himself?

The reading of character, especially your own, is one of the central skills, fascinations and appeals of the game of poker. At its best, it is a form of psychological warfare in which the mind is stretched to extremes. This is the kind of poker played in the movies, where the development of the game itself is usually less important than its effects on the characters of players under pressure. To purists, as a result, even the best poker movies are fatally flawed.

Rarely able to see beyond the poker player as *macho* man, Hollywood has tended to fall foul of a communication problem of its own making. The game of poker may have passed into the Anglo-American language securely enough to have taken a rich array of phrases with it – 'passing the buck', 'upping the ante', 'ace in the hole', 'poker faced' and so on. The average movie audience might even know that a straight flush beats a full house. But the studio bosses have never felt able to assume that the punters were poker players as experienced and subtle as most of the screenplay writers in their employ.

Even a picture as enjoyable as *A Big Hand for the Little*

Lady (1966) is thus robbed of credibility. Henry Fonda, apparently out of his depth in a big-time poker game, collapses of a heart attack in the middle of the hand on which he has staked everything he has left in the world. The entertaining scam at the heart of the story subsequently requires his wife, Joanne Woodward, to take the hand over to the bank as collateral for a loan. Once she has been allowed to take her cards away from the table, the serious poker player will return to his game without watching further. (In Britain, to make matters worse, nervous distributors retitled the film *Big Deal in Dodge City*, although the action clearly takes place in Laredo.)

Even more disappointing is the big hand at the end of Norman Jewison's *The Cincinnati Kid* (1965). Otherwise a classic account of a poker hustler's life, as authentic as the Richard Jessup novel on which it is based, the film blows itself away with a climax still laughed to scorn in card rooms the world over. Not only does the winner, Lancey Howard, alias 'The Man' (Edward G. Robinson) play the hand extremely badly, but the odds against its occurrence would certainly lead the Kid (Steve McQueen) to conclude that the game was fixed.

Playing five-card stud, at which each player receives one concealed card and four 'up' cards, with a betting round between each, Lancey manages to pull a queen-high straight flush against the Kid's full house, aces on tens. The odds against *any* full house being beaten by *any* straight flush, in a two-handed game, are 45,102,784:1; the odds against these two particular hands coinciding are stratospheric. Given that the Kid's full house contains tens, and that one ten is already in his opponent's hand, the chances that *both* of these hands will appear in one deal of two-handed five-card stud have been calculated at a laughable 332,220,508,619:1 – or well over 300 *billion*:1 against. If these two played fifty hands of stud an hour, eight hours a day, five days a week, the situation should arise about once every 443 years.

Even that is a generous assessment, for it is highly unlikely that experts would play these two particular hands to a conclusion. If the player with the pair or trips bet his hand properly, the man with two or three cards to a straight flush can only recognize the hopeless odds against him and fold. After the deal the Kid has an ace on the board and one in the hole. Howard has an eight of diamonds up and a queen of diamonds in the hole. Even if he called the Kid's first bet, which is unlikely, the third card has him looking at a pair while his own hand has not improved. Once the Kid bets again, Howard *must* throw his hand away and hope for a better one, even if he has to wait another 443 years.

In poker terms, the hand is a joke. But even in movie terms, there is no evident moral in the way things turn out. Why should Lancey Howard retain his position as 'The Man'? He hadn't been 'living right' any more than the Kid. Would there be another time, another place, for the Kid to have a crack at him? We are not encouraged to think so: the movie ends with a general sense that the Kid has ideas above his station, that he had his once-in-a-lifetime opportunity – his brief, shining moment – and failed to seize it.

However woolly its celluloid ethics, this is an idea with which poker players *can* feel comfortable. The arbitrariness of things, the lack of justice in an unforgiving world, the fact that sometimes you win even when you *know* you've been living wrong: all these are familiar feelings to players prone to superstition, poker romantics incapable of accepting the fall of the cards as a simple matter of accident-prone mathematics.

During an academic correspondence on the hand in the *Poker Player* newspaper, the columnist Michael Weisenberg came up with two further implausibilities. First, any poker player who had aces full beaten by a straight flush would be sure the deck had been fixed. 'Why didn't the Cincinnati Kid start screaming foul when he got beat? If *you* got beat like that, would you just walk away shaking your head, muttering to yourself "Well, them's the breaks?" I doubt it.' Second, if Howard and Lady Fingers [the dealer] *were* in cahoots, they would have cheated the Kid much more cunningly. 'They'd give the Kid three of a kind, and have Howard fill up two pair on the last card. Or they probably wouldn't even go that strong. They'd give the Kid something like three sevens, and Howard a pair of nines, one of them in the hole, and have him catch the third nine on the last card . . .' By all means read the book, concluded Weisenberg, by all means enjoy the movie, 'so long as you pretend it's three sevens being beaten by three nines'.

Best of all, to my mind, the winner would have *bluffed* the loser out of the climactic pot. Howard's betting would have intimidated the Kid into folding his full house, then rubbed salt in the wound by revealing a much inferior hand. This is how noble spirits can be broken at the poker table. And this is the real purpose of the game: to use whatever cards are on display to bend other wills to your own. No poker player ever earned any respect simply by pulling good cards; the best players are those who can turn indifferent hands into winners through psychological mastery of their opponents.

It is at this level of play, in the Tuesday Night Game as in the movies, that the cards and the chips can seem mere incidentals, no more than the equipment needed to play the game. Money is just the method of keeping score. At this level, as the Crony and I had agreed for twenty years, poker is fun.

But there are grave dangers inherent in enjoying the game this much. Each hand can become a separate challenge to the ego, to an individual's ingenuity – especially in a Tuesday-style Dealer's Choice game, where the varieties of poker played keep changing, each dealer in turn choosing the game in which he is strongest. The player on this kind of a high will come to regard it as a sign of failure rather than of strength, or of self-discipline, to fold. However many hands he may win, he is going to wind up a loser.

It is a simple poker truth, often forgotten by the amateur enthusiast, that the winner is not the player who wins the most pots. The winner is the player who wins the most money.

The consistent winner will play fewer pots than the man who has come for some action. He will develop a thick skin against the irritated mutterings of the other players, some of them his friends, who will shower him in increasingly hostile abuse – relieving themselves of the blame for their own failure by blaming him for his success. He will not feel *embarrassed* about winning, and thus obliged to give the losers a chance to win it back by making some loose calls. However high his stack grows, he will continue to exert the self-discipline to wait, wait, and continue waiting for the right hands, the right odds, the right position, the right situations.

Above all, the consistent winner is the man of strong enough character to grant the most reluctant poker truth of them all: that poker can be – at times, perhaps, should be – *boring*. Nowhere in the world is it more boring than in the London clubs, where my career as a poker pro was doomed to begin.

2

Today one of London's most elegant, high-rent districts, Mayfair began life as one of its most notorious. On the site of Marble Arch once stood the gallows of Tyburn, where public hangings drew huge crowds until late in the eighteenth century. Five hundred years before that, in the reign of King Edward I, the area first took its name from the lusty May Fairs held each year to raise money for the inmates of the nearby Leper Hospital.

What began as a simple week-long cattle market grew by the reign of King James II into a fortnight of revelry that attracted, among other types, 'all the Nobility and Gentry of the town'. Queen Anne's puritanism cleaned things up a bit, but the fairs were back in full swing by the time of King George III – until the Earl of Coventry, who lived nearby, complained about the noise. His Lordship's intervention appeared to signal the end of a 500-year tradition of 'good eating, drinking and merry-making, gambling and revelry of all kinds'.

But the best traditions die hard. Two centuries later Great Brookfield, the thirteen-acre patch of grassland where these revels were held, lies buried beneath the streets of contemporary Mayfair, scene of a stylish twentieth-century version of these ancient rites. Here, within a classy square mile of each other, are London's most elegant gaming clubs – Crockford's, Aspinall's, the Clermont and the Ritz, which play host to the world's highest rollers. This is where Beau Brummel held court, where Princes of Wales exercised their *droit du seigneur*, where Lord Lucan got away with murder. Within these pleasure palaces, in palatial surroundings, you can eat some of the best food in London before trying your luck at roulette, blackjack or *punto banco* (the European name for baccarat). Each night, beneath the timeless splendour of crystal chandeliers, substantial fortunes are made and, more likely, lost.

Gaming *à l'anglaise* was the brainchild of William

Crockford, the father of modern bookmaking, who won so much money from the nineteenth-century English aristocracy that some noble families are said to be suffering still. Born in squalor in 1775, the son of a fishmonger, Crockford was blessed with an uncanny ability to calculate odds faster and more accurately than any of his contemporaries. So lucratively did he milk this talent that the 'Father of Hell and Hazard', as he became known, was soon opening gambling clubs all over London – most notably Crockford's itself, on St James's Street, in 1828.

In this elegant Regency mansion the cream of high society dined sumptuously before lining Crockford's pockets with yet more of the family inheritance. By the time he gave up the management of his club in 1840, after ruining a generation of upper-class Englishmen, it was said that Crockford retired 'much as an Indian chief retires from a hunting country where there is not enough game left for his tribe'.

In a century and a half, you would think that humankind might have learned a thing or two, not least that the odds at all casino games are weighted in the house's favour. But man's capacity for ignoring this simple truth, which first beggared some of England's great aristocratic families 150 years ago, saw British casinos end the 1980s turning collective profits approaching £250 million a year – or about 20 per cent of the 'drop', the money changed for casino chips.

In Thatcher's Britain, where the acquisition of money has become a civic duty, it is no longer the indigenous population which keeps the roulette wheels of the London casinos spinning. The clubs may still preserve an old-fashioned upper-class English lifestyle, but it would seem that the English these days have less gamble in their souls. Oil-rich Saudis, Lebanese, Turks, Greeks and Malaysians have now joined, if not supplanted, their ranks.

The profits of Britain's gaming clubs would be much higher if they did not have to contend with a welter of absurdly stiff regulations. Casinos are not allowed by law to do anything to 'encourage or incite' gambling; they can provide no entertainment, are banned from advertising and can serve no liquor at the gaming tables, which are open only from 2 p.m. to 4 a.m. each day. The law forbids casinos to pay for (or 'comp') high rollers' hotel rooms, a practice taken for granted in America. They are not allowed to accept credit cards, and can cash cheques only by prior agreement.

Above all, first-time gamblers in London come up against the notorious 'forty-eight-hour rule' – designed, like most of Britain's repressive gaming laws, to prevent impulse gambling. Mother England is anxious to keep a Bob Cratchit, as he carries his meagre wages home, from nipping into a casino *en passant* in the forlorn hope of doubling them for his Christmas shopping. Britain's Gaming Board, the Government's statutory watchdog, is equally concerned to stop old Ebenezer Scrooge from having one too many over a five-star dinner, and abandoning the habits of a lifetime with a quick flutter at the nearby tables.

To play at any of these clubs, therefore, it is necessary to visit the premises in person, sign a membership application, and wait forty-eight hours before being allowed to return and place your bets. The only way to avoid the wait is to arrive as the guest of a club member. But he or she must be a bona fide friend – not, as in the old days, your obliging hotel concierge or some such surrogate – and is required to remain on the premises as long as you do. Once secured, membership lasts for life, unless the club's management finds a reason to bar you. As they are not obliged to furnish you with any explanation, winning can often prove as good a reason as any.

Most clubs charge an initial membership fee of anything from £100 to £500 – though this will be graciously waived, and 'honorary' membership bestowed, if you look like a high roller. How much do you have to wager to earn this coveted title? If you need to ask, as they say, you can't afford it. Mayfair estimates vary, but you would probably have to be placing at least £4,000 on each roll of the roulette wheel, £4,000–£8,000 on each hand of blackjack, or £15,000 per 'coup' at *punto banco*. Another London definition of a high roller is someone who would hazard £100,000 in an evening, or £500,000 over a weekend, without blinking too conspicuously. All the clubs have upper limits – in the region of £1,000 per single number at roulette – but the action in London is, per person, the biggest in the world.

At the beginning of my career as a poker pro, this sweeping statement included poker. A nucleus of a dozen or so very rich, very serious gamblers got involved in an open-ended, heavyweight game of 'lowball' – seven-card stud, where the *worst* hand wins – whose reputation went around the world. Americans, Scandinavians, Frenchmen and Germans queued for admission to a charmed circle who were winning and losing in six figures every evening. Pots of fifty, sixty, seventy thousand pounds made even the toughest Vegas pros prick up their ears. So the game, in its turn, began to travel around the world, adding to the attractions of the roving poker circuit.

It began life between the Barracuda Club and the Victoria Casino, then the only two London gaming clubs which hosted poker games. Nowhere in Mayfair's 'golden mile' can you play poker these days – unless you are the Sultan of Brunei and his chums, playing real-life Monopoly for Park Lane properties, in which case they'll lay on a dealer in the *Salle Privée*. Otherwise, as in Las Vegas, British gaming club managements prefer the highest possible return on their square-footage, which means half a dozen more roulette and blackjack tables where the card room might have been. In Vegas, the house takes a percentage of each pot; in England, the clubs charge the players 'table money' by the hour. Either way, they make much less than they do from the casino games – in which players risk their money against the house, attempting to defy unfavourable odds, rather than merely passing it around among each other. Poker takes a revisionist line on the redistribution of wealth, which few casino managements do much to encourage.

I had played at the Victoria, on and off, for years. Many of its *habitués* were refugees from a much smaller, even seedier North London club called the Lyndhurst, raided and closed down when one rash member was reported for running an illegal book on the premises.[1] The vagaries of the British gaming laws had seen the Vic, too, open and close, under constant changes of management, but somehow the Edgware Road card room survived. In the mid-1980s it had come under threat from a flash new establishment called the Barracuda, at Number One Baker Street, whose card room had chandeliers and comfortable chairs. Both began to lay on tournaments. But the players, compared to those with whom I convened every Tuesday, were as solid as the Rock of Gibraltar and as tight as, well, the various unprintable similes they favoured.

They were pleasant enough – though there were plenty of exceptions to that rule, too. The general air of sleaziness seemed to provoke constant rows about the rules, even the occasional fistfight, not to mention the famous night one man

---

[1] Several years later the Lyndhurst has been refurbished and reopened under new management, enjoying a welcome new lease of life.

was thrown out for misbehaviour and soon returned with a 'shooter'. All this was entertaining enough, if only the poker had been too. But here there was little of the table talk which animated the Tuesday Game, less of the genial camaraderie, and none of the risk-taking which made every hand a potential goldmine. The clubs were about the 'rocks' playing the 'nuts' – the style of poker which I had hitherto found ineffably boring, but to which I must now reluctantly adapt. My first attempt to do so cost me £600 – at the time $1,000, or 5 per cent of my bank-roll – when the sheer tedium of it all saw me risk my all with the best available full house. I should have known that the old codger on my left, who hadn't played a hand all evening, would of course be holding four tens.

My second attempt was little better. Priding myself on my professional self-discipline, I would fold hand after hand and watch these anal-retentive vultures beat each other up. Occasionally the hand I folded would turn out to have been a winner; it is agony to throw away 6-9 and see the flop come 6-9-9. But this was another new trick I had to learn: hand in hand with grace under pressure must now go composure at missed opportunities. You were right to throw away 6-9, I had to keep telling myself; you were under the gun, and you would have been wrong to play it.

After an hour or two of this, especially if you've been dealt a gallery of dismal cards all evening, weak hands can begin to look stronger than they really are. Any feeble little sequence – a 5-6 or a 6-7 – can suddenly seem rather exciting, especially if you can limp in late and cheap. King-Queen, when it arrives, looks like a million dollars, even though you know it ranks way down in the textbooks. When the flop comes K-Q-10, you feel inclined to invest your entire stack, on the off chance of the full house coming up, even though you suspect that the noisy Lebanese across the table is already holding the A-J which would give him the top straight. When it transpires that you've read everything right, and lost all your money, you quit the game in shape for nothing but a long winter's hibernation.

There were occasional tournaments at the Barracuda, which brought in the best English players from the regions, and ensured livelier side-games in which the action was more open and fierce. The handful of Brits who frequent Las Vegas would suddenly materialize, and boost my morale with playful remarks about my impressive world ranking (not to mention my King of Diamonds wrist-watch, which was fast becoming my trademark). I even managed to win some money: £300 for a fifth-place finish in a forty-five-strong tournament, and £1,200 with a run of cards in a £5-and-£10 Hold 'em side-game, which got my bank-roll back to quits. But the rest of the time it was the same old faces taking half an hour over £50 calls, slurping their tea at the table, and munching steak sandwiches as they waited for a solid hand. The most fun I had all summer was being fleeced by my sons, three Cincinnati Kids in the making, during our vacation with the Moll's family on Cape Cod.

Poker, I was beginning to realize, doesn't sound right when played in English accents. The regional clubs, I knew from dismal experience, were no better than London. The huge reserves of self-discipline required simply weren't worth the effort; you could spend a whole evening waiting for a pat hand, and wind up with a profit of a few hundred unthrilling quid. The lowball game was way out of my financial league, and was now taking the handful of dashing, high-octane players out of the Hold 'em school. It was an effort to get to the clubs; you had to wear a jacket and tie, and you often had to hang around for a seat in a game in which you didn't want to play. The London clubs made the Tuesday Night Game seem as exotic as Monte Carlo.

Dr Johnson may have said that 'when a man is tired of London, he is tired of life', but Boswell doesn't mention the old boy playing in the £50 stud game at the Vic. My first policy decision as a pro was to visit the London clubs only when no other opportunities were on offer; to treat the Tuesday Game as dangerous fun; and to seek my real fortune abroad. It was time to dive into the shark pool.

5

On Tilt

Get too rough with a pinball machine – let's see that silver orb *really* bounce off those flippers – and it will unilaterally end your game, flashing beside the score a solitary word of explanation: TILT.

The same thing, in poker parlance, can happen to people. No matter how experienced, losers will often get rough with themselves, letting their knowledge of the odds slump into wishful thinking. A guy losing a thousand bucks will often throw away two more trying to win them back. He will climb half out of his hole, get bashed over the head again, and fall back down to find himself stuck even deeper. The word about the desperado playing this way is that he's 'on tilt'.

The word will quickly pass all over town, and people will flock towards a slice of the action. Say 'Tourist on tilt, table five, the Horseshoe', and watch the rail grow thick and sweaty with human greed, with people who'd pay heavily for a stake in the ritual slaughter.

There were to be times, during my year as a poker pro, when I would need my own built-in spirit-level, to check the precise angle of my current self-awareness. Was I a fit person to be in charge of my bank-roll? It is a question a poker pro must keep asking himself, watching for signs of deviation from the norm. As my career began, I felt less like a Rock of Gibraltar than a Leaning Tower of Pisa.

It was perhaps, in retrospect, a mistake to launch myself on the international poker circuit in a fortnight which saw two books published under my name on opposite sides of the Atlantic. But there was nothing to be done about it. The first great event of the new season, the European Poker Championship, was scheduled for Malta in mid-November – a few days after one biography appeared in the United States, a few days before the next was published in Britain. Having already mucked both publishers about somewhat, I was in no position to seek further changes in their schedules. Nor was the subject of one of them, HRH The Prince of Wales, likely to oblige me by postponing his fortieth birthday. So the championships were already a week old when a bleak British November morning saw me check in at Heathrow to the news that Air Malta's flight to Valetta had been indefinitely delayed by fog.

I was on tilt within seconds. Airline officials seemed none too perturbed that a delay of more than two hours might make me miss the starting time of that evening's crucial Texas Hold 'em tournament. The more I ranted, the more they smilingly fed me cheap champagne, with the kind of look they reserve for spoilt little rich kids. I was travelling first class – courtesy of the Tuesday Night boys, who would also be picking up my hotel bill – but the forces of nature have scant respect for the colour of money. As I kicked my heels in Heathrow's Rembrandt Lounge, obsessively recalculating time differences, flight speeds and the distance from the airport to the casino, the real world was too much with me.

It stayed there after the fog had cleared, the flight taken off three hours late, and my fingernails been chewed all the way to Malta – where, even before I had made it through the airport, I immediately encountered a face familiar from the London card rooms, heading home bereft of everything except advice: 'You'll never find the place on your own, Tony. Take a cab. And don't eat the cheese. Everyone's got food poisoning.'

How was the action? 'Pretty good . . . fifty Americans here, those of them still standing.' It was already past 6 p.m., the scheduled starting time for the Hold 'em tournament. Would I make it? 'Oh, I shouldn't worry about that. They never start on time. But the side-action's much better, anyway. If you can pull some cards . . .'

Now he was on the verge of telling me his bad beat stories. Pleading tiredness and haste, I ran for it. As the tiny cab bumped around the Maltese capital with agonizing slowness, I scanned the brochure for the umpteenth time and remembered its stress on the 'dress code' standard in most European casinos: jacket and tie for gentlemen, no shorts or blue jeans, no T-shirts or trainers. The management reserves the right to refuse admission to anyone improperly dressed. So I would have to check into my hotel and change before heading for the casino, delaying me even more. There was no way I could make the tournament.

When I finally stumbled into the Dragonara Casino at 9 p.m., exactly three hours late for the off, the first person I saw was an old friend from Vegas, Frank Cutrona, Eric Drache's Number Two in the Golden Nugget card room. Here in Malta, Frank was tournament director. I told him my sorry tale of London fog, Maltese rain and frustrated ambitions.

'No sweat, Tony,' he grinned. 'The boys are still out eating. We won't get nothing going till at least ten.'

'Is that right?'

'You bet. You've even got time for a satellite if you want one.' I sure did. 'And there's a free buffet over there. But, Tony, don't eat the salad. There's a lot of food poisoning about.'

In the far corner I spotted some familiar British faces from the Victoria and the Barracuda – and some less familiar ones from America, judging from the loud voices, baseball caps, T-shirts and blue jeans. Unused to playing poker in jacket and tie, I felt absurdly overdressed.

'Hey, Frank, what happened to the dress code?'

'Oh, you know what the boys are like, Tony. They disposed of that on Day One.'

I should have known. Americans abroad *en masse* tend to get things their way; if they are poker players, you can be sure that they will. The forty-seven-strong American contingent here, I soon learnt, were not content merely with busting the dress code and dictating the tournament times. The cashier's office at the back was awash with arguments about exchange rates, Maltese pounds and the Government's way of insisting that every transaction be recorded on scraps of paper. The dining room's complimentary buffet had been rejected in favour of 'a good thick steak, buddy, well done, and easy on the gristle'. Bottled water was coming in in crates: 'Ah've been throwin' up all day. Must be the salad dressing.' Even European poker tournament rules had swiftly yielded to the Vegas way of doing things, as had the few Maltese with the nerve to try a modest wager or two in their own casino. One group in evening dress had just been bumped off a blackjack table by a high roller in track suit and sneakers, who proposed to play every seat himself, for $1,000 a hand. That was when the rain started to come through the roof.

The Dragonara Casino, in the little town of St Julian's, was originally built over a century ago as the summer palace of a Maltese bigwig, the Marquis Scicluna, to celebrate his elevation to a papal knighthood. Surrounded on three sides by the

Mediterranean, its fluted Grecian columns and ornate pediments must have hosted many a stylish nineteenth-century summer house party; but it was never meant to host winter poker parties, and its flat stone roof was scarcely designed to survive a century of Maltese rain.

'Hey, what the . . .' yelped the Yank as a large dollop of rainwater, swiftly followed by a larger chunk of plaster ceiling, landed on his number three blackjack hand, which just happened to be two juicy queens to the dealer's eight of clubs. But his Maltese hosts were well accustomed to such emergencies. Without saying a word, three large men in evening dress simply lifted the table and moved it six feet to the left, returning wearily for the high roller – who sat in stunned silence as they picked him up bodily, chair and all, and moved him to his relocated Seat Three with fixed and patient, seen-it-all smiles.

'Sir?' enquired the dealer, who had managed to make his own way to his new position.

'D'you think I'm going to pull to two queens?' yelled the American, as if Maltese insolence knew no bounds.

Carved in stone above the entrance to the casino (and no doubt post-dating the Papal Knight's summer evenings) was a Latin inscription proclaiming DEUS NOBIS HAEC OTIA FECIT. What odds would I get against being the world's only poker pro with a classical education? No bets were taken as I offered a literal English rendering – 'God created these delights for us' – and then translated into American: 'Gambling is the brainchild of the Lord'.

This seemed to go down well enough with everyone except the casino staff, who were used to knowing more about gaming operations than their customers, and the long-suffering employees of the adjacent Dragonara Hotel, who were evidently used to keeping fairly regular hours. Even the 'born-again' contingent, surprisingly numerous among the world's leading poker players, are accustomed to ordering a pastrami on rye – wherever they may be in the world – at four o'clock in the morning. And they expect it to arrive before noon.

For reasons no-one can satisfactorily explain, poker is essentially an act of darkness. By which I mean that it feels odd to play poker in daylight. To professionals abroad, bereft of the timelessness of Las Vegas, and unused to casinos which close at dawn, it thus becomes the norm to play by night and sleep by day. One interesting socio-medical consequence of this is that it is very rare, on either side of the Atlantic, to hear a poker player complaining of jet-lag.

The Maltese, however, are not used to visitors ignoring their sunshine – especially in November, when this rare commodity is the only conceivable reason for visiting their island (which otherwise put me in mind of a giant, disused Second World War aircraft hangar). The Dragonara, therefore, had made no provision for the ordering of blueberry pancakes between the hours of midnight and 6 a.m. As this is one of the few time intervals per day when most American gamblers feel the need for such refreshment, many of them had already checked out of the Dragonara, used their 'funny money' to rent 'dipshit' automobiles, and hied themselves off to the homeliness of the distant Hilton – where, even in Malta, waffles at dawn raise few eyebrows. The Brits, of course, were happy where they were, partly because the bacon, eggs and chips were still available at lunchtime, and partly because the Dragonara was significantly less expensive.

Nor were the locals accustomed to people who expected the Big Fight to be relayed live by satellite from Las Vegas – a matter of far more moment to these itinerant Americans than their presidential election, which happened to be taking place the next day. These particular visitors, in their New World innocence, even expected the phones to work.

One portly, perspiring American abroad had evidently had it with the food, the water, the weather, and the combined facts that the casino didn't open till 6 p.m. and that there was nothing to do all day – not to mention the cards he'd been getting. 'Hey, buddy,' he hailed a passing waiter, 'what's the toll-free number for Air Malta?' There were European sniggers at such colossal colonial naïvety. First off, even if they knew what toll-free numbers were hereabouts, the telephones weren't working within the hotel, let alone across the island. Then, even if you could get a line, you soon discovered that Air Malta is not the world's speediest airline when it comes to answering a telephone. It was quicker, really, to rent a car and drive to the airport, being sure to check the office's limited opening hours in advance. Several people had done all this earlier that very day, only to discover that there wasn't an airplane seat to be had out of the island all week. Not even in first class. We were all stuck there for the duration.

'Don't drink the water, Tony,' warned a familiar voice behind me. 'And take the ice out of your g-n-t. I've had the gutrot ever since I got here.' Roy Houghton, manager of the Barracuda card room, was here more as an observer than a player, spending his days on the tennis courts and his evenings familiarizing himself with how tournaments are run. The Barracuda was planning to stage a series of tournaments, climaxing in an All-England Grand Prix. But was this quite the place to see how things are done?

Terry Rogers, Ireland's leading bookmaker and a popular veteran of the poker circuit, had imported his biannual Irish Eccentrics tournament, to be held the next evening. For now,

as we waited for the American contingent to grace us with
their post-prandial presence, he was busy killing the time by
explaining the rules to all comers. Irritated by the arbitrary
American takeover of the proceedings, Terry had asserted
splendid Irish defiance by posting a list of twelve inflexible
rules, all coined in deliberate contravention of the way the
Yanks liked things done. He was currently reading the entire
notice over the public address system, to the bewilderment of
the indigenous Maltese roulette players. The last rule read:
'Terry Roger's decision is final, even if he is wrong.'

By 10.30 p.m. I was warily nibbling a slice of free buffet
bread (having been warned off the chicken by a passing Nord),
and carefully picking the ice out of my killer Coke, when the
arrival of the heavy mob finally signalled that the action could
commence. There had been, in the end, too few players to
make up a satellite. So tonight's buy-in would set me back
$500 out of the $2,500 I had allowed myself for this trip –
perhaps a tenth of the next highest bank-roll around, but I had
thought it wise to make a cautious start, and leave most of my
money at home. There was a long way to go to the next world
series, and I had yet to find my feet in the big league.

There were sixty starters tonight, making a prize pool of
$30,000. A seat at the final table, and a finish in the top nine,
would set me off on the road to profit. But the omens, in my
first international appearance as a pro, were not good; to my
dismay I was drawn at a table with two former world champions. I could tell from their cursory nods that they had seen
my face somewhere before, but couldn't remember my name
to save their lives. The need for awkward reintroductions was
prevented by the even later arrival of Eric Drache, who greeted
me with that wonderful familiarity of the poker circuit – as if
my presence here sooner or later were inevitable, and it was

just a few hours, rather than six months and ten thousand miles, since we had last seen each other. 'Hey, Tony, just got in? How ya doing?'

The game proceeded in fairly desultory fashion as the late arrivals, anxious looks on their faces, waited for their meal to settle down below with no adverse consequences. After half an hour my own stomach was just beginning to rumble when I found a pair of kings in the hole and a former world champion, 'Gentleman' Jack Keller, betting at me. Everyone else folded, so I decided to go for broke and raise Keller with everything I had in front of me. It set him all-in, too. 'Got a pair?' he asked, as the flop showed K-3-2 – ample confirmation that I was now holding the winning hand, even if he had started with a pair of aces. All his money was in the middle, so there would be no more betting. I was free to show my hand if I so chose. To me, Keller looked anxious lest I had one king, let alone two. Maybe he put me on A-K. I didn't care. I put him on a pair of queens or jacks, and cruelly waited until the dealer had rolled the final two cards – which offered no straight or flush possibilities – before flipping over my set of kings. With a resigned look Keller twirled two queens around in the air, let them fall to earth, and stood staring down at the green baize, in the time-honoured fashion of top players who can't quite believe that they've been busted out by an amateur.

Eric grinned down the table, genuinely enjoying my little moment of triumph. 'So, Tony,' he said, 'the lettuce is eating the rabbits tonight?'

'Hadn't you heard, Eric?' said I, carefully flashing The Watch as I scooped in the pot. 'I just turned pro.' We both knew the remark was aimed at the other players at the table, who had no idea who I was, or whether this was a joke.

'Pro, huh?' said one, on the look-out for information. 'Not hard to be a pro with hands like that.' On a look from Eric, I knew I should ignore this. But it was the first big moment of my new career, and I couldn't resist pushing my luck. 'Well,' I said in no particular direction, as I stacked my chips into satisfying skyscrapers. 'You gotta be there!'

There ensued a rather scary silence. But I was feeling more confident now, perhaps too much so, and a loose call soon saw me handing back too big a slice of the Keller thousands. That lesson learnt, I tightened up sufficiently to survive to the break, having seen off half the field (including Eric and enough other high rollers to start a distractingly big side-game). By way of celebration, I permitted myself to risk a plate of beetroot and onions. Another Coke further bolstered my confidence, though I absent-mindedly gagged on a stray sliver of ice. By 2 a.m., when the field had narrowed to two tables, I was one of only two Britons left alive, along with sixteen Americans, Scandinavians and Germans. But my stack of chips was dwindling fast, and the antes were rising.

Working out the odds at Hold 'em is simpler than at most other poker games, but I was still putting too much mental energy into it. My basic system is to figure how many cards can help you, then divide them into the proportion of the deck available. With a four-flush in hearts after the flop, for instance, you have seen five cards (the two in your hand, plus the three on the table). Of the forty-seven unseen cards, there are nine hearts left to make your flush. The chances against you are therefore 38:9 – which amounts to odds of 3:1, as you should hit your hand one time in four.

The complex systems employed by the pros make these odds even better. Poker boffins, for instance, calculate that a suited ace has a 34.97 per cent chance of becoming a flush on Fifth Street – which, expressed in odds, is a mere 1.86:1. Add in the three aces available to make another powerful hand, and your chances of winning obviously improve further. I have sat in on countless protracted arguments, mostly conducted on the backs of old envelopes, about the way these odds change between Fourth Street and Fifth Street; clearly they are better with two cards to come rather than one, but merely halving or doubling them is far too simple. Suffice it to say that my method – which offers a bleak 4.875:1 against filling an open-ended straight, and 8.25:1 against two pairs becoming a full house – is unduly pessimistic.

Which was just fine by me. When you're out of your depth, it's best to err on the side of caution. To the seasoned pros these percentages are second nature; to this rookie, never a natural at mental arithmetic, they were fast becoming an agonized distraction. The top pros can tell you the odds against being dealt the stronger hands, let alone their chances of improving as the game proceeds. Me, I had seen these figures in the back of various manuals, in indigestible percentage tables, and had come away knowing that a high pair was pretty damn good, and that A-K suited called for a major show of strength before the flop. What I hadn't yet figured was how to be dealt such hands. Playing more on gut instinct than higher maths, I finally busted out in fourteenth place – five off the money, but a lot better than I might have expected for my first pro tournament. Mug up on those manuals, and I might even have a chance.

Too tired and timid to play in the side-games, I contented myself with winning back my entry fee at blackjack before strolling through the delicious Maltese night to the sanctuary of my room. For a while I contemplated the rolling waves from my balcony, thought of my seaside upbringing, and wondered what my parents would make of a second son who had decided to turn professional poker player. Undoubtedly, I concluded, their vote would have gone to their older son, the accountant, who looked after other people's money as carefully as he handled his own.

Missing the Moll like an amputated limb, I read all night and slept all day, until some electronic Maltese miracle enabled the phone to intrude upon my desultory dreams. 'Hey, Tony, Eric Drache. That was a good performance last night. You wanna go eat?'

Among the diverse ranks of professional poker players, Eric Drache (pronounced Drake) is unique unto himself.

You can tell just by looking at him. Eric, for starters, is a snappy dresser, in a Wall Street rather than a western mode, where most of his contemporaries affect the casual, comfortable, usually rather sloppy clothes of the ex-hippy generation. He sports a pudding-basin Beatle haircut stuck in a Sixties time-warp. He is married to an English rose, the daughter of a retired Devon colonel, whom he enjoys escorting on pub crawls around Crediton. While Eric has been playing poker, anywhere from Las Vegas to Malta, Jane has won herself three university degrees (from Columbia and Berkeley) and now works in AIDS research in San Francisco. She is also, of course, a hotshot poker player.

Drache is a sophisticated, cosmopolitan man, with a taste for good food and fine wines. He travelled the world before poker gave him cause, always in the grand style of one to whom cash is just another commodity. All flights must be first class, all hotels five star, all meals embellished by the best wine beneath the cellar cobwebs, and protracted over a succession of exotic liqueurs. Eric is not, however, a materialist; his

Las Vegas home is surprisingly modest; he does not acquire priceless objects, except as gifts; he is acquisitive only about poker pots, and unfailingly generous whether up or down. Whatever the size of Eric's bank-roll from one day to the next, and it can fluctuate wildly, you can be sure he will either spend or risk every penny he has.

Like all the best poker players, Eric maintains a healthy psychological distance between his calculations at the table and his current financial standing in the community. Drache folklore fondly remembers the evening one such dilemma was interrupted by an urgent phone call from his wife, who had just been involved in a car accident.

> *'Are you hurt?' asked Eric.*
> *'No,' said Jane.*
> *'Is anyone else hurt?'*
> *'No.'*
> *'Well, that's all right, then.'*
> *'But I've done $1,500 worth of damage to the side of the car.'*
> *'So call the insurance.'*
> *'But $1,500 damage to our beautiful Jaguar!'*
> *'Honey, I'm stuck four beautiful Jaguars at this moment. Call the insurance.'*

Eric was born in Brooklyn in 1943 and raised in Carlstadt, New Jersey, where gambling appears to have been as urgent and early a priority to him as learning to walk and talk. As a toddler he was rolling marbles and flipping baseball cards; by the age of ten he was playing penny poker. His father had bet horses, but was no longer around to tell young Eric that poker was a game of skill. He played it 'like a shoot-out, without reference to the other hands . . . I'd play against open aces without even a pair, let alone a flush draw . . . I just played.' For years, 'regular as clockwork', he lost his allowance every week.

In high school he took a part-time job to finance his gambling. Then, as now, Eric was always what he calls 'a good creative financier . . . I borrowed from people, but I always managed to pay them back.' He won a chemistry scholarship to Rutgers University, but had dropped out by the day of his final exams, which found him at the racetrack. Come the draft, he was trained as a military policeman and sent to Vietnam, where he sat in an air-conditioned hotel playing poker day and night. 'I was attached', as he puts it, 'to the Pot Limit Seven-Card Stud Division.' Like Richard Nixon, who financed his first political campaign out of wartime poker winnings, Eric says he never had a losing day in the Services. 'I've never smoked, but I reckon I'm still owed about three million packs of cigarettes.'

It was in Vietnam that Eric finally read Herbert Yardley, and realized that poker had a lot to do with his strong suit, mathematics. 'Yardley showed me that if you have three clubs and don't catch one on the turn, you're about a 9:1 dog [underdog] to make the flush. It showed me that poker was a game of skill.' Back in New Jersey, he began to win. He scoured the state for private games, and continued to win. In time, he started hosting his own game, where he could win money as well as charging a rake-off from each pot. But he omitted to 'look after' the local hoods. They tipped off the cops, who one night watched the players go in, then came knocking at the door. 'The dumb girl who lived next door thought they were my friends, and let them in. Like all of a sudden, aged twenty-three, I had eleven friends who wore suits and black shoes!'

That cost him a $2,000 fine and six months in jail, where he further consolidated his notional status as a tobacco millionaire. A couple of years later, after outgrowing the action on his native East Coast, he borrowed $600 and took himself off to Las Vegas for a few days. Six months later he was still there, having parlayed it up to $70,000. He was still there two years later, struggling to pay off debts of $250,000. More at home on the gambler's eternal see-saw than anywhere else, Eric Drache has yet to return to New Jersey, and has long since realized that he never will.

So how long has he been in Vegas? This is one of the few figures on which Eric cannot be precise. 'I don't know exactly when I arrived. Probably somewhere in 1970 or 1971. But the dates don't mean anything, and I've no way of measuring time. What do I know whether it was 1970 or 1971? What difference does it make? It's all one long poker game.'

In those two decades many millions have passed through Eric's fingers, in both directions, won and lost. 'I guess the ratio now is 45:46 – you guess which is which.' For a while, by his own confession, he got disillusioned with poker and lost huge amounts shooting craps. Now he's back to the life of a highly-paid, full-time card-room manager, which pretty much means that of a high-stakes, full-time poker pro. The money he owes, and is owed, never falls below six digits, and Eric has a tough time keeping count. Tracking the figures involved is a job less for an accountant than an astronomer. All that really matters is enough ready cash on the day, at the raising of which he is an unchallenged genius.

Most leading poker players are bright, and many are witty; all are street-wise, though few could be called worldly. Eric is all these things, but uniquely among his peers he likes to apply his lively mind to the world beyond poker, whose very existence few of his peers even acknowledge. For a dedicated gambler, Eric is unusually inquisitive about his fellow man. He seems to see the world as some sort of giant fun palace, inhabited by endlessly fascinating creatures, about whom his judgements are generous to a fault.

If he has another fault, it is a constant failure to take his own advice. Though as shrewd about himself as about others, Eric just won't listen to his own better judgement. Blessed with a rare knowledge of his limitations, he is never happier than when exceeding them. He loves to quote a verdict passed on him by *Gambling Times*, when ranking him sixth in the world at seven-card stud: 'Drache's trouble is that he only plays with the top five.'

Two of them were in evidence when we finally made it to the casino, where Eric's electric energy was soon crackling around the room, trying to whip up a high-stakes game of stud, Hold 'em, anything. I preferred the relative tranquillity of Terry Rogers's Irish Eccentrics tournament, which would also involve me in a strictly limited outlay of $1,000. As he again declaimed his private rules, further to irritate the American contingent, Terry made the Europeans feel more confident, more at home. By the first break, for the second night running, I was again still 'alive' – always a happy index that you must be doing something right – and anxious to appease a friendly Californian at my table, who had just suffered a bad beat at my hands.

'How do you feel about your new leader?' I asked. The previous day had seen the election of a new American president, whose name had by now filtered through even to Malta.

'Hmmm?' he grunted, taking an angry look at my stack. 'You the tournament leader now?' He thought I was trying to be cocky, rub salt in his wound. 'Nope, don't look to me like you can be. Don't much bother me who is. Too early to get fired up about that sort of thing.'

This wasn't quite, I explained, what I had meant.

'Oh yeah. Who won that thing, anyway?' I filled him in on the voting figures. 'You know,' he said after a moment of deep reflection, 'you could get terrific odds against that guy last summer.'

This sparked a heated discussion of the other guy's brief summer lead in the polls, and pocket calculators were soon deployed to calculate just how much of a 'dog' the eventual winner had been at that pre-convention stage. If poker players hold political views, which few do, they are either shaped by politics as a sporting event, on which money can be made, and/or blindly right-wing. The tournament had already recommenced when a battered copy of the *International Herald Tribune* was discovered beneath Seat Six, open at the sports page. As soon as they were out of the hand, people studied a graph of the two candidates' developing fortunes, so that the summer odds could be precisely evaluated.

'Hey, lemme see that.' A portly latecomer, still chewing whatever he had decided was safe to eat, snatched the paper from the hands of Seat Six, and disappeared behind it in Seat Two. 'Ah wanna read abaht that purrezzidunt thaing.' There ensued some ten minutes in which he re-emerged only to check his hole cards, fold them, and retire behind the *Trib* again. When finally he rejoined us, discarding the paper on the floor behind him, the stranger announced: 'Ah'm from Kentucky. Ah see Kentucky has gone to the Republicans.' There was a pause, during which the general disinterest at this news did not seem to deter him. 'But Massachusetts went to the Democrats. If ah lived in Massachusetts – which ah never have, and ah never would – ah'd move out.'

I eventually outdrew Kentucky and came tenth out of fifty starters that night, one off the money. 'The worst result you could get,' Eric cheerfully told me. 'You've worked hard all that time, you've played well, and what have you got to show for it? You've lost your $1,000 entry fee. That's not good pay for five hours' work.

'If you'd finished one place higher, you'd have got your money back. That's better, but not much. If you wanna be a pro, you've gotta come and play in a *real* game.'

And so I did – but not his. Eric, as always, was involved in the biggest game in the room: $100–$200 seven-card stud, in which eight players were regularly building a pot well into four figures before they had received even the fourth of their seven cards, with four betting rounds to go. The biggest stack of chips – and didn't he let them know it – belonged at the time to the youngest player, Phil Hellmuth Jr, at twenty-three a rising star of the American poker scene.

'I got another ace down here, pardner,' yelled Hellmuth's shrill, not-so-small voice as he dropped his chin to the table and squeezed out the two hole cards beneath a visible A-K. 'I'm going to have to bump this baby a little bit.' So saying, he duly raised the maximum. But Hellmuth's braggadocio did not impress an older, impassive opponent rendered more inscrutable by mirrorized dark glasses. The pot had reached six thousand dollars, and Hellmuth was showing A-K-3-J, to his opponent's two small pairs, before the showdown followed the final down card. There was no second ace in Hellmuth's hole. He had pulled a top straight in six cards, and disguised it with sheer bluster. A less harassed opponent might have raised Hellmuth out of contention earlier on – or, at the least, wondered how the heck Hellmuth could call, let alone raise, with no pair visible.

The kid was on a roll. He had just won his first major title in the Diamond Jim Brady tournament at Los Angeles' Bicycle Club, and he figured this was his year to win the World Series. 'I'm the best all-round poker player in the world,' was his constant boast, and there was only the rolling towards the heavens of older and wiser eyes to gainsay him.

Hellmuth, like Drache, is a college dropout – the added edge in his case being that his father was the Dean. Phil was reading accountancy at the University of his native Madison, Wisconsin, when he discovered – to his father's considerable dismay – that the delights of poker accountancy exceeded those of bookkeeping. After only some two years on the circuit, playing regularly in Vegas and the California clubs, he had tangled with the big boys regularly enough to win several of their tournaments, and successfully enough to buy himself a Cadillac. 'This is going to be my year,' he told all listeners in Malta. 'The first of many.'

Wishing that I had the bank-roll to try my mettle against him, I was forced to settle for a little $10–$20 PLO. In poker circles – even as close to the Middle East as Malta – PLO stands not so much for Palestinian Liberation Organization as Pot Limit Omaha.

Omaha is a variant of Texas Hold 'em in which each player is dealt *four* hole cards, two of which he must use to improve on the communal cards. After the dry, intellectual disciplines of Hold 'em, Omaha seems like a country-and-western knees-up, so many and various are the possibilities which unfold before you, and so much broader the risks people are prepared to take. The chips fly much more loosely, and you must be prepared to reach double-or-quits in double-quick time. Like Brits in Las Vegas, however, Americans abroad tend to play a tad more conservatively than at home, aware that they must measure the limitations of their travelling bank-roll against the assumed ineptitude of all foreign players. Twenty-forty players, moreover, are in these situations the tightest of the lot, as they are also by definition the poorest. So this particular game was not so much a square-dance as a gentleman's excuse-me. Every time anyone bet, the rest folded *en masse*.

You can steal a few pots that way, taking advantage of your position when the chance comes, but you soon get sussed out. Thereafter you can very rarely bluff, as there are bound to be such good hands out against you.

My trouble was (and still is) that to me every Omaha hand looks like a good one. I can't stay out of a pot. If you've never played the game, think about it. A pair of aces, both suited, for instance, is an indisputably good hand; but many players would rather have A-K-Q-J, and some believe K-Q-J-10 or Q-J-10-9 even better than that, so strong are the possibilities of a straight. So 3-4-5-6 suddenly becomes a pretty good hand before the flop – much better if it brings a few low cards. Normal poker values are often inverted at Omaha. High pairs can look very sick very suddenly, and two pairs should often be thrown away if the pot is raised before the flop. The worst hand you can be dealt is trips – in most other games, the best. And so on.

I was doing reasonably well, showing a profit of some $400, when I was suddenly dealt A-A-A-K, two of them diamonds. The hand looked so dazzling that I actually lifted it bodily off the table – something of a breech of Omaha etiquette – to contemplate it awhile. I really couldn't bring myself to throw it. At any other game of poker it would be enough to bet your house on; at Omaha it was a hand you should chuck at the first sign of a raise. I stayed for the flop, which brought 3-4-4, two of them spades. For a moment my hand looked rather better – aces up, with the remote chance of a full house. Then I realized just how remote were the chances of that full house, and how likely it was that someone else was already holding trips, probably a house themselves. When four people called an opening bet of $40 before me, there were clearly some stunning low cards out there. So I sadly parted with my A-A-A-K, only to see the turn bring a third four, and the river the case ace.

The odds against that card appearing were, I had figured, 47:1 before the flop. I would have had the best available full house at the end, though I would have been terrified by the prospect of four fours around the table somewhere. The plethora of possible combinations makes other hands much harder to read at Omaha than at Hold 'em. Why would someone have stayed in, before the flop, with a four? I'll tell you why. Maybe because it was matched by a suited king, and his other two cards were K-3 of hearts, giving him a pair of kings, two strong flush possibilities, and a straight shot. See what I mean?

The hand was indeed won by the fourth four, played with a suited king. Winners are obliged to display all four cards at Omaha, so I was able to see why that player had stayed in before the flop: his other two cards were Q-J of the same suit. The card he had regarded before the flop as his worst, and which he had least expected to come into play, had turned into a decisive and substantial winner.

Though a much less exact science than Hold 'em, Omaha is now the fastest-growing poker game for this very reason: the bewildering array of possibilities both before and after the flop make for some very lively action. So lively, in fact, that I fluctuated all night between a $2,000 profit and the verge of bankruptcy. I must, I kept telling myself, hang on to my $500 entry fee for the following night's tournament, the European Hold 'em Championships, brought forward from the weekend as so many Americans were desperate to get the hell out of Malta. The news was manna from heaven for me, as I had to leave on Thursday morning, to be back in London for the hoop-la attending the publication of my new book.

The mere thought of London and books sent my spirits slumping, so I waited for another decent pot, yawned my way conspicuously through a few folded hands, and got up to cash in $1,200 ahead. I had won back my Irish Eccentrics entry fee, but was wishing I'd brought a bigger bank-roll with me. A $1,200 win the previous Tuesday had covered the costs of this first trip; but even so that $17,500 safely stashed away at home suddenly seemed nothing like enough to sustain my ambitions. Confining my sophomore activities to tournaments and little-league side-action would ensure limited liability; but these tournaments were fairly small-scale beside those stretching ahead of me. Once the circuit hit the States, entry fees alone would come to more than my entire bank-roll. Yet even here, in rinkydink Malta, the money I had been able to bring gave me too little room for manoeuvre. Where could I hustle up some more? And why did my ex-life have to keep getting in the way?

The Maltese dawn was unfolding with such splendour that I mooned my way around the beach for another hour and more – a hopelessly self-pitying figure, fancying myself a Hamlet fetched up on an alien shore, contemplating the rottenness of something in the kingdom to which he must shortly return. There being no Horatios, gravediggers or skulls with whom to share these thoughts, I finally felt my bleary way back to my room and again slept right through the day – the last I was likely to spend in the Mediterranean for many more moons.

My flight was due to leave horribly early the next morning; and, with a day of radio and television interviews lined up, I was more than anxious not to lose my seat. There were horror stories of would-be departees being bumped off their flights all week, and I had been advised to check in at 6 a.m. for an 8.30 a.m. take-off. So I was somewhat alarmed, not to say astonished, to find myself still a contender for the European Hold 'em title as 2 a.m. became 2.30, 2.30 turned into three, and three showed every sign of heading towards four.

We were again down to the last two tables, or eighteen players, out of sixty-three starters; so this thing was not over yet. I was far from being the tournament leader, but I was far from dead either. Instead of concentrating on the cards, however, and the calculation of odds and pot returns which I found such hard work, I was deeply into the statistics of the travelling time to the airport, with due allowance for getting lost in my rented car, and the latest moment I dare arrive without losing my precious seat.

At 3.45 a.m., when desperation was setting in, there came a hand which at last gave me the chance to act decisively. Either I was going to get busted out now, and head off to the airport with reasonably steady blood pressure; or I was going to win a pot so big that I would get into the money, with a shot at the title – and the tournament would end in time to give me an hour or two, while failing to get through on the phone to London, to come up with an excuse for my publishers.

In late position I was dealt A-K suited, my favourite Hold 'em hand apart from aces wired, and duly made it tough for the others before the flop. With three players calling the big blind, I was hoping for at least one or two callers when I bet $2,000, a little under half my stack of almost five thousand notional plastic dollars. After long thought by the dealer and the first caller, who both eventually folded, I got one call from a wily old bird in Seat Three, chewing calmly on a toothpick as he hovered over a stack of chips considerably taller than mine. The flop came A-K-10. The bird checked to me, which made me dismiss the outside chance that he had come all that way with Q-J, which would of course mean that a miracle flop had given him the unbeatable top straight. There were no flush draws in sight. Even if there had been, a pro's gotta do what a pro's gotta do. My heart beating with a rhythm and intensity which would have impressed Wagner, I bet the rest of my stack, over $2,500, and expected him to fold.

While he pondered my offer, or appeared to, I began to calculate where a $10,000 pot would put me in the current rankings, and started to formulate the first in a series of vivid excuses to London about the shortcomings of Air Malta. But I got my answer rather more swiftly and brutally than I had bargained for, when the Bird called my bet with a cry of 'Wish you'd got more money there, London', and flipped over a pair of tens.

I needed an ace or a king to survive. The odds against it were so high that the only satisfaction remaining to me, while the fourth and fifth cards were rolled, was to refrain from showing the Bird my own hole cards, and let him sweat on a possible pair of aces or kings. The dealer thumped the table twice with his fist, to indicate that the betting was complete, burnt a card and rolled the three of clubs. No help. Another double thump, another burn and there appeared the jack of diamonds. Now old Bird looked a mite worried: a queen in the pocket would have given me the pot. Not wishing to appear a bad loser, I began to rise as I tossed my A-K down on the table in front of him.

With a strangled cry of 'Good hand' – and a mistimed one, too, for this is what a good loser says when the caller reveals better cards than he has shown – I donned my jacket and left the table to a smattering of applause. All that remained was to take a quick farewell of Eric, slumped across the room in yet another all-night stud marathon, and hit the Maltese night air for the last time with Phil Hellmuth's shrill voice ringing in my ears: 'Another dead Brit?'

He may be dead for tonight, I thought, and he may be going home $700 to the bad. But he's now officially ranked the thirteenth-best poker player in Europe.

6

The Hall Of Fame

♥ ♣ ♦ ♠

Early one May morning in the mid-1980s, patrons of the coffee shop of the Golden Nugget Hotel and Casino, Las Vegas, were confronted by the unusual sight of a lone figure at the breakfast bar reading a black-backed Penguin Classic over his oatmeal and waffles.

I had arrived on my annual birthday visit determined upon an experiment. Commissioned by a British newspaper to write a discursive meditation upon the psychology of gambling, I had decided to re-read Dostoevsky's short story, *The Gambler*. But I had delayed doing so until this trip, to see if it read any *differently* in the gambling capital of the world. Las Vegas is scarcely Wiesbaden; but it is surely beyond challenge as the latter-day Roulettenburg.

Three stools down from me sat another lone figure, chain-smoking over his umpteenth black coffee – another all-night punter down on his luck, it seemed, brooding on life's verities before squaring up to the day ahead. Normally I would have welcomed his company, the camaraderie of the coffee shop bar being one of my favourite offshoots of the American dream. In England, a stranger looking to strike up a conversation in a diner would most likely be arrested; in the United States, it is almost illegal not to. Today, however, I wanted to read my book, in which my nose was deeply buried in brazen British defiance of western saloon-bar ethics.

'Reading, huh?' My tactics, I should have known, were hopeless. His opening conversational gambit was as direct as it was inevitable. 'What's that you're reading?'

'Oh, just a book about gambling.' Instinctively, my *amour propre* would rather have me thought a gambler than an egghead.

'Yeah? What's it called? My name's Harry, by the way.'

'Tony.' We leant over and shook hands. 'It's called *The Gambler*.' I showed him the jacket, hoping that it would de-wimp me in my companion's eyes, and playing a hunch that the author's name would mean nothing to him.

'*The Gambler*? Don't know that one. New manual, huh? Who's it by?'

'No, it's not really a manual, Harry, it's a novel. Well, a short story. By a guy called Dostoevsky . . .?' There was no flicker of recognition. 'A Russian,' I added helpfully. 'A roulette freak. He's dead now.'

'A red, huh? A *dead* red?' He laughed, and so did I. 'Any good?'

I was still working out how to answer that one when a third party came to my rescue. Another solitary caffeine addict, sitting opposite, he had evidently been following these exchanges with interest and awaiting his cue to join in.

'Dostoevsky? Did you say *Dostoevsky*? You're reading Dostoevsky in *Las Vegas*?'

I mumbled my assent, and Harry leant towards the interloper, sensing that there was something here he was missing out on — maybe some secret new numbers system we would share with him. 'What's so strange about that?' he asked him.

'Well, Dostoevsky, he's big stuff. That's real literature. Not the kind of thing you see people reading here in Vegas.'

This, to all of us, seemed a truth too solemn to bear further discussion. We sat in silence for a moment before the new arrival continued his train of thought, addressing himself directly at me with the utmost gravity. 'You know,' he said, 'I'd be prepared to bet that you just might be the only person in the history of Las Vegas to have read Dostoevsky in Las Vegas.'

'That so?' said Harry, his eyes brightening. 'What odds d'you want on that?'

Hopeful Harry had given me the perfect way in to my article. He is now, as he deserves to be, immortalized in my candidate for the definitive anecdote about Las Vegas, a town where nothing is definitive, or ultimate, and where every experience, every yarn, every statistic can always be capped.

The Binions are living proof. As I arrived back six months after the World Series, to embark on my first American tournaments as a poker pro, workmen were busy erecting a new $2 million neon sign atop the Horseshoe – the biggest in town, using more wattage than any other light in the world. Binion's Horseshoe had just bought out its next-door neighbour, the Mint Hotel and Casino, a transaction swiftly symbolized by the arrival of a helicopter to remove the old Mint sign from the summit of the hotel's 25-storey, 300-feet tower, and replace it with an electronic, revolving gold horseshoe 30 feet tall. The Horseshoe now colonized an entire block of Glitter Gulch. When a hole was driven through the party wall downstairs, it was as if a dam had burst. The Mint side of the complex, hitherto rather sparsely populated, was teeming with activity within seconds, as if all these punters had never been anywhere else.

To drive in yet more off the street, Jack Binion literally cemented this lucrative merger at the point of its junction, with a $150,000 panel of fibre-optic 'living lights' set into the sidewalk – hearts, diamonds, clubs, spades and, of course, another golden horseshoe, all winking and blinking their way towards the entrance, willing the passers-by to change course and follow their hypnotic progress towards the gaming floor. 'We're sticking with Benny Binion's original concept,' said his son in a rare public statement, officially meaning, 'Something You Folks Can't Find Back Home In Iowa.'

What did it mean unofficially? Jack nostalgically recalled his father's days as a Dallas boot-legger. 'Benny was never really into figures. He made the booze in gallon jars and counted up the dollars. But he had a partner who went around totting up bits of paper and generally doing the accounts. Well, somehow, at the end of it all, there wasn't as much money as Benny figured there ought to have been. So one day he just kicked his partner out. What counted to Benny was gallons and dollars. Gallons and dollars was my dad's way, and gallons and dollars is my way.' Since the acquisition of the Mint, meanwhile, the official, public Jack was reaching back to 'the kind of glitter that made Vegas famous. We Binions hope it'll knock your socks off!'

Poker-playing ankles were already naked. More stunning than anything the Binions could dream up was the news from across the road that Steve Wynn, owner of the Golden Nugget, was closing down its card room. I had discovered this quite by accident, having strolled over from my complimentary suite in the new Horseshoe tower, in my usual state of jet-lagged anticipation, to come up against an apparent mirage: row upon row of ugly, shrieking, state-of-the-art slot machines where once the poker gods held court. It was as if I had turned my back for a moment, and Buckingham Palace had become a supermarket. 'But where' – I spluttered to a passing pitboss – 'where's the card room?'

'Gawn,' was all he said. 'Try over the road.'

Over the road was where I had come from – Binion's Horseshoe – shrewd enough, as I thought, to host poker games for only three weeks of the year. Benny and Jack thrilled to the music of the slots, not the moans and groans of tight-fisted poker players, risking their money against each other rather than handing it over to the house.

But a quick dash back across Fremont Street revealed that the Nugget's card room, as if bodily transplanted, had indeed been uncannily re-created in the Horseshoe, right beside the hole Jack had opened up to the Mint. There were the same dealers, the same floormen, the same shift bosses – even, as I was soon to discover, the same tables and chairs. The Binions had used a corner of their new empire to capitalize on Steve Wynn's shock decision – which became less of a shock on discovering that Wynn was planning to open a bigger and better card room, with Eric Drache still presiding, in a new hotel–casino complex he was building on the Strip, next to Caesar's Palace. At a cost of some $600 million, it would open within a year as – surprise, surprise – the biggest hotel in the world, to be called the Mirage. Plans included a permanently erupting volcano beside the main entrance, and a shark pool in the reception area. In the meantime, he had ceded poker dominance to the Binions.

Back home, post-Malta, I had criss-crossed the Atlantic four times in four weeks without a single game of poker. Two different book tours, for two different books, from coast to coast of the United States and Canada, had only helped me grow more depressed about the size of my bank-roll. It took the Moll, in her own unique way, to tell me what a *klutz* I was. 'The time to get depressed,' she said with some force, 'is when you've lost it all.' It was a point I had to concede, especially when she followed up with a stroke of seasonal genius: an air ticket from London to Vegas – and back, if I insisted – as my Christmas present. I could count on being 'comped' at the Horseshoe, so the trip would cost me merely petty cash. Given the American tax authorities' rule that travellers register amounts of $10,000 or more, I decided that $9,999 was the perfect amount to take along for the free ride.

So, thanks to the Moll and Jack Binion, I was winning before I even set out for the Horseshoe's pre-Christmas bonanza – a new tournament to replace the Golden Nugget's defunct Grand Prix of Poker, traditionally regarded as the big mid-term moment in the poker year, second only in scale and status to the World Series. With Steve Wynn and the Nugget in a state of flux, the Grand Prix had this year been replaced by Binion's Hall of Fame Poker Classic, held in honour of the select few inducted into a gallery of all-time poker greats.

The Poker Hall of Fame was founded in 1979, to add yet more lustre to the burgeoning World Series, and to cement the Horseshoe's claim to be the world headquarters of high-stakes poker. If, hitherto, there had been no poker played there the rest of the year, it had simply re-emphasized that the high rollers were elsewhere – on the road, hustling up their entry fee for next year – and that Binion's was not the place for small fry. But the times they were a-changing. Now the Horseshoe was opening its doors to smaller-stakes poker players, refugees from Steve Wynn's heedless imperialism. And here was a whole new tournament to prove it, dedicated to the memory of poker's all-time greats.

Inclusion in the Hall of Fame is based on five heavy-duty criteria, to which many aspire but few are chosen. They require candidates to have played 'consistently well . . . for high stakes

. . . against acknowledged top competitors', maintaining 'the respect of their peers' in the process. The committee's choice must also have 'passed the test of time, maintaining a high standard of excellence over the years'.

Of the seven founder-members, the only living one was the Grand Old Man, Johnny Moss, still unmatched as three-time world champion. The others ranged from Moss's most famous opponent, Nick 'the Greek' Dandalos, to 'Wild Bill' Hickok, who achieved poker immortality in 1876 when he was shot in the back while holding two pairs, aces and eights (ever thereafter known as Dead Man's Hand). Joining them were three of the greatest recent high-stakes players: 'Red' Winn, cited as 'the quintessential all-round poker player'; Sid Wyman, 'a high-stakes player who was instrumental in developing Las Vegas as the gaming capital of the world'; and Felton 'Corky' McCorquodale, 'a classic no-limit player', who introduced Hold 'em to Las Vegas in 1963. Also included was Edmond 'According to' Hoyle, who never actually played poker, but laid down for most card games rules which have lasted since the eighteenth century.

Each subsequent year saw one new player inducted, usually posthumously. Chronologically, from 1980, the new faces in poker's Mount Rushmore were such local legends as 'Blondie' Forbes, Bill Boyd, Tom Abdo, Joe Bernstein, Murph Harrold, Red Hodges and Henry Green. 1987 saw Walter Clyde 'Puggy' Pearson, like Bill Boyd before him, join the immortals while still alive to feel good about it, as the following year did their friend and contemporary Doyle 'Texas Dolly' Brunson. Photographic portraits of these sixteen poker giants graced the walls of the Horseshoe's new card room, now the Hall of Fame's official home.

It was beneath their stern gaze, still reeling from all these unexpected developments, that I embarked upon what was now becoming my perennial first-night-in-Vegas tradition. Jet-lagged, well-wined, and good only for sleep, I could not resist entering a $150 satellite for the next day's $1,500-entry-fee Limit Omaha tournament. Again playing with the vim and venom of a man who doesn't really know where he is, but somewhere deep down knows how to play poker, even how to riffle chips, I saw eight of the ten players eliminated and entered the heads-up showdown leading $1,000 to $500. This looked like it was going to be a repeat of my freakish entry into the World Series in May. I refused the carve-up offered by my opponent, and then managed to lose to him. Don't ask me how. It was so irritating that I promptly entered a second satellite, and was the first to bust out. And so to bed, $300 to the bad, and cursing my carelessness.

In the next day's tournament, however, I played like a demon, and wound up thirtieth out of 144 entrants in the $1,500 Omaha tournament. Though way off the prize money – the $70,800 pot would be divided among the first nine – this seemed a pretty good result for my first Vegas tournament since the World Series, and appeared to bode well for the trials ahead. I had to confess that Lady Luck had been with me when I needed her, no fewer than six times was I forced to go all-in, and five of them I survived.

At my table was the Grand Old Man of Poker himself, Johnny Moss, with whom I reluctantly found myself tangling early on in the proceedings. With two hearts on the board, and A-4 of hearts in my hand, I was intrigued to find the GOM betting at me. It was with some trepidation that I raised him the limit. This was Omaha, not Hold 'em: for Moss to bet at an ace flush draw – which I must assume him to have read correctly – he might already have trips, and his hand (unlike mine) must have ways of improving. The board could yet pair up, making a full house a very strong possibility. Those lizard eyes bore down on me around the dealer – Moss was on the dealer's left in Seat One, I on his right in Seat Nine – and registered stern disapproval at my whipper-snapper temerity. Even through the dealer, I felt like a quivering mass of tells. But fate was with me: though the fifth heart emerged on Fourth Street, and no pair materialized on the river, he continued to call my bets through the showdown, when Moss revealed a king-high heart flush. From the look in his eyes, the Grand Old Man was not going to forget my impertinence. He *knew* I was an amateur masquerading as a pro, and that inexperience would tell sooner or later.

My trouble was that I agreed with him. It was around 7 p.m., after six hours of play, that I made the serious mistake of tangling with Moss again. This time he saw me off with (it has to be said) a lucky straight on Fifth Street; I had (unluckily) failed to improve on my three kings from the flop. My contribution to the Moss funds made him the tournament leader at the time of my departure, but even he eventually failed to come in the money. The $35,000 winner turned out to be José Rosenkrantz, one of a posse of sprightly Costa Ricans who have recently made their presence felt in high-stakes Vegas circles. Though José gave his occupation as shirt manufacturer, telling the press, 'I feel fantastic! It's like a dream! I love America!', few Vegas heavies would regard Rosenkrantz as anything but a pro. Moss, however, still saw him as a shirt manufacturer. 'Damned amateurs,' was his withering verdict. 'Ah've played with that guy, and ah *know* he don't have the first goddam clue about Omaha. Riles me up . . .

'Hey, even *you* could whup those South Americans. To prove it, ah'll pay your entry into the next tournament.'

So saying, Mr Moss turned on his heel and went to seethe elsewhere, in more familiar company. Had he said 'Ah'll' or 'Ah'd' pay my next entry fee? This apparent promise had me in heady mood for the next few hours, though I regret to record that it was one on which he eventually failed to deliver, and to which I felt it rather low to hold him.

Drained by a day's competition, I felt in need of some swift action. At times like this I have to watch myself, for impatience can prove expensive. If there's a long line of names waiting to play Hold 'em or Omaha in the limit side-games, I can all too easily turn to the instant gratification of the blackjack tables, whose high limits suddenly look very seductive. For years I have made my pocket money in Vegas at blackjack: I reckon I can *guarantee* winning a few hundred dollars for taxis, meals, etc., the catch being that it requires risking a larger percentage of your bank-roll than you would at poker. Set yourself modest limits at blackjack, however, and it takes an extremely bad run of cards to stop you realizing them.

I have friends who are professional blackjack 'counters', who can memorize each passing card even in a six-deck shoe, and adjust their play accordingly. The best I can manage is to count the tens and court cards; which is just as well, for up there beyond the ceiling, watching our every move on close-circuit television, are casino eyes trained to spot 'counters' and have them removed before they swing the odds too far their way. The rest of my system is, by comparison, blushfully amateur. Depending on my mood and the state of my bank-roll, it is to play $500 or $1,000 in $50 or $100 units; to play ultra-cautiously; and to quit when I've doubled my original stake. No lesser amounts will provide the thrill necessary to impose self-discipline. The point is that blackjack, unlike poker, is not fun. Nor is it even *about* fun; it is entirely about money. Today, according to plan, I started with $1,000, played at $100 a pop, and quit immediately I had managed to work it up to $2,000.

If you have only a few thousand with you, and a week of poker ahead, the process requires some nerve. At one point I was down to $300 out of my original $1,000. There's nothing too unusual about that. But I have firm rules to deal with this aberration, as blackjack is the one casino game to which I sometimes allow circumstances to tempt me. Had I lost the whole lot, I would have stopped at once and made myself win it all back at low-limit poker – which might take a day or two, compared to the ten or fifteen minutes it took to lose. The other critical discipline is to pick up the money and run as soon as you have doubled your original stake. Blackjack moves so fast that this can be difficult. Keeping a track of your chips, especially while trying to count cards as well, can trip you into wrong decisions.

One motivation for today's win was a spangly sweatshirt I had spotted in the window of the Golden Nugget's absurdly tempting gift store, and immediately marked down as a minor Christmas present for the Moll. At $178 – which, after twenty-four hours in Vegas, seems like pocket money – I could simply and easily have paid for it, cash on the nail. But the satisfaction of winning it twenty yards away at the blackjack tables, first left past the World's Largest Golden Nugget, more than doubled its value. Now it was duly stashed away in my hotel room, and I still had more than enough for a stake at the $10–$20 table – if ever a seat came free – as well as buying dinner for two friends to whom this gesture was long overdue.

It is so easy to score free meals in Las Vegas that actually paying for one involves a certain amount of effort. For a start you have to leave the hotel for the first time in days, thus forfeiting your place in various poker queues, to secure the sense of occasion provided by a restaurant. Then you have to persuade your guests to make the same sacrifice. If a dinner date is made even hours, let alone days in advance, it is entirely dependent on the state of the game in which host or guest might be playing at the appointed hour. A meal may have been planned weeks ahead; participants may have flown thousands of miles to be there; yet it is taken for granted that anyone badly 'stuck' in a game, or indeed blessed with a tourist on tilt, has much more important priorities. If you all actually make it to a restaurant in the Vegas 'burbs, all these complications duly redouble the resonance of the gesture you wish to make by paying – even if the ritziest meal still costs less than the Moll's sweatshirt, or less than nothing in the global scheme of things.

At Cosmo's uptown branch, over some sizzling clams with Eric Drache and Henri Bollinger, there was much talk of ring players, marked cards and other forms of card-room misdemeanour. Most of them concerned games in California. As card-room manager of the Nugget, it was Eric's job to police and punish any irregularities, which rarely went this far. Just occasionally you find a dealer in cahoots with a player, perhaps tilting the deck towards him as he deals to his opponents. In Las Vegas there are countless tales of 'cold' decks and fixed games all over the rest of the world; and it seems depressingly true that there are few places left on earth where a stranger can sit down entirely sure that the game will be straight. To a pro it is par for the course, all part of looking after himself. In the public card rooms of Vegas, I was discovering, if nowhere else in the world, you can generally rely on an honest game.

Then there is etiquette – in poker, a sub-branch of the rules. Only by playing for a hundred years can you master every nuance of proper procedure. Day after day disputes still break out, even among people who know those procedures backwards. A cry of 'Floorman, Table Three' usually means that a hand has been stalled by an intractable argument, where neither player will give way about the other's inexcusable conduct. The real point, of course, is that one of them is losing, and his inner turmoil has taken control. It is up to Eric and his staff, from dealers to shift bosses, to make the rulings.

Dealers are a long-suffering race, whom players tend to blame for their own ill-fortune. Minimally paid, they can be handsomely tipped by good-hearted winners, and scorchingly abused by bad-mouthing losers. Actually distributing the cards is only a minor part of their job. They have to run (or in their word 'protect') the table, maintaining order and discipline, often at times when players are going through life and death extremities. Above all, the dealers must know the rules.

Dealer stories are legion – everyone knows the names of the famous players they like least – but I was able to tell Eric and Henri one they hadn't heard before. The friend who told it to me was the dealer in question, when a hand went badly wrong for a former world champion. A bad loser at the best of times, the ex-champ's way of conceding the hand was to throw his hole cards at the dealer, off whose shoulder they bounced onto the floor. There ensued an embarrassed silence, during which the dealer got on with shuffling the deck. When no comment, let alone apology, proved forthcoming, he calmly proceeded to deal the next hand.

'Hey,' foamed the ex-champ. 'You can't deal those cards! That's not a full deck! Two of them's on the floor!'

'That's quite right, sir,' said the dealer. 'If you would kindly fetch them for me, I will be pleased to deal a full deck. Until then, I'm obliged to carry on like this.'

All hell, of course, broke out, with everyone summoned from floorman to shift boss to card-room manager to casino owner. The ex-champ was a big shot, and he wasn't going to take this kind of shit from a two-bit dealer. The dispute ended, however, with the big shot on his knees, grovelling to retrieve the cards. The dealer was deemed to be proceeding quite correctly. There are rules for every poker eventuality and these, the best dealers in the world, know them all.

Having learnt the kinds of trick to look out for, I proceeded to raise the delicate question of aces in the hole. Here, it seemed to me, was a definitive symbol of the difference between tournament poker and real-money poker. Indisputably the best hand before the flop, aces can quickly go wrong after it, as I had already learned to my cost. The most seasoned tournament players, as far as I could see, only ever bet their *entire* stack on a certainty. OK, make it difficult for the others, and most of the time they will fold. I would certainly bet the maximum on aces in a real game. But surely tournaments require an extra degree of caution? Eric laughed me to scorn. To prove his point, after blinding me with poker science, he 'bought' a third of me in the following day's $1,500 No Limit Hold 'em tournament; in other words, he put up $500 of my entry money, which would entitle him to one-third of any prize money I might win. But he did so on one condition: that if I ever find myself holding aces in the hole, I bet my entire stack.

These precepts duly lodged, it cost me a mere $1,000 of my own money, plus Eric's $500, to find myself starting the next day's tournament at the same table as my old sparring-partner from May, the two-time world champion Stu 'the Kid'

Ungar. Lady Luck, it transpired, was in mischievous mood.

In the very first round of the tournament – it was only the third hand – I found myself in possession of a pair of aces in the hole. Ungar, of all people, had already raised the blind. When the betting reached me, in comfortably late position, I felt honour-bound by my agreement with Eric to re-raise the Kid's bet with everything I had in front of me. I didn't even bother to count it out, just flashed The Watch for luck as I shoved in my entire stack in the apparent belief that no-one would even think about calling it.

Ungar did. He thought long and hard; then he called it.

We were both all-in. To force me to show my hand, Ungar displayed his: a pair of jacks. Again – these people really ought to develop better memories for faces – he seemed to assume that I was some amateur without a clue what game we were playing. When I showed him my two aces he was already half out of his seat. The flop was moderately agonizing; one jack, and I would have been a loser worthy of sympathetic applause. But it followed the odds, offering no card to improve either hand. Ungar was out; I had doubled my stack; and I couldn't wait to tell Eric how right he was.

That day I was all-in a mere four times, finishing a very respectable (but profitless) twenty-third out of 198 starters, just five off the money. My stack had dwindled to emergency levels by the time I was dealt the K-9 of clubs, an all-in hand if ever I saw one. I was called by the A-3 of diamonds. The flop brought Q-10-8-2-4, all of them spades or hearts, making the lone ace the winner.

I was beginning to see how tough it was going to be to win any money in a Las Vegas poker tournament. I could play really well by my standards – patient, disciplined, aggressive when need be – and still find myself struggling to make the last session. I had yet to win back an entry fee, let alone finish within a chip's throw of the final table, where the *real* money was contested: today's winner netted $118,800 of a total pool of $297,000. To punish myself, I reverted irrelevantly to the role of press man, and attended the post-tournament briefing in self-imposed sackcloth. It is always fun to see how the winners wrestle reluctantly with the need to give an occupation which may appear in the newspapers. This guy, a New Yorker, was not the first big money winner to describe himself as being 'in import-export'. Of what? Other people's bucks?

Depressed and suddenly lonely, I was in need of some sort of fillip. This is not the state in which to play poker, where self-confidence is half the battle. This week's big tournament, No Limit Hold 'em with a $5,000 buy-in, was beginning to look beyond my reach. I had played long, hard and reasonably well, and all I had to show for it was the loss of $2,800 in tournament and satellite entry fees. Of the $1,000 won back at blackjack, half had gone on gifts, meals and tips. Currently showing a $2,300 deficit on the trip, my $9,999 was dwindling fast. It would be folly, therefore, to play in the following day's seven-card stud tournament. Sometimes these events were cheap practice, a way of improving my game without risking too much real money. The $2,500 buy-in, however, amounted to a term's school fees for just one of my three children, and it seemed better spent on their education than on mine.

To catch myself breaking one of my cardinal rules – equating my bank-roll with 'real world' expenditure – was to realize just how low my morale had slumped. At moments like this Vegas begins to loosen its grip, and the world outside to trickle back into view – a dismal horizon fraught with problems, nearly all of them financial. Most, it is true, could be solved by the simple expedient of placing the entire bank-roll on red at roulette, and winning; look, there is a quiet table right over there, just waiting for me to choose the right roll. Get thee behind me, Vegas. Such thoughts, praise be, still come back-to-back with their flip side; a heavy shudder at the consequences of losing, to a gambler still vaguely in control of his emotions, is a wonderfully strong antidote to temptation.

Rescue, as I was about to discover for the umpteenth time, can often lie in the very fickleness of the male ego, which takes remarkably little to bounce back into contention with anything Dame Fortune may care to chuck at it.

When Jack Binion passes by and asks you how you're doing, he is the last person who actually wants to know the answer. Like a campaigning politician, or the Pope going walkabout, Jack is merely working the crowd, distributing his blessing. When you consider that he owns this joint, and that it has the highest return per square foot in Las Vegas, it should be enough merely to touch the hem of his garment. Tonight, however, I told Jack just how I *was* doing. Times were so hard that I had given myself the next day off poker to do my Christmas shopping. 'That bad, huh?' he said absently, his eyes moving around the room behind me. 'Well, er . . . take a limo.' At which point I was paged, and Henri Bollinger told me the local paper wanted to interview me.

Twenty-four hours later, London Tony was a transformed figure. He had spent the day cruising Vegas in style and comfort, piling high the Binion's stretched limousine with gifts for his loved ones, wondering at the driver's courtesy and patience as he bobbed from shopping mall to remote baseball card stores, from Toys R Us to the Gambler's Book Club. Then he had seen the early editions of the *Las Vegas Review-Journal*, across a full half-page, complete with presentable photograph, declare him to be 'among the world's leading poker players'. If they want to or need to badly enough, even professional journalists can believe that something must be true because it says so in a newspaper.

Bubbling with *bonhomie*, I dined again that night with Henri, in the Horseshoe's Italian restaurant, and drowned him in anecdotes about my poker prowess. When he finally made an excuse and left, I hooked up with the guy sitting alone at the next table, one 'Billy Mac' from New Orleans, who told me of the joys of the Cajun Cup tournament in Louisiana, tentatively on my schedule for the following Easter. Never, he promised, would I again see so many pigeons. Vying with each other in the ebullience stakes, amply fuelled by excellent Italian red wine, we decided that there must be some pigeons downstairs right now. Why not hit the $4–$8 Omaha tables and ruffle their feathers? We seemed to be slightly tipsy – so why not *act* even drunker, raise the old 'rocks' more than they are used to, and mop up?

We had a riotous time. The gaunt faces in the $4–$8 chain gang never knew what hit them. There they had been all evening, playing a quiet, calculated game of poker, when this double tornado arrived and took the table over. Sauced, by the look of it, wisecracking wildly, playing almost every hand and raising most of them. It is amazing, in the cold light of the following morn, how often this technique works. A couple of lucky wins, and you have them completely fazed. It took me ninety minutes or so to win $500, sober up, and realize that satellites were under way for the next day's $2,500 Pot Limit Omaha tournament. My brain having made the adjustment from Hold 'em to Omaha, and appearing to be firing on all pistons, I bid Billy Mac a fond farewell and headed for the tournament area.

The top professionals dislike the whole idea of satellites, as they take the mugs out of the real money games. For a maximum $250 entry fee, enthusiastic amateurs can get some high-level Omaha practice without losing their shirts, which the pros feel ought to be shed in the side-games. All the more satisfaction, therefore, is to be had from a good run in this corner of the arena – where my professional career, after all, had been born the previous May. With such limited liability, and the chance to try again within minutes, the satellite was at this stage my only hope of playing like a real pro.

That night I began to prove it, making bold but accurate decisions which I might have funked in the do-or-die context of a tournament, and certainly would have in the this-could-go-expensively-wrong terror of a high-stakes real money game. In the first satellite I played, I reached the last two, the 'head-to-head', almost exactly equal with my opponent. So desperate was he to win, and so unclear as to my abilities, that he offered me a deal: if I were to concede, he would give me $1,250 in cash, the equivalent of the chips in front of me at the time. From his point of view, this meant that he would secure entry in a $2,500 tournament for just $1,500. The satellite would have been worthwhile for both of us. Rather than one of us losing a sudden death play-off, we would each receive financial recognition for our achievement in besting the eight other starters.

Suddenly I saw a whole new avenue of poker pleasure opening up. I accepted with alacrity, pocketed my $1,000 profit, and put my name down for the next satellite. This seemed to me to be a new route to quick gains – an enjoyable and skill-sharpening method of parlaying small risks into big profits. My self-confidence was reflected in my play, which again saw me reach the head-to-head. This time it was I, though marginally ahead in chips, who offered the deal to my startled opponent. I would let him win, and secure his entry for the next day's tournament, if he gave me – let's see now – $1,500 cash. This guy, as I thought, was a tourist who had never come across the suggestion before. I explained his options. (1) Pay me $1,500 now, in which case he would have entered a $2,500 tournament for $1,750, thus saving himself $750. (2) Play on and lose, in which case his tournament entry would have already cost him $250 more than the $2,500. (3) Play on and win – a saving of $2,250. But I was ahead in chips, the antes were rising, and the head-to-head is always a bit of a crapshoot. My only motive in offering the carve-up was that I enjoyed playing satellites.

'Yeah,' he growled suspiciously, 'and I seen your face in the paper this morning. OK, you gotta deal.' Even though my head was fizzing, this struck me as something of a non-sequitur. I was still trying to work it out – if he thought I was taking him for a ride, why pay up? – as I trousered the $1,500. Two satellites played, and a $2,250 profit scored. This was fun.

The next one saw me in over-confident mood, blowing my $250 entry fee in double-quick time on an absurdly optimistic drawing hand. Cursing this one lapse in my otherwise fierce concentration, I looked at The Watch and realized it was after three. The tournament in which I supposedly wished to play began at noon. If I wanted to be in any kind of shape for it, I must think about sleep soon. By the time this thought process had taken shape, I was already committed to the next satellite, my fourth. Energized by my earlier advances, I was the only player alert enough to see that everyone else was getting tired. Several were also deeply downcast, attempting their last satellite before giving up and abandoning all hope of playing in the tournament. Once you've played five, after all, you've spent half the tournament entry fee.

During a spate of cautious folds, I began working out a new thesis. The top players were no longer involved in these satellites; they had either won one already, or weren't bothering to try. Most of the stragglers, by definition, were players so short of cash that they could play in the tournament only by winning a satellite. To lose half a dozen, and still stump up the entry fee, you had to be some kind of eccentric; even if loaded, no gambler likes to pay $4,000 to enter a $2,500 tournament. It thus followed to my tingling wits that I was not merely the most shrewdly calculating player in this game; I must also be the best. The powers of self-persuasion – aided on this occasion by a newspaper accolade – saw me again to the head-to-head. This time I was neither offering nor accepting deals. This time, I *knew*, I was going to win.

And so I did, barely restraining an exhilarated whoop of triumph until alone in an empty elevator. In six hours of play that evening I had scored a cash profit of $2,250 and won free entry into a $2,500 tournament. I was $50 down on the trip so far, which in Vegas feels like a profit. Even the Christmas shopping was accounted for. The bank-roll was back in shape.

Too elated to sleep, I ordered an alarm call for 11 a.m. and settled down in bed with a crucial volume I had been saving for this moment. *How To Win at Poker Tournaments*, by the 1983 world champion, Tom McEvoy, explains in great detail how tournament play differs from 'real' play. There are sections on slow, medium and fast action in limit and no-limit tournaments – the advice changing as the event progresses from early through middle to its late stages – as well as heads-up matchplay, re-buy strategies and other such mysteries. Like all recent poker gurus, McEvoy places great stress on position, and offers lists of hands you should and should not play at progressive stages, urging you to commit them to memory, and warning against an array of possible pitfalls so diverse that I was surprised to find no mention of road and weather conditions. After a while, reading these books sets the head spinning, evoking potent memories of schoolboy algebra lessons. The dreams they provoke are of poker played with flow charts, slide-rules and pocket calculators.

But I must have slept soundly enough, for the next thing I knew it was 1.30 p.m. Disaster! The alarm call had either failed to materialize or failed to wake me, and the tournament had already been under way downstairs for an hour and more. Sprinting down half-dressed, and hoping that some unforeseen delay would enable me to slide into my seat unobserved, I was dismayed to see tables already being removed. If that many players had already been eliminated, I could only pray that the tournament director, Jack McClelland, had noticed my absence, allotted me a seat, and told the dealer to ante me away until I turned up. Otherwise my hard-won entry fee would be forfeit.

A quiet word with Jack, and I discovered that Eric Drache had wandered through and indeed wondered where I was. 'Next time, Tony,' said Jack, 'get the tournament desk to call you. They're the best alarm service around here.'

But the situation was still a trifle delicate. Players who have been hard at it for a while resent a lazy latecomer, so Jack picked up my pile of chips and made it look as if I were a player from a broken-up table, reassigned to another. Eventually I found myself gestured into a seat next to . . . Tom McEvoy, the man who had consigned me to such a deep and dream-ridden sleep. I felt as if I knew him like a brother.

I also felt as if I knew his style of play as well as my own.

The pros often joke about the books they produce, wondering why they should give away their trade secrets to potential suckers, and now I began to see their point. The most celebrated example is the great Doyle Brunson, whose 656-page textbook *Super/System* can be said to have altered the game's history. Originally published in 1978 (under the title *How I Made Over $1,000,000 Playing Poker*, which even Doyle eventually deemed a mite gawdy), it was read and re-read so universally as to raise standards of play all over the world. Tourists like me thought the excess baggage payable on this hefty tome, the first book since Yardley to be acclaimed as 'the Bible', more than worth the improvement it brought to our game. Doyle himself now ruefully admits that some of its ideas have become out of date, so widely have they been put into practice. 'It's become a Frankenstein's Monster,' he told me. 'For years I kept comin' up against people playin' like me. I had to think up a few new moves of my own, and I sure ain't puttin' those in no goddam book.'

The only book since Brunson's to influence Hold 'em play at the highest levels is a handbook 'for advanced players' put out by two academic professionals, David Sklansky and Mason Malmuth. Alongside 'Mad' Mike Caro, whose computer analyses, manuals, even videos have a cult following among middle-rank players, Sklansky is perhaps the game's current leading theorist, with a host of publications to his name. Fellow pros like to jest that they have yet to see him win the world title, but it is impossible to hold your own in the card rooms of Nevada or California without being aware of Sklansky's very rigorous principles of play. For 'rigorous', in fact, read 'tight' – so tight that if I'd been observing Sklansky rules I'd scarcely have played a hand all week.

McEvoy's handbook was even more recent, especially for

someone who had spent the night with his nose literally buried in it. To me, for a glorious few hours, the 1983 world champ played, as it were, like an open book. I could tell when he was slow-playing the boss hand, over-playing a weak hand, using late position to creep in 'on the come'. I could almost hear his thought processes, as he gave himself his own familiar advice. After a somewhat drowsy start, I, too, began to play with the calm, confident self-assurance which is McEvoy's hallmark. When a few more casualties saw our table in turn dispersed, and I found myself relocated opposite him, I felt uncomfortably like a mirror image.

Thanks to my late arrival, my compulsory antes had been dwindling my stack for nearly ninety minutes. You can stay in a tournament quite a long time that way, as if folding every hand, but you sure ain't going to win it. I needed to rebuild my pile urgently, and reassert myself at a table already settled into a mutually wary rhythm. As much as I wanted to upset that rhythm, exploiting the accident of my lateness by being caught in a few eccentric plays, I forced myself to assert world class self-control. Sklansky would have been proud of my studied inactivity.

Few poker pros ever open a newspaper, so my face was still usefully unfamiliar. Thanks to this morning's article, however, I was now due on local television later that day, as the guest interviewee who provides light relief amid the gloom of the nightly news. This tended to coincide with each tournament's evening dinner break, and was apparently watched by large numbers of players resting in their rooms before the evening's action. My comparative anonymity being my greatest asset – as some friends, rather unflatteringly, had reminded me – this was my last chance to play the innocent.

Behind my innocence, however, lurked the knowledge that

all these manuals have produced a new breed of stereotyped poker player, who expects fellow professionals to play in certain orthodox ways. A 4-5 off suit, for instance, is a text-book fold in early and middle positions; but the experts suggest that you can 'creep in' with a low sequence in late position as long as the pot has not been raised.

So this was precisely what I did, quite early on, only to see the flop come A-2-3, two of them diamonds. At Omaha, this can produce serious dangers of a higher straight emerging as the flop progresses, or of a flush outdrawing them both. So calling Seat Three's maximum bet, already called by Seats Five and Six, was not an option. Thanks to Brunson, McEvoy and other former world champs – visitors to Sinai generous enough to *publish* their tablets of stone – I knew that these were probably all drawing hands, at best trips. My only alter-natives were to fold pathetically, or to scare the hell out of them (and myself) by raising all I had. In this situation, I knew that the others, thanks to the textbooks, would probably read me right; the only seat in which I could still be in the pot with 4-5 was the one in which I was sitting. My bet, moreover, was big enough for any drawing hand to have to defy the odds to call me. Sure enough, they all folded, and I scooped in a pot big enough to compensate for oversleeping.

Now I had enough ammunition to vary my play a little, and act unpredictable, making them wonder if I had read the text-books after all. I lasted long enough to be forced to postpone the television appearance, as I, too, would be watching the evening news in my room during a restorative dinner break. All too soon thereafter, however, I invested my entire stack on a top straight on the flop, only to see it beaten by a 10-1 full house on the river. Sklansky might have frowned on such boldness, but I could permit myself no regrets. Twenty-second out of seventy-three starters, I was just four off the money, which today totalled $182,500.

It was another decent result on paper, but none too helpful to the bank-roll. Without pausing to eat, I headed for the satellite zone, where $150 shoot-outs were in progress for the next day's $1,500 Pot Limit Hold 'em tournament. Again, the illusion of starting at the final table did wonders for my play. With only nine players to beat, instead of a hundred or more, my entire poker metabolism seemed to change.

Make that eight, in fact, for I again made the doing of deals my strategy as I played four satellites in four hours. Heads-up in the first, leading in chips by a margin of 2:1, I let my surprised opponent buy me out for $1,000. In the second I failed early. In the third I again reached the head-to-head, this time a considerable underdog, and was lucky to be bought out for $600. The fourth I won. 'Satellite Sam', as Satellite Betty had taken to calling me, had done it again. I had won a place in the next day's $1,500 event for an outlay of $600 in entry fees, against a profit of $1,600 in carve-ups. My $1,000 cash profit on the evening at last put me back in profit for the trip.

Forty-eight hours ago I had been a broken reed $2,300 down; now I had $950 more than the $9,999 I had arrived with, even after accounting for more than $8,000 worth of tournament and satellite entry fees. Merely holding my own, at this level, again had me absurdly elated. Being a poker pro, to me, was fast becoming a matter of damage containment rather than early retirement.

Consolation could always be found in the immortal words of Jack Straus: 'If the Lord had wanted you to hold on to your money, he'd have made it with handles on.' One of my oldest friends among the top pros, and a popular world champion in

1982, Jack had stunned us all the previous August by dropping dead of a heart attack, at the age of only fifty-eight, in the middle of a high-stakes poker game in California. He had often said, as they all do, that he would like to die at the table – but only Jack could have added that he hoped he'd be losing at the time.

The word 'heart' carries a particular meaning in the poker player's vocabulary. Fiendishly hard to define, but a lot more than mere grace under pressure, it has to do with courage and ingenuity, nerve and self-possession. 'Heart' is what you need to take your life in your hands, to back your own instincts against the whims of fate, in the toughest, coldest, most fearless company. Jack Straus himself defined it as 'intestinal fortitude'. Heart, to me, was what defined Jack, both as a man and a player. After so many years displaying such vast quantities of the stuff, and putting such pressure on his own, it was really no surprise that it finally registered the ultimate protest.

'I have only a limited amount of time on this earth,' Jack would say, 'and I want to live every second of it. That's why I'm willing to play anyone in the world for any amount. It doesn't matter who they are. Once they have a hundred or two hundred thousand dollars' worth of chips in front of them, they all look the same to me. They all look like dragons, and I want to slay 'em.'

Jack was a lifelong dragon-slayer. At sixteen, in a high-school poker game, he won a car before he could drive. At six-feet-seven – hence his long-standing nickname of 'Treetop' – he was a college basketball star who went on, like Doyle Brunson, to vent his competitiveness at the poker table, where Jack's refusal to quit became legendary. In 1970, for instance, a lousy run at one point reduced him to his last $40. Far from quitting, he took it over to the blackjack table and ran it up to $500, which he took back to the poker table and converted into $4,000. Back at blackjack, he transformed this into $10,000, all of which he proceeded to bet on the Superbowl, taking the Kansas City Chiefs at 2:1 against. The Chiefs won, converting Jack's original $40 into $30,000 in less than twenty-four hours.

This was an episode of considerable magnificence. Not once had Jack compromised; at every opportunity he had studied the odds, kept nothing in reserve, and gone for all-or-bust. This was the quality which had won Straus, always a better player for real money than in tournaments, the 1982 world championship. Down to his last $500 on the first day, he had bluffed his way back from the dead, then gone on to win the title and $520,000. It was a performance typical of his life-long refusal to give up; but Jack's unique skill was an uncanny way of turning unplayable cards into winners. The Crony once witnessed a timeless example:

At No Limit Hold 'em, Straus was dealt 7-2 offsuit, the worst hand in the deck. But he was 'on a rush', so he raised anyway, and only one other player stayed with him. The flop was dealt: 7-3-3, giving Jack two pairs. He bet again, but as he did so he saw his opponent's hand reach quickly for his chips, and he knew he had made a mistake. The other guy, Jack realized, had a big pair in the hole (it was, in fact, two jacks); with great confidence, he raised Jack's $5,000. At that point, the logical move was to fold, since Jack was certain he was beaten and only a bluff could save him. But he called, thereby sowing doubt in the other player's mind.

The dealer turned over the fourth card: a deuce. It paired Jack's second hole card, but did not improve his hand, since there was already a communal pair of threes on the board. In

other words, he knew he was still losing. Without hesitating,
Jack bet $18,000. There was a long, long silence while the
other man considered the implications of the bet. Then Jack
leaned forward, smiling his most charming, lop-sided smile.
'I'll tell you what,' he said. 'You give me one of those little
twenty-five-dollar chips of yours, and you can see either of
my cards, whichever you choose.' Another silence. Finally, the
man tossed over a yellow-and-green chip and pointed to one
of the cards in front of Jack. Jack turned it over: a deuce.
Another long silence. The only logical explanation for Jack's
offer was that the two cards in front of him were the same, so
the flop gave him a full house of deuces. The other man folded
his winning hand.

'It's just a matter of simple psychology,' Jack said later. But
Al thought it was a lot more than that: 'It wasn't just simple
psychology, nor was it merely a matter of bluff. It was a *play*
in the true sense: a kind of wit, stylish, elegant and full of
imagination.'

The Crony and I once went into business with Jack Straus,
promoting a million-dollar poker game aboard the *QE2*. The
idea came to us while climbing a mountain in the Isle of Man,
during a break from a summer tournament there. It seemed a
good money-making idea at the time, and proved the fore-
runner of today's highly successful poker cruises; but we were
all such inept business men, even when Eric Drache added his
own unique ambassadorial skills, that we were lucky to break
even. Tuesday Night Ltd, as we cheerily called ourselves, never
quite reached the stockmarket flotation its directors had in
mind.

The *Las Vegas Review-Journal*'s obituary of Jack credited
him with 'helping to dispel the negative image of poker'. He

helped to dispel a lot else besides. The last time I had seen him turned out to be the night my mother died, a few days after my father's funeral. He had spent much of the evening offering characteristically shrewd, worldly *aperçus* on the loss of one's father; a few days later I had a letter from him addressing the death of one's mother (with a postscript worthy of a Nevadan Oscar Wilde on the loss of both parents inside a week). It is uncommon, not to say unheard of, for poker players to write letters, so I was doubly touched. When I heard of Jack's own death, his own words of comfort naturally came immediately to my mind, only to be elbowed aside by my favourite Straus story, which perfectly captures the man's zany generosity and fellow-feeling.

In 1985 Jack was taken to court by the Internal Revenue Service, who claimed that he owed the Government three million dollars. Flat broke after a disastrous run at sports betting, he had no way of paying up if he lost. Jack arrived at court early, and sat at the back with his lawyer as the previous case wound up. The defendant owed a mere $35,000 in back taxes, but was also unable to pay. He was asking the judge for time, pleading that otherwise he wouldn't be able to house or feed his family: 'We'll all be on the street, your honour. It'll break up our lives.' When Jack heard all this, he felt so sorry for the guy that he stood up at the back of the court and yelled, 'It's OK, your honour, just stick it on my tab!'

This immensely lovable man, one of the few poker players who would be genuinely missed, was now to be the latest posthumous addition to the Horseshoe's Hall of Fame. We took a break from the final stages of the Limit Hold 'em tournament for Jack Binion to do the honours, describing Jack as 'a gambler's gambler'. At that precise moment I had just been forced to go all-in, with A-K in the hole. After speeches remembering Jack, the flop came 5-5-A-A-K. It is the nearest I have ever come to a religious experience.

Thanks, no doubt, to Jack, whom I could feel rooting for me from the great green baize beyond the clouds, I proceeded to my best tournament finish yet in Vegas, twentieth out of 142 – still two off the money, but good enough to feel I was displaying the skills of a seasoned pro.

For the last two hours, to catcalls on all sides, I had in fact been playing in two tournaments at once, as Henri Bollinger had been obliged to start the media event without me. 'Just ante me away,' I had cried cockily from the main arena. 'I'll join you when I've won this one.' Peter Alson of *Esquire* magazine undertook to look after my interests, responding cheerily to my show-off shouts across the room of 'How'm I doing?' By the time Hans 'Tuna' Lund's pair of aces beat out my A-K of hearts, and I teetered across the room from one championship to another, I had 'lost' only $75 out of a notional $500. Twenty-two of the fifty-five starters had already been eliminated; but tournament fatigue soon set in, and I didn't last much longer. Who won? It was a matter of total indifference to me.

There was time during that evening's dinner break to make it to the television studios for my postponed cameo appearance. The British biographer-turned-poker-pro made good copy for Vegas's local news, but my thoughts were still stuck in the tournament arena. Eric Drache, who happened to be watching at home, literally fell out of bed laughing when I was asked which professional poker player I found most interesting. Would I, wondered Eric, choose Johnny Chan or Doyle Brunson? Johnny Moss or Stu Ungar? Perhaps even Eric Drache?

'D'you know what you said, Tony?' I couldn't remember. Eric again collapsed with laughter. 'You said . . . Me. I thought you were going to say Amarillo Slim, and you said Tony Holden!'

Back at the Horseshoe, it was astonishing how many people, as predicted, had been watching. At the cage, on the casino floor, even in the elevator, people wished me luck and beamed generous fellow-feeling. But they were the amateurs. The pros grinned knowingly, and nudged each other as I went by. In the coffee shop I could enjoy my statutory Warhol quarter-hour of celebrity; but in the card room my cover was irrevocably blown. Five thousand bucks now seemed far too much to risk in the Hall of Fame tournament's main No Limit Hold 'em event the following day. With barely twice that much in my pocket, it was time to take a realistic look at myself and my developing skills, and acknowledge that neither was really worth the investment. Better to let Johnny Chan win yet another title (as indeed he did, without my having had the *nous* to back him), and try to run the bank-roll up in some last-night, high-stakes, real-money action.

But what, in my book, were now high stakes? This was the crunch calculation: to balance ego against self-awareness, throw in a bit of humility, spice with greed, and decide between the $20–$40 rockface and the perils of Pot Limit. This was a bottle-of-decent-wine decision – to be made over a room service television dinner with the Kenny Rogers–Dolly Parton Christmas special, punctuated by further calls to the Moll and the Crony, whose advice was to go for broke. Knowing them both to be canny politicians, who figure the best advice to give people is the advice they want to hear, I realized that the decision had in fact long been made, and was simply awaiting this little ritual of self-assurance to be acted upon.

At the cage I decided to leave half my wad in the deposit box, and made for the card room with a heady $5,000 in my pocket – precisely the entry fee for the next day's big tournament. The $500 satellites were full of heavies busily saving themselves a routine $4,500 before getting down to the serious business of the side-action. This ruled out much chance of any prolonged parlaying on my part, but I allowed myself to attempt just one. It was peopled by various leading pros including the egregious T.J. Cloutier, a former pro football player who is now one of the toughest – and nicest – of the world's top players. If I had to have a nemesis, TJ would do me just fine.

From the start, I had the curious sensation that I was playing only him, and that the other participants were irrelevant. Only later did I discover this to be a standard tactic among tournament pros: pick out your man, Chan or Tourist, and play him and his money rather than the cards. But I felt the truth of it fairly early on, when I called a large pre-flop bet of TJ's, then set myself all-in with a nervous pair of queens in the pocket. The grizzled giant thought for a long time, stared hard at me for even longer, then folded with a cry of, 'Good bet, England!' It turned out to be even truer when one by one the others dropped, and I was left with Cloutier in the head-to-head. He was ahead 2:1 in chips, so he wasn't making any offers, even without knowing that in my mind I had already conceded, regardless of what the crapshoot might hold. Even so, I lost in style. Setting myself in with A-A in the hole, I found myself called by the 10-J of diamonds, and watched the flop come 5-10-10-J-J. TJ whistled, stared at the hands and commiserated. So much for Eric's system. Somehow I was unsurprised, even by so extraordinary an ending. It didn't even occur to me to whine about the bad beat, which made TJ think me an even finer ambassador for Britain than he had in the first place. He has had a smile and a kind word for me ever since.

But that was enough of that. It was my last night here, and I was intent on serious action. I found it in a $5–$10 Pot Limit Hold 'em game in which my bottle-of-wine decision was to prove ruinously expensive. Perhaps, for once, I should recognize that it might have been the bottle of wine itself. There are times when my biorhythms tell me that alcohol can sharpen my poker-playing faculties, giving me an extra edge of insight and aggression. That much had surely been proved right by my satellite performance. But now it had me playing fast and loose, for real money, which is a dangerous way to take on high-limit players in town for a major tournament. So pleased was I with the number of pots I could steal this way, raising the more calculating players out of playing medium hands, that I began to grow bumptious. My come-uppance was not long in arriving.

It was a small error, but mine own, and a costly one. In early position, with a pair of kings in the hole, I raised the maximum – $250 – before the flop. Seat Eight, a wealthy Scandinavian whose play I didn't much rate, took the chance to raise me back $1,000. Could he have a pair of aces? I didn't think so. He had been playing fast and loose himself – largely, I figured, because the money meant nothing to him. Judging by his previous play, I put him on a suited ace with a high kicker, and re-raised another $1,000. It could – perhaps should – have been $2,000; but I had sat down with only $4,500, and now had some $6,000 in front of me, while he had over ten on display, and plenty more in his pocket. I wanted him in.

He just called, and we saw the flop come Ah-Kc-3s. As it emerged, I watched him watching it, and thought I saw something in his eyes to confirm my view about that ace he was holding. So now I had three kings, but he had a pair of aces. First to bet, I checked to feign weakness, to seem scared of his ace. Slow-playing my three kings seemed to me a super-crafty professional manœuvre, designed to result in a check-raise. I expected him to read me as a pair of queens or jacks, and bet his aces, giving me the chance to re-raise the max. But he, too, checked.

This was enough of a setback in itself, but the next card was another club. Could that be his suit? Already I could feel things going wrong, and I checked again. This time he bet the lot, challenging me to call for the full $3,750 I had left. Now it was my turn to think.

Out of the blue, as I did so, he said with a grin: 'You looked good on TV!' This convinced me that he was weak in the hole. It is standard, if slightly sharp practice to distract a brooding opponent with irrelevant small talk. A reply can be very reveal-ing. The player who is bluffing will stammer inanities; the man with the lock hand will talk relaxed sense. I said noth-ing, still convinced that he couldn't have a concealed pair of aces. He may be pulling to a club flush, but I was still winning. There was also an outside chance that the river – internal cries of 'pair the board!' – would give me a full house, though four kings would be too much to hope for. Maybe, after my two checks, he simply figured that a lone ace was winning it? I called, wishing I had enough to re-raise.

The last card was the seven of clubs. I rolled over my kings – out of turn, as the Scandinavian was the one who had been called – to watch him turn the A-10 of clubs. I'd been stuffed, and it was entirely my own fault. I had let him improve his hand for free, then bully me when my funds were low. If I had bet the maximum after the flop, a sound player would have known the odds against him, and found it very hard to call. The way he had echoed my check, moreover, proved him to be a sound player. He had been extraordinarily lucky to pull that winning flush on the last two cards. But I had both misjudged my opponent and misplayed my hand.

That was enough. As the complacent Nord raked in my cash – an awful lot of my cash – I left the table without a word, closed down my safe deposit box and headed upstairs to pack. What a disastrous end to a helter-skelter of a trip. Now I had to face a long journey back to London rendered miserable by one moment of weakness – one moment that, by ignoring everything I had spent all this time learning, was sending me home for Christmas with $5,000 in my pocket instead of $10,000, let alone $100,000. No matter that I had paid off my $700 Malta deficit, saved four thousand notional dollars in cut-price satellite entries into tournaments, and managed a run of consistently good results in my début on the American tour. The bottom line was not good. Six whole months to go to the World Series, and my bank-roll was down by 25 per cent. I had only $5,000 left – exactly what I had just lost in one hand – over the $10,000 needed to defend my cherished world ranking.

So much for my supposed self-knowledge. So much for hours and hours of tournament tutelage. So much for my 'lucky' *diamanté* wrist-watch, which I now solemnly discarded. Maybe, after all, I should be reading Dostoevsky rather than Doyle Brunson.

Maybe, come to that, I should take a tip from Dostoevsky, and seek out my own private Sigmund Freud. I certainly couldn't face the cosy camaraderie of Gamblers Anonymous. Once back in London, I resolved, I would swallow my pride, stifle my misgivings, and throw myself upon the mercy of a shrink.

7

Enter The Shrink

♥ ♣ ♦ ♠

It is a perfect summer evening in the early 1970s, in the side streets of Salzburg, city of Mozart and *festspielen*.

Two young Englishmen, respectable enough looking in their jackets and ties, can be seen accosting passers-by and offering them large amounts of money, in ready cash, for their shoes. For an hour and more, they are firmly rebuffed. Finally, with a wild surmise in their eyes, they fall upon an astonished Indian hiker, beneath whose regulation shorts, khaki shirt and mountainous knapsack lurk the most elegant, shiny pair of brown brogues which these two young Englishmen ever did see.

One of them (the bearded one) removes the sandals he is wearing, and begins to praise their sturdy German qualities to the bemused long-distance traveller. After some heated exchanges, marked by much incredulous Indian gesticulation, this unlikely trio eventually disappear into a nearby youth hostel. Some minutes later the two Englishmen re-emerge at speed, the bearded one wearing the brogues. The Indian stares forlornly after them, then gazes down at the German sandals on his feet, as they disappear in the direction of the Salzburg casino.

It happened like this. Summering in Austria with my friend John David Morley, then an unemployed expatriate Briton, now a novelist of some renown, I had discovered the addictive allure of roulette in the fashionable casino at Kitzbühel. Operating as a team, employing different but compatible systems, Morley and I had managed to work up a fat profit – by our then standards – of some £300. Next day, dragooned by music-loving companions into an excursion to Salzburg, we had inevitably packed our winnings, taken a rain-check on Mozart and presented ourselves on the stroke of opening time at this, one of the grandest casinos in Europe.

As we climbed its ornate, chandeliered staircase, we were prepared for the usual scornful looks. Though decked out in the statutory jackets and ties, and duly armed with our passports, we looked all too much like the students we had until recently been. Our hair, it has to be said, was less kempt than they like it in such establishments, unless atop recognizable stars of stage, screen or song. The major-domos at these joints tend to prefer sleek high rollers. This one kept a malevolent eye on us all the way up the staircase, seeking out some chink in our threadbare tourist armour. When we smugly presented him with the passports, his eyes were still searching for some reason to deny us entry. Eventually he leaned over his desk, looked down at our feet, and spotted Morley's sandals. Triumphantly he declared this kind of footwear '*verboten*', and pointed us back down the staircase. My partner's lengthy and vehement protests, for all his fluent dialect-German, were wholly in vain.

We still had five minutes until the shops closed, and the Austrian equivalent of £300 in our pockets. Down the stairs and into the street we sprinted, arriving at the nearest shoe-shop just as it was locking its doors. No amount of banging on the window and waving of banknotes would persuade them to reopen for us. It was then that we realized our only remaining option: to buy someone's shoes off his feet.

For all our desperation, we found much innocent enjoyment in the discovery of a new branch of social anthropology: measuring people entirely in terms of their shoes. Smart leathers with laces tended to wax indignant, even threaten to call the *polizei*; slip-ons were friendlier, listening to the precise terms of our offer before deciding we were crazy; boots were beyond our means, sandals and trainers naturally beneath consideration. One pair of winkle-pickers proved a near miss; picking his teeth at the entrance to a low-life dive, their owner heard us out impassively before wearily shaking his head and gesturing us on our way.

It was then that this magnificent Indian, or rather his magnificent shoes, rounded the corner, like a walk-on in a Nevada desert mirage. By this time, life was too short for pleasantries. He was brusquely told to remove the brogues and take the money. We even agreed to pay for his night at the hostel; hence the brief diversion from our purpose.

When we reclimbed the casino stairs, the same major-domo again leaned over the same desk, and again looked us over from head to toe, but this time could find no pretext for excluding us. After brief early advances, it need scarcely be added, we lost every *pfennig* we had. The management then proved curiously reluctant to let us wager the Indian's shoes on *impair* and *rouge* respectively. Just as well, for the next roll came up *pair* et *noir*.

Back to Kitzbühel we stumbled, broke but fulfilled, Morley convincing himself at some length that the Indian brogues (which we were henceforth to share, alternately, year by year) were more than worth the investment. We had taken, in our own terms, the ultimate risk; we had gone to unusual lengths to do so; and the loss of all our worldly goods seemed a small price to pay for so inspiriting an adventure. We were both, in short, clinical archetypes of the compulsive gambler. Losing everything had swiftly become a thrilling confirmation of the size of the risk we had taken. It was a sensation quite as life-enhancing as winning.

On the way to Salzburg, I had commended to Morley a letter written by Dostoevsky to his sister-in-law in 1863, asking her to forward to his wife some money he had won at Wiesbaden, *en route* to Paris:

> *Please don't think I am so pleased with myself for not losing that I am showing off when I say that I know the secret of how not to lose but win. I really do know the secret; it is terribly silly and simple and consists of keeping one's head the whole time, whatever the state of the game, and not getting excited. That is all, and it makes losing simply impossible and winning a certainty.*

On the way back, I read him the next paragraph:

> *But that is not the point; the point is whether, having grasped the secret, a man knows how to make use of it and is fit to do so. A man can be as wise as Solomon and have an iron character and still be carried away . . . Therefore blessed are they who do not play, and regard the roulette wheel with loathing as the greatest of stupidities.*

A week later Dostoevsky, too, had lost the lot, and was busy wiring home for funds. We both decided that *The Gambler* was perhaps a better story than we had at first thought. Who cares if it is sloppily written, long-winded and rambling? The roulette passages capture the thrill of the 'pleasure principle' behind compulsive gambling – even if they fail, revealingly, to rationalize or explain it; and old Fyodor had anyway dashed the whole thing off in six weeks to pay his debts. Now we were with him all the way, not least because our own folly would oblige each of us to drown in at least six *months* of punitive hackwork.

During the rest of the 1970s I indulged occasionally in roulette, blackjack and horse-racing, losing consistently before wising up to the better odds offered by poker, which also tends to give you a longer run for your money. During my first six months as a professional poker player, however, there were times I felt the old gambler in me resurfacing. Poker, I had always argued, was not a form of gambling; on the contrary, gambling was a *style* of playing poker – a loose and losing style, at that. Had I failed to heed my own warning? Was that clumsy loss at the end of my Christmas visit to Vegas a sign that I was on the slide, that I could not sustain the self-discipline to cope with my deep-seated need for action?

Or was I just screwed up? The received wisdom on compulsive gamblers begins with Freud's essay on Dostoevsky, published in 1928. After discussing the writer's feelings of associated guilt about the murder of his father, and reminding us of his own Oedipal theories (in terms of Sophocles' *Oedipus Rex*, Shakespeare's *Hamlet* and Dostoevsky's *The Brothers Karamazov*), Freud dismisses Dostoevsky's compulsion to gamble as a substitute for masturbation.

> *The 'vice' of masturbation is replaced by the addiction to gambling; and the emphasis laid upon the passionate activity of the hands betrays this derivation . . . The passion for play is an equivalent of the old compulsion to masturbate.*

An American pupil of Freud, Edmund Bergler, took the idea several stages further in an influential essay called 'The

Psychology of the Gambler', first published in *Imago* in 1936, only eight years after Freud's thoughts on Dostoevsky. The neurotic gambler, Bergler argued, suffers feelings of unconscious guilt about his childhood resentment of his parents, the first people to introduce the notion of refusal into his life, to squash a child's instinctive megalomania. This guilt has the gambler unconsciously intent on punishing himself. He knows that the odds are stacked against him; his persistence in attempting to defy them is a last-ditch plea for forgiveness from the authorities (either or both of his parents). Even if he wins at first, he will not be content until he has lost. Losing amounts to self-punishment for his early transgressions against authority. The compulsive gambler, in other words, *wants to lose*.

At his bluntest, Bergler argued that 'gambling is not a profession. It is a dangerous neurosis.' Losing was 'essential to [the gambler's] psychic equilibrium. It is the price he pays for his neurotic aggression, and, at the same time, it makes it possible for him to continue gambling.'

It was an idea whose time had come. America's popular press had such fun with Bergler's basic thesis – 'Unconsciously, the gambler wants to LOSE!' – that he felt obliged to reinforce it with detailed clinical evidence in a book which became even more influential, *The Psychology of Gambling*, published in 1957. The gambler's basic problem, according to Bergler, was 'psychic masochism'. He summarized the compulsive (or neurotic) gambler's inner feelings as follows:

First, unconscious aggression [against parents]; second, an unconscious tendency towards self-punishment because of that aggression. The self-punishing factor, which is always present,

is almost never recognized except in psychoanalytic treatment.
Thus the childlike, unconscious neurotic misunderstanding of
the whole gambling process creates a vicious, and endless,
circle. Hence the inner necessity to lose.

Though often misattributed to Freud, Bergler's theory has
gained sufficient renown over the years to become the butt of
many a nervous joke in casinos from London to Las Vegas. It
was the first notion I wanted to thrash out with the Shrink,
whom I found lurking on the edge of my current circle of
acquaintance. He had sons at the same school; we had met
over the dinner tables of mutual friends; he knew the outlines
of my professional career, and had formed an impression of
my character. Though psychiatry and socializing are not
supposed to mix, it occurred to the gambler in me that some
prior knowledge, albeit of the surface variety, might save me
a bit of time . . . and money.

From the smoky clatter of a casino floor to the clinical
spareness of a hospital consulting room: this was not quite
the road I had thought to travel on turning poker pro. As he
perused the clipboard on his knee, the Shrink's formal, busi-
ness-like air rather scared me. This was not the genial fellow
I had met at school sherry parties; this was a grave professional, whose knowing looks and silent nods gave him an
immediate edge. Could he really know things about me I
didn't know? If so, would he share them with me, or would
the men in white coats arrive first? I had expected him, I now
realized, to say something like: 'There's nothing wrong with
you, Mr Holden. We all have our needs, our little voices.
They're just pressure-valves.' Instead he seemed to be
contemplating a committal order.

My ego and my sexuality, two wholly-owned subsidiaries

to which I am rather attached, both seemed to be at stake until we could fight our way free of the textbooks. I started in a gush, insisting that I did not regard myself as a compulsive gambler, and thus considered the Freud–Bergler thesis irrelevant to my case. Poker, when played properly, was the most controlled form of gambling available. What did Freud mean, anyway, by relating gambling to masturbation? Surely the old boy was talking about some ill-defined thrill *akin* to sexual excitement, which for some may even amount to a surrogate sexual experience?

And surely Bergler's thesis must these days be qualified? I knew people who proved his point – who were somehow purged, even fulfilled, by losing – but I had never experienced this sensation myself, nor ever expected to . . .

'Quite so.' The Shrink's first move was to call a halt to these defensive ramblings. He wanted to start (as Freud, I gloomily presumed, would have wished) by hearing about my parents. As I wandered through the highlights of my childhood – the card playing, the prohibition on poker, being sent away to school at the age of eight, growing away from my parents after reaching university – the Shrink seemed particularly struck by my father's hard luck story. Not the one about losing £50 on the way back from the war. The one about the rotten hand subsequently dealt him by life.

My father was born the second son of a Lancashire cotton millionaire: Sir John Holden, second baronet, of the Firs. He grew up in a house so big that it is now a hospital; breakfast was served from silver platters by butlers. My father's father, like his father before him, was the mayor of Leigh – the youngest British mayor on record, and the only one to be *invited*, rather than elected, into that office. He was such a major local figure that one of Leigh's main thoroughfares was renamed, and is still called, Holden Road. After a public school education, at the same school as his father before him (and the Crony and me after him), my father was destined to join the family business, walking straight into a plum job on the Manchester cotton exchange.

Shortly before the Second World War, however, my grandfather suffered a serious stock market reverse, and dropped dead of a heart attack at the age of forty-seven. By the time his son came home again – penniless, as we have seen, because of poker – the family assets (including the house) were being auctioned, and there was no Manchester cotton exchange, no family business. He was forced to start from scratch, in the Lancashire resort of Southport, as a trainee jack-of-all-trades in a garage. Subsequently, for reasons I have never quite fathomed, he went to work in a wire mesh factory in Manchester. But he hated it so much that in 1953, when he was thirty-five (and I was six), he threw it all up, borrowed some money from his father-in-law, and opened a sports shop in Southport, which he ran for the rest of his working life.

My father loved sport, and was happy enough to spend six days a week behind the counter of his sports shop, staying on after it closed to keep his own books. But the rest of the time he moved in middle-class, golf-club society, where most of his circle of friends were better off, and rather more than shopkeepers. Dad found it hard work keeping up with them financially. He was regarded, for instance, as a figure of sufficient popularity and probity to have taken his turn, like all his peers, as Captain of the Golf Club, the height of social achievement thereabouts; but he could never have afforded the entertaining involved, and was thus discreetly passed over. An enthusiastic and conscientious chairman of the Greens Committee, notably when the Ryder Cup came to town, was more his mark. Though he was happily married for forty-five years, and proud of the emergent careers of his two sons, I believe that in many other ways he died a quietly disappointed man. He was too much of a gentleman ever to say so himself, but I suspect he felt that life could have dealt him a better hand.

What would Freud and Bergler have made of all this? I was, as I now told the Shrink, devoted to my father. Apart from my youthful defiance of his poker ban (for which I had long since won his indulgence), I felt no conscious guilt about my dealings with him. We had parted suddenly and all too prematurely, but on the best of terms. My feelings about my mother might perhaps have been more complex, but for my late father (*pace* my subconscious) I felt nothing but the simplest and deepest affection.

The Shrink declared himself 'enthralled' – all this, to him, was rich new pasture – then asked for a brief résumé of my career in journalism, with particular reference to the extent to which I had achieved my own desires and ambitions. After listening in silence, the Shrink saw off Freud and Bergler in one stunning pronouncement: 'What strikes me is not so much your will to lose as your will to *win*.'

That sent me off to that night's Tuesday Game in high enough spirits to mop up through sheer willpower. And so it continued, in much the same vein, for my next two sessions with the Shrink – some random burbling from me, much head-nodding and note-taking from him, rather in the manner of Sherlock Holmes unravelling a particularly untidy sequence of clues. To sense him divining hidden meanings in my every spoken thought was not unlike playing an especially uncomfortable poker hand. Before we had begun, I had secretly doubted that any shrink could tell me much about myself that I didn't already know. By the end of our third long, intense session, however, this one came up with an *aperçu* which knocked me sideways.

There was a direct correlation, he suggested, between my sense of my father as a somehow defeated man and the development in me of a stubbornly powerful will to win – in life as in poker.

What I was up to, it seemed to him, was *avenging my father's hard luck story*.

2

The name of Toledo, Ohio, an otherwise unexceptional outpost of the American Midwest, is forever tarnished in poker circles by the fact that it sired the game of 'jackpots'.

Until an indeterminate point in the mid-eighteenth century, in Toledo, Ohio, as elsewhere, before and since, good poker players had been the consistent winners and poor poker players the consistent losers. There is a simple reason for this. For the good poker player, as one wag put it, 'the fact that a player does not have to bet on every hand in pure poker is tantamount to a block of General Motors stock'. The good player, in other words, will know to drop out of a pot, without parting with any money, when the cards in his hand are no good; the poorer player will pay to play on, in the hope of drawing the miraculous cards needed to improve his hand. When the good player's cards are good, of course, he will play – as again will the poorer player, in the hope that his luck will change. It never does.

It was in Toledo, Ohio, that one of these poorer players

decided one day that this emphasis on skill was rather unfair, and that the poorer players should have more of an edge. So he invented the game of jackpots, a form of draw poker in which every player is forced to ante before the deal, but only a player holding a pair of jacks or better can open the betting. Thus was the random fall of the cards increased in value and importance, at the expense of the psychological skill at the heart of the game. From here it was but a small step to wild cards and jokers, Mexican Flip, Fiery Cross, Spit in the Ocean, and the seemingly infinite array of deviant games now played in amateur poker schools the world over. These variants are known to professionals as 'Mickey Mouse games', and have been wearily described by one old hand as 'the desecrations of people tired of drawing moustaches on the Mona Lisa'.

The Tuesday Night Game plays more than its fair share of Mickey Mouse poker, baffling newcomers with such home-grown products as The Don's Game (hole card and all like it wild if paired), The Thinking Man's Game (five-card stud with a change at the end), and even Big Cross (a king-size version of Fiery Cross, amounting to Omaha with five cards in the hand, and two flops). In the grey New Year, following my return from the Hall of Fame tournament at Binion's, the latest Tuesday fad was a variant of draw called Levy's Game, after the London player who invented it.

In Levy's Game, as in pure draw poker, you are dealt five concealed cards; there is then one betting round, after which the survivors may change as many cards as they like. Instead of ending things with another round of betting, in the good old-fashioned way, Levy's demands *five* more rounds. After the draw, players arrange their cards in the order in which they wish to reveal them, and roll them one by one, with a bet between each roll.

Even that is not enough. Once the fourth exposed card has
been bet, players may *change* any one card, up or down. Oh
yes, and Levy's is high-low. After the final round of betting
come declarations, and the pot will be split between the highest and the lowest hands. The 'wheel' works – which means
that straights or flushes can count high and/or low, the best
low hand being A-2-3-4-5. To go 'both ways', and win the
whole pot, however, you must win both the high and the low
hands outright. The player who goes both ways and shares
either end – usually with another perfect low – forfeits the
lot.

I was still grumbling about the absurdity of all this one
Tuesday when I found myself holding the A-2-4-5 of
diamonds after a deal of Levy's Game, with the ten of spades.
This hand, of course, is likely to involve me in a lot of action,
for these are already four perfect up-cards to play, regardless
of what I might draw to them. Even if my change proves
useless, I can leave it in the hole and still look good; then I
will have a chance to change it again at the end if the situation so demands. This is the kind of hand that can prove
extremely expensive, if you draw badly both times and someone decides to go against you at the showdown. I was silently
cursing the temptations of the hand when I changed my ten
of spades for a . . . three of diamonds.

I was holding the perfect high-low straight flush, an object
of such extreme rarity that I had to stop myself staring at it.
The point now was to maximize its value.

Cunningly, as I thought, I left the ace in the hole, and started
by rolling the five. The low heart on my left bet, and got three
callers, including me. It was too early as yet to raise; I didn't
want to frighten them out, and I wanted the guy on my left
to continue setting the pace. The next bet, after I had rolled

the four of diamonds, also came from him, and was already in three figures. By the time all four of our 'up' cards were on display, there were three of us left, I was still slow-playing my hand, and we had already reached the school's maximum bet of £500. On my left was an apparent high hand, four un-related hearts including the ace, and to my right an apparent low hand: 2-3-4 . . . 6! Thanks to that six, I already knew that I had won this hand both ways, with two rounds of betting, before and after the change, to come.

Things couldn't be going better. The heart flush had hith-erto done all the betting for me. I had wanted to keep them in, and be sure I had them both beaten; so not until the round immediately before the change did I lob in my first raise – the maximum, of course – to 'give them something to think about'.

Not to change in these circumstances is often a bluff, or a safe play from someone with a seven-ish low. When I declined to change my hole card, the others looked at me long and hard, then decided not to change theirs either. The ace-high flush, it seemed, was genuine; the low hand also a straight, wondering if either or both of his opponents were bluffing. The flush duly bet again, the maximum, called by the 2-3-4-6, who must have been wondering if he had this huge pot won both ways. When I raised again, they both seemed for the first time to fear the worst, but called nevertheless.

As I declared both ways, and showed the concealed ace which gave me the perfect, unbeatable high-low hand, there were gasps from the onlookers and cries of, 'Thank God I wasn't in *that* hand'. The pot I proceeded to haul in totalled £9,340, over six thousand of which was clear profit. It was the biggest single pot in the history of the Tuesday Game – enough to put Vegas in the shade – and simply proved my point about Mickey Mouse poker: that if he happens to draw the nuts, and Lady Luck gives a couple of other players good hands, a robot can't lose. That's my kind of gambling.

The odds against my being dealt that hand were, as we have seen, 64,973 to 1. I spent the rest of the evening calculating that, after fifteen years in the game, this was probably just about the 64,974th hand I had played. My *real* luck was that two punters had come all that way for the ride. While making these calculations, of course, I also clung to my winnings as to life itself, and went home £6,000 to the good.

All of which is a lengthy (but, oh, so nostalgic) diversion to explain why our scene now shifts to a sun-baked beach on the Caribbean island of St Lucia, where the Moll and I spent mid-January enjoying a straight flush of a vacation, and pondering the Shrink's early findings over a banana daiquiri or three. A self-indulgent dent in the bank-roll this may have been, but it was proving a good investment. All around us was living proof of the extent to which people gamble with their lives. The corporate executive openly flaunting his mistress; the Wall Street broker, never without his mobile phone, incessantly trading from the poolside; the minor politician savouring the Inauguration Day of a new American president; each was a visual aid to my theories about the games people play.

The spouses who cheat on their partners, for instance, embark upon a game of chance involving fine calculations. In the circumstances, they have the odds on their side. Both have played the game of co-habitation long enough to know how much they can get away with. They also know what they have to do – it may be as simple as a bunch of flowers – to divert attention from their aberrant behaviour. They are becoming proficient practitioners of the art of bluff.

Like seasoned poker players, they are playing the person

they know rather than the hand that person is holding – playing 'the man rather than the cards'. But then, like the weak poker player, they become overconfident. The unfaithful spouses have no problem reconciling their infidelity with their own conscience. They persuade themselves that they are justified, that the occasional betrayal is of no relevance to the state of their marriage. In this, of course, they are deceived, as is the punter who bets into a pat hand. The odds strongly suggest that both will be found out, and pay heavily for it, in the end.

Bluffing, however, is not merely slyness. In life, as in poker, it is usually an act of aggression. Big business deals – takeovers, mergers, flotations, affecting the personal finances of countless innocent shareholders – are inevitably conducted like poker games, with one side raising the stakes and the other wondering whether this latest move is a bluff, whether to call or fold.

For most 'white-collar' professionals, wheeling and dealing their way towards the top, the art of bluff is an everyday occupational hazard. To politicians, it is an essential part of their bag of tricks. The most successful politicians, by definition, are those who have bluffed most effectively, perhaps most often, and have been 'called' least.

It is no coincidence that many American presidents have been expert poker players. On the evidence of one or two episodes from recent history, the game might well be written into the constitution as required vocational training.

3

Ever since George Washington kept a ledger page headed 'Cards and Other Play', listing a profit of £6 3s 3d in the three years to 1 January 1775, expertise at America's favourite game has become an all but essential qualification to aspire to its leadership. As one of Richard Nixon's teachers at Whittier College, California, put it: 'A man who can't hold a hand in a first-class poker game is not fit to be President of the United States.'

Nixon seems to have heeded the advice, learning his poker in the Navy, and playing with characteristic determination and guile. According to one of his fellow officers, 'Nick' Nixon one day asked him if there was any sure way to win at poker. 'I explained that I didn't know of a sure way to win, but I had a theory for playing draw poker. It was that one must never stay in unless he knows he has everyone at the table beaten at the time of the draw. "Nick" liked what I said. I gave him his first lessons. We played two-handed poker without money for four or five days, until he had learned the various plays. Soon his playing became tops. He never raised unless he was convinced he had the best hand.'

Dwight Eisenhower, a solid poker player from childhood, once recalled how uneasy he felt about winning money off fellow soldiers: 'When I found officers around me losing more money than they could afford, I stopped.' Not so his future vice-president. Nixon won $6,000 in his first two months in the Navy, and kept on winning. 'Nick was as good a poker player as, if not better than, anyone we had ever seen,' testified one of his victims. 'He played a quiet game, but wasn't afraid of taking chances. He wasn't afraid of running a bluff. Sometimes the stakes were pretty big, but Nick had daring and a flair for knowing what to do.' Nixon later revealed that his Navy winnings enabled him to finance his first political campaign, when he ran for Congress against Jerry Voorhis in 1946. Poker, in other words, provided the launch-pad for Nixon's political career.

It was also, you might say, his undoing. During the Watergate crisis of 1973–4, Nixon should have remembered his poker precepts: never stay in the hand unless you have everyone beaten before the draw, never raise unless sure you are holding the best cards. The Watergate cover-up was self-evidently the biggest bluff Nixon had ever attempted. His strategy was nothing if not aggressive: if he staked the power and prestige of the presidency itself on the cover-up, he calculated, the odds were that Congress would not dare to 'see' him.

But there was a fatal flaw in Nixon's thinking. Poker players who bluff successfully never, by definition, reveal their cards to the other players, let alone make a record of them for posterity. David Spanier, himself a Washington correspondent at the time, divined this basic error in his book *Total Poker*:

The bluff failed in the end because the hands were recorded in the form of the [White House] tapes. That was why the cover-up was ultimately exposed. If the tapes had been destroyed instead of being doctored, the probability is that Congress would not have nerved itself to bring in a Bill of Impeachment, and Richard Nixon's greatest bluff would have 'held'.

Poker was also the backdrop to one of the most momentous presidential decisions of the twentieth century. Returning from the 1945 Potsdam conference, while agonizing whether to drop the first atomic bomb on Japan, Harry Truman relaxed by fleecing the White House reporters crossing the Atlantic with him aboard the cruiser *Augusta*. 'Why in the world don't you men leave the President alone?' demanded the Secretary of

State, James F. Byrnes, of the press corps. 'Give him time to do something besides play poker?'

'Leave *him* alone?' replied the United Press correspondent, Merriman Smith. 'We don't start those games. He does.'

Truman, who had been in office less than four months, and was now exhausted from weeks of tense negotiations, wanted to relax while weighing his apocalyptic decision. Byrnes, he knew, was in violent disagreement with him. In his report of the trip, Smith explained that for most of that week Truman 'was running a straight stud filibuster against his own Secretary of State', using a deck of cards and a stack of chips to avoid having extended conversations with Byrnes, a strong-willed South Carolinian, who later split with the President 'in a sunburst of political fireworks'.

Truman played poker with the press corps 'morning, noon and night'. The stakes were high – pot limit – and frequently reached hundreds of dollars. Byrnes, meanwhile, 'waited in the wings for a chance to talk extensively with the President, but Mr Truman's only free time was early in the morning before breakfast, or at meal times'.

The shipboard games apparently started as early as 8.30 a.m. and went right through to midnight, stopping only for lunch and dinner. One morning, a Marine orderly turned the pressmen out of bed before 8 a.m., with an order to report to Truman's cabin in fifteen minutes. 'Good Lord,' complained one reporter, 'why don't we play all night instead of starting out at this awful hour?' But this particular summons was not about poker. 'The President instead reviewed in great detail the development of the atomic bomb, and the forthcoming first drop on Hiroshima. Once this graphic secret was told to us for later publication, out came the cards and chips.'

Truman was the big winner. But Smith divined 'a basic

streak of kindness' in the President. Playing with comparatively low-salaried reporters, Truman became embarrassed when he won heavily, and would play impossible hands in an effort to plough his winnings back into the game. His luck was so good, however, that while trying to give money back he sometimes hit inside straights, and thus won even more.

'I never,' wrote Smith, 'saw him lose badly.' The reporter learnt a great deal else about Truman from his style at the poker table, drawing conclusions as to how he would later handle political problems. 'He did not hesitate to take calculated risks. He played a forthright, hard-hitting game and seemed to bluff only out of playful mischief or boredom resulting from a long run of mediocre cards. His game was based more on analysis of the other players than strictly on the cards themselves.' In a wry afterthought, Smith added: 'I know of no-one who ever got any state secrets or information from Mr Truman in a poker game, unless it was the chilling fact that aces beat kings.'

John Kennedy seems to have been one of the few presidents in the *macho* mould not to have been much of a poker player. But the other great trauma of the modern presidency, the Cuban missile crisis of October 1962, can be analysed in almost uncanny detail as a slowly developing hand, involving bluff and counter-bluff, with stakes as high as they go.

Khrushchev, like Truman and all the best poker players, was playing the man rather than his hand. He and Kennedy had played an earlier game at their Vienna summit, where the Russian leader had 'read' the new American president as young, inexperienced and easy to push around. His subsequent *chutzpah* in placing nuclear missile sites on Cuba was essentially based on this assessment; Khrushchev believed that Kennedy would prove too weak to respond.

He had read his man wrong. When U-2 reconnaissance planes spotted the missiles ninety miles off the Florida coast, Kennedy quickly imposed a blockade to prevent Russian ships ferrying nuclear warheads to the launch sites. The best poker players bluff, or raise the maximum, to give their opponents 'something to think about'; this is precisely what Kennedy had done as he coolly kept to his pre-arranged domestic schedule, leaving Khrushchev to make the next move.

Neither country wanted nuclear war. Both, in effect, were bluffing. But the Americans were bluffing with the better hand, in terms of nuclear superiority. Though obviously aware of this, Khrushchev could not lose face. He ordered twenty-five merchant vessels then *en route* to Cuba to continue, with an escort of nuclear submarines. The chips were down, and the kibitzing world watched in agony as the showdown approached.

Which man would back down? In especially large pots, when two good players have too much at stake to leave the result to destiny, they sometimes negotiate a settlement based on the power of their respective hands. In exactly the same way, tense backstage diplomacy struggled to find a way out – a way, in effect, for the weaker side to fold without loss of face. Kennedy proved shrewd enough to see that he had to help Khrushchev to withdraw; the alternative was an American victory which might spell the world's doom. By agreeing not to invade Cuba, in return for the withdrawal of the Russian missile sites, he gave Khrushchev a dignified 'out'. The Russian fleet was immediately recalled.

Before the game began, the odds had been almost too close to call. By its end Khrushchev had, in effect, folded his hand and conceded the pot. The true cunning of Kennedy's route to victory was to enable his opponent to lose without being humiliated. The alternative might have proved a decidedly pyrrhic victory.

4

Back home, I put it to the Shrink that lesser mortals take as many chances, quite as nerve-racking on their own personal scales, every day of their lives, many involving psychological calculations quite as delicate as Kennedy's. To improve their lot, whether at work or at home, human beings will not hesitate to misrepresent the hand they are holding, to make out that it is stronger than it is; and often they will win, or have their own way. Proxy gambling runs deep in the human spirit. Big businessmen juggle figures; politicians have affairs; husbands and wives conduct a permanent form of domestic guerrilla warfare; children exploit their parents. In Dr Eric Berne's *Games People Play* there is a classic textbook proof, if proof be needed, that human beings conduct their relationships as a series of games of chance, often for high stakes. Only the limits are up to the players.

I had always admired people who took risks, who ran their lives with a decent sense of danger about the decisions which came their way. I had to admit, however, that most of them appeared to derive enough stimulus from their everyday lives, without resorting to the more overt and obvious dangers of gambling. Does a penchant for gambling, poker included, necessarily assume some black hole in the rest of the gambler's life? Or is he merely a breed apart?

Almost all the poker players I have known, from the hardened pros of Las Vegas to my amateur Tuesday Night brethren in London, have had one specific characteristic in common:

they were all people who liked to feel that they had bucked the system. They were determined to live life on their own terms. In a worldly sense, therefore, they were people who had rarely held down a regular job since compelled to by the indigence of youth. If ever they had since been obliged to do so, or to attempt to do so, they had extricated themselves from it, regardless of the consequences, with all possible speed.

I had only to look at my own journalistic career – rarely in the same job for more than eighteen months, maximum three years, all of them voluntarily surrendered when I was doing just fine – to find a classic case. It wasn't just that I always wished I were doing something else. It was more a loathing of being an *employee*, fiddling away my life at some-one else's pleasure.

When my last employer issued me with a radio-controlled bleeper, to be worn at all times, it was supposed to be a compli-ment, a sign of seniority, of indispensability; to me, suddenly at his beck and call twenty-four hours a day, even while asleep, on the lavatory, *at the poker table*, it was merely the most demeaning symbol of my servitude.

Apart from that one twelve-month aberration, moreover, it had now for almost a decade been my proudest boast that this son of a culture-free northern household, not a book in the house during his childhood, could earn his living by his pen, no longer answerable to the baronial slave-drivers of Fleet Street – master of his own hours, and thus of his own over-draft. It was a fact of which I was inordinately proud.

All this, to the Shrink, fitted a pattern. It was evident that I sct an unusually high value on attaining the greatest possi-ble personal freedoms; but I had also set up some prickly defence mechanisms against the consequent dangers of loss. He would need more input to develop this thesis in the weeks ahead. In the meantime, he rested content with a dissertation on male bonding. The all-male Tuesday poker group, for instance, presented a classic case of male 'affiliation'. It was almost a secret society, with its own unique code of behaviour – a set of rules which even imposed a form of etiquette on men otherwise resistant to the very word. It scoffed at the workaday world in a pretty self-satisfied way. It had its own set of values about non-members, most of them fairly cynical, if not downright dismissive. Being an insider in this group, able to sneer at the outsiders, was a useful piece of self-imagery.

This forum gave its inner circle a chance to work out their various hang-ups in ways acceptable to their own pride and *amour propre*. Poker, for instance, gave the Tuesday boys an acceptable way to *lose*. Losing is one of life's most difficult challenges, often causing deep psychological problems. However much human beings may hate it, even the most upwardly mobile still need to have the freedom to lose in some department of their life. As with Kennedy and Khrushchev, whoever loses at the poker table – and it helps that every game, by definition, must have both winners and losers – is likely to be treated as a winner *manqué*.

In a social game like ours the other players will pat him on the back, say, 'Bad Luck,' and generally make him feel it wasn't his fault. He took a commendable risk; he played his cards right; it was just that the odds don't always conform to the rulebook, and old so-and-so was lucky to pull that miracle card against him. Old so-and-so, in fact, will be the first to say so – and not just because he wants to be thought a gracious winner. False modesty can all too quickly curdle into hypocrisy. Though believing it was his skill which made him a winner, rather than a fortunate distribution of the cards, he is prepared to pretend the opposite in the hope of making the loser play on while at a financial and psychological disadvantage.

The annals of the Tuesday Night Game record that one cheery December evening I suggested taking a pound out of each pot, and using the resulting few hundred to go out for a major Christmas luncheon. The notion was greeted with blank expressions of disbelief. Someone pointed out that we would have nothing at all to say to each other, beyond talking about the game; and that the logical step from talking about it was playing it. Why not have a Christmas *game* instead?

However touching, my seasonal suggestion was absurd. To take ourselves out to lunch would be to rob our group of its *ratio vivendi*. Although, on the whole, we all liked each other, we had no wish to foregather for any reason other than the game of poker which had initially brought us together. We felt so little need to meet up for any other reason that the idea was laughable. In passing, this also seemed to deal with the Moll's occasional neo-Freudian quip that we were, deep down, a bunch of latent homosexuals. But which of us, if any, thought hard enough about his poker performance to learn deeper truths about himself? If I were to try, with the Shrink's help, would I go to the game with a built-in advantage?

'Character . . . is what the game of poker is about,' to the American writer David Mamet, a keen player since his college days. 'Most of us, from time to time, try to escape a blunt fact which may not tally with our self-image. When we are depressed, we recreate the world around us to rationalize our mood. We are then likely to overlook or misinterpret happy circumstances. At the poker table, this can be expensive, for opportunity may knock, but it seldom nags . . .'

In a witty, perceptive essay entitled 'Things I Have Learned Playing Poker on the Hill', Mamet explains: 'Many bad players . . . cannot bear the notion that everything they do is done for a reason. The bad player will not deign to determine what he thinks by watching what he does.' To do so might, and frequently would, reveal certain aspects of himself of which he would rather live in ignorance.

This, to the Shrink and me, was core material. We much preferred Mamet's version of Freud to Freud's. Too few people, we agreed, choose to acknowledge that their every move, at work or at home, derives from a set of psychological needs lodged in them since childhood. In adult life, as at the poker table, these needs translate into ploys, which will in the end make or break them.

Charlie, let's say, had a forceful father in the habit of acting 'cruel to be kind'. Charlie's dad thought his wife over-indulgent to the children; though a loving parent, he would therefore impose sanctions where he thought them due. Charlie in turn loved his father, but he also feared him.

This is why Charlie will prove a weak poker player. He will keep betting into the best hand – because of his need to have Daddy relent, and let him win. Nine times out of ten, now as then, Daddy won't. Continuing to seek his father's indulgence, in adulthood as in childhood, is going to cost Charlie a fortune.

The child is the father of the man. Since his schooldays, Fred's friends have known him as 'a bit of a rebel'. He enjoys challenging authority. In which case, Fred is more than welcome to visit our Tuesday game. His need to take on his betters, preferably for all to see, will see him constantly calling superior hands. As he loses heavily, Fred will take consolation in feeling hard done by. He will rail against authority

– in this case, the odds he is wilfully defying – until he goes broke.

Bill, the out-of-work actor, is nice to everybody. He is kind to animals, and helps old ladies across the street. Bill has a desperate need to be loved. Well, the Tuesday Night Boys will love Bill to pieces. He will keep on playing four-flushes, and drawing to inside straights, in the hope that Dame Fortune, too, will show how much she loves him. The rest of us know that she'll smile on old Bill once in 4.5 and eleven attempts respectively.

So could the Shrink help me find my own poker programming? He read out a note from his clipboard, quoting me as saying in Session One that in my childhood home dissent of any kind had been strongly discouraged. My parents had such a horror of disagreement within the family that even political discussions were avoided, or killed off at birth, for fear that they would develop into rows. There were of course, as in any family, generational differences in attitude and outlook, but they were never allowed to reach the surface. Growing up was a matter of conforming to parental values.

This had given me insufficient leeway for the private rebellions every teenager needs. Such inhibitions were seemingly redoubled by a fondness for my father, many of whose personal views and values were naturally at odds with my own. It was perhaps not until the death of both my parents, when I was thirty-six years old, that I had finally begun to get in touch with certain aspects of myself which had hitherto lain buried – 'with a potential,' in his words, 'which you had previously chosen to ignore'.

Thus far, to the Shrink, the lid had been held down on my private Pandora's Box, which then burst open with a vengeance. For one thing, my natural combativeness now sought adult outlets with redoubled ferocity. It was no surprise that I had turned out to be strongly competitive by nature, in my career as in my personal relationships, and that this had recently grown in intensity. Hitherto, what's more, I seemed to have been insufficiently aware of the sheer nastiness lurking within me, as in all of us.

Poker gave all these traits the exercise they needed, which was of course both desirable and healthy. It fulfilled a 'fundamental human need' in a thoroughly acceptable manner. Better to beat up my poker buddies than my loved ones. Often in his work the Shrink found recourse to a syndrome he privately dubbed, 'Whatever turns you on'. A captain of industry might feel embarrassed and concerned about his need to don leather and seek exotic sexual adventures; a jetsetting VIP might habitually reroute via Bangkok because of a craving for various services uniquely accessible there. In the Shrink's view they worried too much about these apparent aberrations; in fact they were basic needs best gratified, so long as they were causing no harm to others.

I was reminded of my first foreign assignment for *The Sunday Times*, who sent me all the way across the English Channel to an ineffably boring EEC conference at the time of one of the great British sex scandals. While I attempted to interview a French government minister, he was much more concerned to grill me about why a British cabinet minister's relationship with a prostitute should enforce his resignation. 'In France,' he protested, 'we get worried when our government ministers *don't* have mistresses!'

'Quite so,' said the Shrink again, then loosed another of his surprise attacks on my spiritual solar plexus. 'We've identified some of the reasons why you enjoy poker so much, and some of the needs it fulfils for you. We've agreed that it offers a necessary and healthy release for deep-seated aspects of your character. But there's a potentially serious problem in the way it can blot out other, equally important priorities, whether practical or spiritual. People who regard life as time to be killed between Tuesday Night poker games are in trouble.

'We must now examine why the role of poker in your own life has grown quite so dangerously out of proportion.'

8

Amarillo Slim's Superbowl

'Creation's OK,' said Steve Wynn, Developer of the $630 million Mirage Hotel on the Las Vegas strip. 'But if God'd had money, he woulda done this.'

The rapid growth of the Mirage from site to skeleton to slab to mini-city measured my comings and goings from Vegas all year. 'Capital,' said Wynn, as his costs spiralled past half a billion, 'is not an issue.' With a grin you could screen a movie on, he summarized his financial philosophy. 'If one of my staff tells me we need to spend more to get something right, maybe fifteen, twenty or thirty million dollars more, I say OK. No hesitation. Most businesses are revenue-driven. The Mirage is cost-driven.'

The mere name had set him back half a million in pay-offs to two low-rent motels with the good fortune to have thought of it first. Now a permanently erupting volcano was under construction outside the main entrance, itself soon to be lost deep in a man-made, 100-acre tropical rainforest. Some thirty million was being spent on landscaping alone – more than the entire cost in 1966 of the Mirage's monumental next-door neighbour, Caesar's Palace, on which God has presumably long since paid off His mortgage.

If Vegas has an archetypal fun palace, symbol of American vulgarity at its most shamelessly inspirational, it must surely be Caesar's, pioneer of the gold bath-tap and the sunken jacuzzi, the heart-shaped waterbed and the mirrored ceiling. Across the Strip, the bulbous oriental towers of the Aladdin hide a magic realm in which you can rub your lamp and see Raquel Welch dance and sing; a few blocks down at Circus Circus, you can gamble away an arm and a leg as trapeze artists take similar risks overhead. But none can quite cap Caesar's, a plastic extravaganza of Greco-Roman confusion whose mobile walkways sweep you right off the street, through the air, into an ancient world where credit cards are welcome along the Appian Way, Dean Martin sings in the Circus Maximus, and Caesar himself is on hand to help you find your way out of the deep-pile carpet to Cleopatra's Barge, where the Martinis are mixed and served by the Muses.

This is a world to make Hieronymus Bosch blink, to make Coleridge awake and find himself in Xanadu. And this, thanks to my former life, was my next port of call. My past came to the rescue of my *vita nuova* early in the New Year, when my American publishers wanted to fly me to Los Angeles to guest on CNN's Larry King Show. A West Coast air ticket for half an hour on television seemed to me like a bargain – doubly so when the date coincided with Amarillo Slim's Superbowl of Poker at Caesar's Palace.

They weren't too keen on my insistence on Business Class, but Larry King was Larry King, the programme which sold more books than any other coast-to-coast talk show. It does wonders for a dwindling bank-roll to sit free in the front of a 747, even if you are the passenger singled out to complete British Airways' latest eight-page questionnaire, an ordeal only made more acute by the offer of a free Patrick Lichfield print for your pains. Minus my luggage, which was said to be making a valiant attempt to find me, I checked into the Four Seasons, collared the hotel limo, and headed straight down the

Long Beach Freeway to Bell Gardens and 'The Bike'. I was only twenty-four hours from Vegas, one day away from Cleo's arms, but I couldn't wait any longer.

'The Bike' is its *habitués*' name for the Bicycle Club, the world's largest card room, with two hundred action-packed poker tables stretching almost to the crack of doom. Its vastness has all but eclipsed the traditional California card rooms of the neighbouring city of Gardena, the first to find a way around century-old local ordinances prohibiting all gambling games – specifically including 'stud-horse poker', a term so precise (and, these days, unintelligible) as positively to encourage evasion. Since rewriting the rule book in 1936, soon after Gardena's incorporation as a city, famous old clubs such as the Eldorado, the Normandie and the Horseshoe have been offering the locals the rangy lifestyle well captured in Robert Altman's 1974 movie *California Split*, in which Elliot Gould and George Segal learn California poker the hard way. The clubs pay city taxes vast enough to ensure that local standards of living, notably the percentage of homeowners, are among the highest in the United States.

But the recent arrival down the road of more flashy, Vegas-style card clubs such as the Commerce, and vastly bigger ones like the Bicycle, have undermined the monopoly of the Gardena pioneers. The Bicycle in particular has been so successful that it now accounts for almost a quarter of Bell Gardens' entire annual tax income. It favours a warm, old-West atmosphere, epitomized each summer in its Diamond Jim Brady tournament, rather than the clinical, chrome-and-glass glitz of the nearby Commerce, with its fancy restaurant and floor shows. Southern Los Angeles was originally colonized by immigrants from the East, and it is no coincidence that the Bicycle and Commerce alike devote a large acreage to Oriental gambling games, notably a wild game of pure chance called Pai Gau Poker, in specially set-aside areas where the action is fast and furious even among the three-deep crowd of spectators.

In my time I had sampled them all, limo-hopping from the Commerce to the Huntington Park, the Normandie to the Eldorado, the Horseshoe to the Bell, only to confirm that the 'Bike' was still the place for me. So pleased was I to be there now that I soon forgot I had started this longish day in London, and managed to lose $1,000 in a dazed spell at the $10–$20 Hold 'em table before deciding it was time to get my act together for Mr King. Either I clocked a little sleep, or the nation would see me looking, feeling (and probably talking) like a waxwork on tilt.

Twenty-four hours later, the show safely in the can, I was back in Vegas, my bankroll still smarting from last night, but bullish enough to deal with the trials ahead. What *could* the Shrink have meant? The sheer gusto with which life is lived here in this latter-day Ancient Rome made mock of his innu-endo that I could find better things to do with my time. I was in just the mood for Caesar's Palace, itself more abuzz than ever since hosting Dustin Hoffman and Tom Cruise for the blackjack sequence in *Rain Man*. One other Englishman turned out to be in residence for professional reasons: the boxer Lloyd Honeyghan, due to defend his WBC world welterweight title here at the weekend. My spirits, dazed but climbing, soared even higher on reading the letter awaiting my arrival in a complimentary *petite suite*: 'I, Caesar, welcome you to Caesar's Palace. My royal wonderland has been created solely for your pleasure. My noble staff and I aim to provide you, our royal guest, only the very best in quality vacational and recreational services . . .'

'Hail Caesar!' I cried heretically upon arriving in the card room, to salute the imperial bulk of Jack McClelland, director of this tournament as of so many others. 'Hold up, centurion,' he replied, 'I've got news for you.'

Jack settled a heated dispute on Table Six, then returned to tell me that he had just seen the proofs of the brochure for the forthcoming World Series. 'You're gonna love it, Tony. There's a colour spread saying you're a leading contender for the world title.'

Bemused, flattered and elated in a moment, I muttered something conveying my thanks, on the assumption that this was all down to Jack. 'Don't thank me, Tony. Nothing to do with me. And I don't think you should be too pleased about it, either.'

'Oh no? How come?'

'Because that's your cover blown. Come May, that glossy's gonna be in every card room in America, and then some. You'll find it tough to get a game.'

'That's right, pardner,' said a familiar voice at my shoulder. I looked round, then up, to see a huge and welcoming grin on the face of my eponymous tournament host, the most famous poker player alive.

Many of today's younger poker pros, physical as well as mental athletes, belie the game's unhealthy image by arriving at the table in track suit and trainers, fresh from the squash court or the jogging track. The rest get fat. And then there's Amarillo Slim.

Forget yon Cassius' lean and hungry look. Slim is so tall and thin that even his friends say he looks like the advance man for a famine. 'Slim?' says the man himself. 'Hell, when I was a kid, I had to get out of the bathtub before they pulled the plug.'

Thomas Austin Preston, surely the only Arkansan christened for one Texas town and nicknamed after another, weighs 170 pounds and stands six-feet-four – six-nine or more if you count the huge stetson which never leaves his head. You can see Slim coming two blocks away – and hear him, too, for 'Amarillo' is one of poker's greatest talkers. This is not just his natural *joie de vivre*. Table-talk, to Slim, is a wily tactic, designed to throw his opponents off their game. Variations on such themes as, 'Hey, neighbour, you better not call that big bet o' mine, I got six little titties [three queens] down here', or, 'This man's slower than a mule with three broken legs', or (if there are no ladies present), 'This sucker's tighter than a nun's doodah' have won Slim a handsome fortune for years, and helped to make him the most celebrated poker player of his time.

When challenged to take on the world's top woman player, *à la* Bobby Riggs vs. Billie-Jean King, Slim accepted with glee, forecasting that 'a woman would have a better chance of putting a wildcat in a tobacco sack than she would of beating me'. Betty Carey, then the reigning women's world champion, allowed herself to be table-talked to defeat. She had arrived demurely dressed, but Slim claimed after the game that, 'ah could see that left little titty of hers throbbin' every time she tried a bluff.' A rematch was arranged, for which Betty arrived displaying a little cleavage. 'All the easier to see that tell o' yours,' cried Slim repeatedly, throughout the game, and won again. For the third and final contest Betty arrived with a dramatic *décolletage* – and, more to the point, a Sony Walkman to shut out Slim's ceaseless chatter. This time she won.

Slim's own victory in the 1972 World Series of Poker surprised even him: 'Neighbour, at one point I had a better chance of getting a date with the Statue of Liberty than I did of winning that tournament.' But he put it to extremely good effect. A wise-cracking appearance on the Johnny Carson Show, swiftly followed by a bestselling poker manual, made him poker's only household name since 'Wild Bill' Hickok. These days he may no longer be the best player alive, but he is certainly the best known. Home-town card-sharps making their first, wide-eyed visit to Vegas nudge each other, point and whisper excitedly as Slim lopes by. Even those who have tired of his antics at the table concede that he has been a great ambassador for poker over the years. Anywhere he is invited he will go – 'My passport looks like a chicken scratched on it' – so long as the terms are right. When, to this day, amateur enthusiasts hail Slim as 'Mr Poker', few of his fellow professionals can find it in themselves to protest.

Born in Johnson, Arkansas, some seventy years ago – he is one of the few poker pros to be bashful about his age – Slim was less than a year old when his folks 'saw the error of their ways' and moved to Texas. There was no gambling at all in the Preston family background. 'My parents were average, church-going, hard-working people. Daddy had some cafés and ran a used-car business in Amarillo for many years.' Today, likewise, the private Slim is very much the family man on his huge spread outside Amarillo. He travels in the winter, and stays home in summer to be with his family. 'So far as I know, my wife, Helen Elizabeth, has never played a game of chance in her life. She thinks a king is the ruler of a country and a queen is his bedmate.'

In that chicken-scratched passport, to this day, Amarillo Slim lists his occupation as 'professional pool player', which is indeed how his career began. In high school, young Preston used to cut sixth-period study, head for the pool hall and 'bust everybody in sight'. He graduated from pool to cards at about sixteen, though his pool skills continued to come in handy. In the Navy he hustled his way up and down the West Coast, using an official car when off-duty as a captain's yeoman and chauffeur. On one famous occasion, so the story goes, he won five Cadillacs in San Francisco after cleaning his opponents out of cash. 'I came out of the Navy with over $100,000 in my pocket. I was still a kid, just twenty, and I thought it was all the money in the world. I lost it all within a year.'

When war came Slim travelled Europe giving pool exhibitions as a civilian member of the US Special Services. Though he could never beat England's legendary world snooker champion, Joe Davis, he bested America's equally legendary Minnesota Fats in two out of three public challenges. Or so he says. Fats has always disputed Slim's memories of these occasions; but they have long since passed, like many another story too good to check, into the Preston folklore.

These days, the US Statute of Declarations also enables Slim to reminisce gleefully about the lucrative blackmarket trade he ran among Allied troops in Europe. 'Them GIs were just *amazed* what they could find in the back of my wagon.' By war's end pool-hustling was no longer a gravy train rich enough to sustain his taste for the high life, so Slim shifted his centre of gravity to poker. In the fifties he went on the road in a playing partnership with Doyle Brunson and Brian 'Sailor' Roberts, sharing their wins and their losses as they chased action all over the western United States. 'When we moved on, the town looked like a vacuum had been through it.'

Another of Slim's ploys was to hang around in the early mornings in the bars outside state prisons. Newly released prisoners, their savings ripe for the plucking, would head here first in search of a drink and a woman; and here they would find Slim and a partner playing a deceptively amateur game of dominoes, the only gambling game allowed in American jails. Challenges would inevitably be issued. Slim would let the jailbirds win a couple of small games, innocently offer to up the stakes, and ruthlessly clean them out.

Doubters of this particular legend – including, to his cost, Steve Wynn, owner of the Golden Nugget – were silenced only recently, when Slim accepted and won a dominoes challenge from a celebrated ex-con then appearing in the Nugget's showroom, the country-and-western singer Willie Nelson. Celebrities seem to love taking a crack at Slim. A few years ago it cost Larry Flint, the proprieter of *Hustler* magazine, nearly two million dollars to find out that Slim really *can* talk his way to victory in a two-handed poker game – especially with the kind of pots he loves best, 'higher than a dawg could jump over'.

Poker pros tend not to penetrate each other's homes, but it doesn't take much persuading for Slim to tell you about the Waterford crystal chandeliers which adorn his lavish Texas ranch, or the head of cattle wandering about outside, within sight of the Olympic-size swimming pool. He used to own a string of thoroughbred racehorses, but 'you should never have a hobby that eats'. Most yarns emanating from Slim's home on the range carry glancing references to the stockmen who tend his herds, the grooms who care for his horses, the hands who ride for days without leaving the Preston patch. It was one of these who loyally killed and skinned the rattlesnake which bit Slim ten years back, and now winds for eternity around his stetson, its emerald-green eyes matching the large, uncut rocks with which he buttons his monogrammed shirts.

You don't believe him? He'll show you the rattler's bitemark on his hand. You've never seen him win? He'll offer you a (modest) discount at one of the chain of fast food stores for which he owns the franchise in three western states. Then he'll tell you how much he paid for the dead-weight of jewellery which sets off his tailor-made western suits. The Imelda Marcos of poker footwear, Slim wears five-figure boots of calf, alligator, lizard, even ostrich, kangaroo and anteater skin. 'I know I live high on the hog, but it's something you've got to do when you're hunting high-stakes poker . . .

'It never hurts for potential opponents to think you're more than a little stupid, and can hardly count all the money in your hip pocket, much less hold on to it. That's one reason I wear a big cowboy hat, cowboy boots and western duds – especially when I'm globe-trotting and looking for high action. People everywhere assume that anyone from Texas in a ten-gallon hat is not only a billionaire, but an easy mark. That's just fine with me, because that's the impression I'm trying to give. This approach puts those dudes in the category of guessers, and guessers are losers. That's my meat, to make the other guy guess.'

'Live high on the hog' – that was Slim's first piece of advice when I sought a few tricks of his trade. The finery, moreover, is functional: 'Why d'you think I like to wear this big-brimmed Stetson o' mine? A man's eyes show 90 per cent of what he's thinking. When I'm wearing my hat, you can only see my eyes when I want you to.'

Having tried on the hat, which weighed a couple of tons, I decided to go for dark glasses. Headgear, to Slim, is even a source of poker metaphors. 'Just as important for home-town players as for the World Series pros are things like psychology, position, the percentages and trappin'. Ah love to trap – and it ain't all trappers wear fur caps.'

Slim offered me a lexicon of poker advice too eloquent to hug to my chest. For starters, he confirmed one of my pet theses: that although poker is an institutionalized form of dishonesty, the relationships between its regular players are among the most honest to be found in this murky world. 'Tony,' he said with feeling, 'I've got two or three cigar boxes full of bad checks I've been given by businessmen, but I ain't got one from a professional gambler.'

There followed Slim on the need to be observant: 'You want to be able to see a gnat's keester at a hundred yards or hear a mouse wet on cotton.' Slim on knowing whom you can trust: 'In this game, if a true friend tells you that a goose will pull a plow, then hook him up, because he'll damn sure move it out . . .'

On feeling pity for friends who are losing: 'I like you, Tony, but I'll put a rattlesnake in your pocket, and ask you for a match.' On going for the kill: 'You can shear a sheep many times, but you can only skin him once.' Slim on optimism: 'I'm kinda like that guy who got a big box of horse shit from some joker for his birthday, and when this optimist opens it up, he's happy as hell and starts digging in all that horse dung – looking for the horse.'

Slim knows how to make the most of a strong hand: 'You don't come in like a wildcat gusher. Wait till you think you've got this cat, then introduce him to Mr More.' He chooses his opponents carefully: 'Ah'd rather have early frost on my peaches than play stud with that guy.' He knows when to quit: 'You can damn sure stick a fork in me because ah'm done. Ah'm slicker than a wet gut.' And he knows how to take defeat philosophically: 'Sometimes the lambs slaughter the butcher.'

One of Slim's best lines, however, distils the art of the dignified exit: 'If they ask you where you're goin', just tell 'em:

"No-one knows where the hobo goes when it snows".'

Before the week was through, ah was to find out.

Despite my St Lucian extravagance, that one immortal hand of Levy's Game had covered enough costs to shore up the bank-roll at $15,000, three-quarters of its original pristine self. Again a free air ticket had fallen into my lap; and again, of course, I was living free in Vegas. But I was already out $1,000 at the Bike, and this week's tournament entry fees were hefty. If I was going to risk some side-action as well, my statutory $9,999 wasn't going to get me too far unless I could win a satellite or two. Once Slim had found another arrival to drown in wisecracks, I got straight down to work, with a $150 shot at the next day's $1,500 Limit Hold 'em event.

On the first hand, I was dealt A-6 of spades and bet it. There were three callers. The flop brought 5-7-8, two of them spades. Now a guy with a lucky rabbit's foot in front of him bet the max; the next two folded; I raised Rabbit's Foot, and he called. The turn brought a nine, so now I had a straight made, complete with a nut flush draw. He bet; I raised; he called. I didn't believe 6-10 would still be there by this stage; so the only hand which could beat me at that moment was 10-J, which would have raised me back. Despite the rabbit's foot, which was getting to me a bit, I was feeling good about this until the river brought a ten. When he checked it, I bet everything I had left. To my surprise, he called, setting us both all-in.

When I showed my straight, Rabbit's Foot threw away his cards; but thcy flipped over just short of the muck to reveal a pair of jacks. The dealer took a long, slow look at them while the loser shrugged his shoulders, picked up his rabbit's foot and prepared to leave. He thought he had a pair of jacks.

In fact he had wound up with a straight higher than mine. At this game, as they say, 'cards speak', so the dealer did his duty and pointed out to the departing stranger that he had just won a pot big enough to make him the satellite leader. Me, I was out on the first hand.

Ah well, them's the breaks. Never, as they also say, play with mugs. Maybe I should get myself a rabbit's foot? Some of the coolest, most rational poker pros will admit to superstitions: they like particular seat numbers; they believe in certain 'lucky' cards; after a bad run of cards they will call for a 'set-up' – a new deck – in the genuine belief that it will make some difference. Even Johnny Chan has his lucky orange. Maybe it was time for me to give The Watch another chance? I decided to try one more satellite, just one more, and nipped up to my room to change wrist-gear.

This time, for once, I found myself at a table where I didn't know a single face. In the early stages I was disconcerted by a woman who could riffle eight chips at once *on top of* a pile of twenty, without any mishaps – enough to discourage any further attempts on my part. This game, I figured, might prove a good chance to practise spotting 'tells'; but I soon found myself tangling regularly with a tough, aggressive Oriental in Seat Five whose face yielded absolutely no information at all – before, during or after the pots between us. His was the ultimate poker face – inscrutability personified. For a long time he had me terrified, but I was managing to hold my own, even matching him from time to time in the cool self-assurance of his play. After an hour, when I was $700 up on my original $1,000, I intuitively backed a loser – bet the maximum on absolute rags in the hole – and had the satisfaction of seeing everyone fold. So I was getting some respect! It was a rare and very pleasant sensation.

It was at times like these, in the midst of these prolonged poker sessions in Vegas, that I began to see the true import of intuition to a poker player. Play all day every day, rather than once a week with the world on your mind, and you develop a sixth sense not just about the cards, but about opportunities, situations, the people you are up against. Figuring the odds becomes almost subconscious, as perhaps it should, leaving your mind free to rove around the mood of the game, the private agonies of the other players, the fickleness of fate, the irrelevance of all other activities. If a heedless autopilot takes over, as it can, you're headed for trouble. If, however, you find yourself making correct decisions, relying as much on instinct as on logic, you can enjoy brief communion with the Poker Gods. The pros tend to scoff at such romantic notions, insisting on a ruthless, remorseless adherence to poker science; but most of them also know moments when the game blossoms into an art form, offering powers of insight which can feel divine. Would that I were playing in a bigger league, for this was turning into one of those moments.

When an ace came up on the next flop I let the Chinaman's bet take the pot, even though I figured he had nothing. I was holding J-J, but what the heck. Now I was dealing and he was in late position, perfect for the kind of 'steal' I had just pulled off myself, but it wasn't worth risking my all to expose him. I had moved into that comfortably serene cruising zone, when a quiet, undramatic self-confidence emerges from nowhere and imperceptibly takes over. At times like this – there is no explaining it – the law of averages just melts away and you *know* that you are going to win this thing if only you can play carefully. Even when it reached heads-up between me and the Chinaman, I found my hands steady, my play unflustered, my patience unprecedented. Wait, wait, wait long enough, I kept telling myself, and the cards will come. Following my own advice was as tough as ever – but I did, and I won.

Had The Watch finally come good? I couldn't let myself think so. All I knew was that for an outlay of $300, instead of $1,500, I found myself still wearing it next morning as one of 128 starters in Amarillo Slim's Limit Hold 'em tournament, which offered prize money totalling $192,000. By the first break, at 1.20 p.m., I was still alive, though down to $1,200. A pair of sixes held up for me to bust out Seat Three and put me back to $1,500. Now there were only six players at our table. There was a brief delay as Jack McClelland told us: 'Sit tight. There's more fresh meat on the way.'

Sitting here hour after hour, day after day, waiting, waiting, waiting for the right hand, the right situation to come along, I confess to letting my mind wander from time to time. Sit with Stu Ungar or Johnny Chan, and you will see them making use of the time they have to kill after folding; they will study everyone else's play, base judgements upon their betting patterns, scour their faces for tells, even watch the shuffle and deal with minute attention. Any clue, any hint of a clue, gives them an edge. Me, I'm often so bored that I get the same impulse which occasionally comes over me at tedious dinner parties: to do something wild, maybe scandalize the gathering with some foul language, or flash at the droning dowager duchess on my left. Here there is plenty of action beyond the rails to occupy the wandering mind – and there is always the thought that a pro would not let his mind wander in the first place. Watch the play, study the faces, try and see whereabouts in the deck that glimpsed king of hearts winds up after the shuffle.

Was I still playing too many hands? Probably. There was only one way to find out: take notes on my progress, and analyse them later.

1.45 p.m.: Playing J-10 on my small blind gets me back up to $1,725 when the big blind goes against me with a K-2 flush draw – and pulls two diamonds on the flop. But the odds hold, and no more come up. Close shave. I'm in Seat One; my neck aches from craning around the dealer; and I don't like not being able to see the dealer's name, written on his or her lapel badge, when a new one arrives every twenty minutes. When I talk to them, I like to emulate the local habit of addressing them by name.

2.00 p.m.: After some sloppily loose calls, I creep back to $1,300 (again on my small blind) by busting out the big blind. He has 8-6; my pair of eights is enough to see him off.

2.05 p.m.: Comes a hand in which I'm not sure what I did right. I have A-Q unsuited and call lots of raises – wrongly, I suspect – until the end, where the table champ checks; I bet, and he (to my astonishment and relief) folds. There was a queen on the board to give me comfort; I suspect he was testing my mettle. Anyway, he's helped me up to $3,025.

2.10 p.m.: K-K in the pocket gets me up to $3,600. One caller throughout. 'Rags' on the board. In the next hand, some loose play against what turns out to be a pair of aces – I had a pair of tens – takes me down to $3,200.

2.30 p.m.: Tough beat. K-J unsuited beats my K-10 of spades after a king and two spades on the flop. I'm down to $1,800 as the blinds go up to $100–$200.

2.35 p.m.: It's my big blind and I'm holding 6-7. The flop comes 8-9-10-bet-J-bet-bet-Q. Split the pot! Back to $2,500.

2.50 p.m.: My big blind again, and I'm holding 5-5. Lyle Berman, whom I know to be a very good player, raises before the flop; I call. Flop brings A-A-3. He bets; for some reason, instinct rather than merely bad play, I call. The turn brings a five – I check-raise; he calls. Last card is a ten. He checks; I bet; he folds. This is the only full house I've seen all day. It takes me back up to $4,000.

2.55 p.m.: I'm hungry. I ask the cocktail waitress to bring me a chocolate bar. It takes forty minutes to arrive.

3.00 p.m.: My small blind, holding A-2, both spades. Flop brings A-A-3-4-7. Beaten by A-Q. Down to $2,500.

3.05 p.m.: A-Q suited beaten by 10-10 after pre-flop raise. Down to $1,500.

3.10 p.m.: Moved to Table Eight. Of 128 starters, thirty-five players are left at four tables. I have $1,500.

3.15 p.m.: Things are getting desperate. After one round of blinds, I have only $1,200 left. Now the blinds are going up to $150–$250, so that's enough for three rounds, which at this table means twenty-four hands. Thirty-one players left. Ten minutes to the next break.

3.20 p.m.: Worse. J-10 costs me $400. Zilch on the flop. $800 left.

3.25 p.m.: I've seen no cards at all since I moved tables. When the end comes, it comes fast. Thirty players left; I have $600. One hand should do it.

3.45 p.m.: On the first hand after the break, I'm forced to go all-in ($500) on my big blind, holding the wonderful hand of 9-3. The flop brings 3-5-6. My pair of threes winds up beating a cheeky concealed pair of twos. Still alive, just, with $1,200. Moved again.

3.50 p.m.: The big blind is now $1,000. Players are dropping like flies – there are only twenty-seven left, at three tables – so I'm moved yet again. Now I'm at Table One, Seat One, and immediately cop the small blind. I have $1,200 left after half an hour (which seems like a year) of living dangerously. Still no cards come. Everyone is playing cautiously to get in the money, the top eighteen, now that there are only twenty-five players left. Do I have enough to hang in there?

4.00 p.m.: You betcha. Oh, for more money, as I behold a pair of black aces in the hole, set myself in, and get two callers. The flop brings three diamonds. Seat Three bets, and Seat Five folds. Three rolls over a pair of kings, also both black, and sighs when he sees my aces. The turn brings the ten of diamonds, the river . . . a decidedly pesky five of diamonds. The board has won. Neither of us has a diamond with which to improve on the freak flush before us, so we split the pot. In other words, we carve up Seat Five's measly $1,200. And it should *all* have been mine.

4.05 p.m.: The big blind forces me to go all-in on 'rags'. My jack high is beaten by a full house! I finish twenty-second out of 128 – four off the money, dammit.

Studying my notes over a well-deserved glass of Chablis, I reckoned to have played fourteen hands to a conclusion in two hours twenty minutes. One every ten minutes is still, by local standards, too antsy. The trouble is that those ten-minute intervals seem like hours.

I needed to relax, so put my name down for a few cheap satellites for the next day's Pot Limit Omaha tournament. At a mere $30 entry fee, however, it was hard to take them seriously.

In the first hand of my first satellite, I was holding Ac-Kc-Ad-10d; I bet $40, and the entire table called. The flop came 4-5-6, two of them clubs. This guy set himself in to the tune of $160. I called. Up came 8-4, neither of them clubs. My opponent was holding two sixes, giving him trips. Any club or any ace would have won me a $720 pot on the first hand. Instead, out I went.

I had quickly frittered away two more $30 satellite fees before my first attempt at calling it a night. It says 'lots of tough beats' in my notebook, but I suspect that I was kidding myself. In that hand I was losing all along, and my opponent had the odds on his side. Tighter pros would not have called his all-in bet; but at $30, with a chance of dominating the table, I still don't think mine too bad a call. A 'bad beat' has to be a *really* unlucky defeat: when you are playing the correct odds, and some jerk beats you by pulling a flukey card. Most poker players will tell you 'bad beat' stories which are quite the opposite, merely revealing what bad players – not to mention bad losers – they are.

I won $300 in a $15–$30 Limit Hold 'em side-game, recouping all but $90 of my losses since the Bike, before turning in early. Slim's PLO tournament next morning had an unusual, potentially very expensive structure, which I wanted to sleep on. The entry fee was only $200. But for the first two hours of play, people who were busted out could buy their way back into the tournament. 'Rebuys' normally cost the same as the original entry fee; professionals hate them, rightly saying that the tournament proper does not begin until the rebuy period is over. But they sure swell the prize money; today's rebuys will inflate it ferociously. The first one costs $500, after which you can 'buy back in' as often as you like – at $1,000 a time.

During the night, I made a strategic decision to let the others do all the rebuying. If I can't make my $200 last until the break, I'll go find something better to do.

So it's not surprising that I make an over-cautious start, watching what would have been two winning hands go by without me; in one of them, my K-Q would have become a full house, kings on queens. But I'm much too grown up these days to let these things get to me. Out of 155 starters, it is just my luck to have pulled an enthusiastic amateur on my left, who keeps asking the rules, then winning flukey pots. These guys are dangerous. They make me wonder whether I'd have done better to retain my amateur status. But . . .

11.55 a.m.: K-K gives me a full house, with a flop of 5-5-8-8-5, and me all-in for $150 with two callers! Pushes my original $200 up to more than $400. Then I steal one from the amateur, and I'm up to $520.

12.05 p.m.: All the others at my table have already rebought for their $500. Suddenly I'm the tight-ass round here. The Tuesday boys would never believe it.

12.08 p.m.: I hate to admit it, but I just caught a glimpse of the amateur's hand. The flop is 10-10-6-5 and he's bet $200 with merely a six in the hole. Somehow I wish I had rags, but

I have a ten. Everyone else folds, I win a huge (by current standards) pot, and the amateur rebuys for $1,000.

12.15 p.m.: God, Omaha makes Hold 'em seem so austere. I find it very hard to fold before any flop, and am certainly seeing some cards. This time, a full house on the river: I have K-K-10-9 in the hole, and the flop comes J-J-x-x-K. Lucky to outpull that jack, I know, but it takes me up to $855.

12.20 p.m.: I'm getting a lot of satisfaction here in avoiding – as yet – the rebuys. My object is to survive the three hours until they are over. But will it be worth the effort?

12.45 p.m.: Suddenly I'm next to 1986 world champion Berry Johnston, who has arrived ninety minutes late. After being 'anted away' in his absence, he has $120 left. He goes all-in on the first hand, gets beat and rebuys for $500. My original two hundred, now over nine, feels even better.

12.50 p.m.: A couple of late-position steals put me up to $1,200. I'm playing confidently and well.

1 p.m.: Up to $1,530, thanks to a worryingly low full house: playing 6-3-4-4 in my hand is rewarded with a 6-2-4 flop, and a 2 on the river.

1.10 p.m.: Break due in five minutes. I have the satisfaction of making some small change out of two $500 chips (alias 'nickels') for the champ on my right. But pride comes before . . .

We've reached the first break. One more hour, and the rebuy

period will be over. (So far seventy entrants have paid at least $1,500 on top of their original $200 to continue playing.) But before the tournament proper proceeds, every player still alive is entitled to make one last $1,000 rebuy – known as the 'add-on' – regardless of the amount in front of them. I seek advice from the tournament director, Jack McClelland, who is kind enough to step out of his impartial role and suggest that $2,000 will be about the average chip position at the time of the add-on. If I have more than that, it's really not worth it. At the moment, after a loose call just before the break, I have $1,315.

1.30 p.m.: First hand after the break. I have Ad-Kh-4s-6s; the flop comes Ah-3h-5h. In early position I cockily bet the maximum, $300, and get one caller. The turn brings a 7c, filling my open-ended straight. I go all-in. He thinks a while, then folds. This takes me up to $2,050.

1.40 p.m.: A pair of aces on the river jacks me up to $2,250.

1.55 p.m.: After three wasted calls of $100 each, I am holding Kc-Kd-Qd-4d, and the flop brings 2-5-6, all of them diamonds. I am 'under the gun', the first to speak, so I check in the hope of later action. Seat Nine bets $400; I call, wondering if he could have the ace-high flush. The turn brings the seven of hearts. I check in the hope that he'll bet again. He doesn't. Another seven comes on the river. So I check again lest he has a full house. He checks, too, making me sure I've won, and wondering whether I should have bet on the end. It turns out he was holding a straight. My K-high flush takes me up to $2,750.

2.35 p.m.: Finally, after a dull half-hour in which I saw no cards worth major risks, we reach the three-hour break. This is the end of the rebuys. I'm at $2,225 without having rebought, and mighty good that makes me feel. Fifty-four players are left.

Perry Green, a genial Alaskan with whom I share a fondness for chewing toothpicks during play, advises me to take up the $1,000 add-on. The advantage, to his mind, is the extra thousand one would have in an all-in pot with several callers. 'After all, Tony, it's only a G-note.' Jack McClelland, who knows better than Perry how much a grand means to me, repeats his advice not to. I resolve not to.

One minute before play is due to recommence, five of the nine people at my table impulsively decide to take up the offer. Suddenly, for all my patience over my original $200, I'm behind them in chips, and feeling vulnerable. So I hear myself call for the add-on people. Jack McClelland frowns at me, then grins, as if there were some inevitability about that decision. So I restart with $3,225.

3.00 p.m.: The only other Englishman in this event, whom I know from the Rubicon Club in Wolverhampton, is busted out at my table, so now I'm the only Brit left. While patting myself on the back I miss a winning pot. With the Ah-3h-3d-2d in the pocket, I am driven out by heavy betting before the flop, which then brings a three and two hearts. The turn is the seven of hearts, the river the seven of spades. I would have held the nut flush, then a full house, threes on sevens. More irritated than I should let myself be, I play the next hand stupidly and lose it. Am I suddenly in danger of going on tilt? It seems hours since I won a hand.

3.15 p.m.: Suddenly I notice that the table leader is wearing not merely a diamond horseshoe ring but *The Watch* – yes, the self-same, cheapo *diamanté*-studded king of diamonds who had yet to convince me that he was earning his keep. How could I have been playing with the guy all this time, supposedly studying his every move, appraising his every nervous tic, and not have noticed? It is a cruel indication of how amateur a player I still am. In the next hand he promptly beats me out of $300. Good hand but lousy flop. CONCENTRATE!

3.25 p.m.: I've spent the last ten minutes making a firm decision no longer to regard The Watch as any kind of talisman; that way madness lies. It is simply a timepiece, and from now on I will wear it as such, regardless of the consequences. So I cannot blame it now for two more bad-ish beats, and a distinct slump in morale. To my chagrin it is suddenly role reversal time; I have to ask the guy in Seat Five to change my 'nickel'. He gives me the lowest denomination chips available, while offering bigger ones to Berry Johnston. I protest jocularly that this is unfair: 'You trying to tell me somethin'?' He is unmoved.

3.30 p.m.: Berry Johnston is busted out beside me. Suddenly, after my early run of cards, it's happening for everyone here except me. I have $2,325 left, and I've got to go for something or I'm dead. The two big boys at my table (with $6,000–$7,000 each) are bullying their way through every pot. Small change to them is life or death to the rest of us. I feel an urgent need of a hand to be dramatic with.

3.45 p.m.: Who should take Berry Johnston's seat on my right (Number One) but the reigning back-to-back world champion, Johnny Chan! He's got about $6,000; I have $2,250. Chan seems to be in a mean mood. Immediately he is irritated at walking straight into the big blind. 'I've been moved three times in five minutes,' he scowls, to no-one in particular. 'I mean, I get more exercise here than I do at home. Know what I'm sayin'?' A cheap crack from the Oriental Express, followed by a rare smile, wrings a sycophantic laugh from the lads.

3.50 p.m.: Will my extra $1,000 help? I'm still brooding about that prodigal add-on. I'll tell you when I'm all in with it. Which will have to be any minute now.

After a bad beat Chan gets even meaner. How can he (the guy on my left) call? We discuss it. I tell Chan that the amateur has been doing it all day. Then Chan is rude to the dealer; he wants to see all the cards in the muck. Abe, the dealer, says, 'That's how I teach it in dealers' school.' Chan replies: 'Well, we're not at dealers' school now.' Boy, is he steaming.

As I note down this exchange, my hands beneath the table, Chan stares at me, leans over to see what's going on down there, and testily asks the question no-one else has ventured all year: 'What you doin'? Writin' a book or somethin'?' There's no answer to that.

4 p.m.: My cards have grown cold, and my bladder weak. I've been in and out of here three times during this tournament, which is not good for the concentration. As his stack grows ever smaller, so Chan's mood grows fouler; he is hideous to another dealer when she leaves the table during a 'race' for the odd chips. Then there are amazingly piercing shrieks five yards to our left as someone wins the daily slots jackpot. Chan is the only one at the table to remain completely unmoved. As the dealer leaves in tears, we calm down and resume play. Thirty players are left, out of 155 starters.

4.10 p.m.: Johnny Chan is busted out . . . by little ol' me. Well, who'd have thought it? He's been on tilt for a while, trying to get back at the amateur; when the hand began, we were both holding about $1,500 in chips. The flop brings A-J-7. I have a pair of sevens in the pocket. Chan, first to bet, sets himself all-in. Naturally, I have to call, also all-in. It turns out he is holding A-J-Q-K, but the rest of the board helps neither of us. As he snatches up his possessions and wanders off, as if he had just been killing time before doing something *real*, my triumph is spoilt by a long mental list of my poker friends – precisely 100 per cent of them – who were not here to see me floor the world champ.

4.15 p.m.: I am holding Kd-Kc-2d-2c, and raise before the flop. One caller. Flop brings Q-x-x (two diamonds). Do or die stuff now, I reckon, so I try to look powerful by betting the maximum, $800. The other guy has a long think, then calls and raises me my remaining $1,600. My kings fail to improve, while he catches a straight on the last card.

So I'm out in twenty-ninth place, which gives me the chance to go and apologize to Jack. 'The extra thou didn't make the slightest difference. You were dead right. It was a complete waste of a good K.' My tournament diary reads: 'Depressed again. Any pro reading this and looking at my results will tell me I lack the killer instinct. And he'd be right . . . I seem to become too chary, increasingly so, as the field thins and I try to hang on . . . I tend to pass good hands, and play better ones which go wrong.' I moan down the phone to the Moll in Boston, where she has dropped in on her mother and sisters to divide up the family jewellery. Not even I can cast down her spirits, however, as she has just cornered a gold bracelet on which she had set her heart. 'That's great,' I tell her. 'Can you hock it on the way here?' And so to the big fight.

How to get that maddening $1,000 back? After another good tournament run, but another finish short of the money, my add-on folly was really hurting. I took my Chablis round the corner from the tournament area to the vast 'Sports Book' of Caesar's Palace, a dazzling complex of giant screens and electronic scoreboards straight out of *Star Wars*. A patriotic bet on Lloyd Honeyghan? Forget it. He was −250 (5:2 on) against +200 (2:1) for his opponent, Marlon Starling. That, in one of my favourite new poker phrases, wasn't going to win me diddley-squat.

Unfamiliar with the American system of fixing sports odds, I sought advice from a seasoned-looking punter who peered furtively around, lowered his voice, and offered a colonial cousin a hot tip. In the supporting bout, the American welterweight Mark Breland was heavily fancied at −600 (6:1 on) to beat an unknown Korean called Seung Soun Lee. Though Breland won gold at the Los Angeles Olympics, he was now, according to my conspiratorial friend, 'over the hill'. At +400 (4:1) 'the Chinaman' (as he insisted on calling the Korean) was 'a terrific bet'. Knowing absolutely nothing about boxing, and never having heard of either of them, I was more struck by the neat equation of wagering $250 on the Chinaman to win back my lost thou.

Having placed the bet, I set off through Caesar's vast expanses in the remote hope of finding the sports arena. Legionnaires were wandering about everywhere, their spears in constant danger of causing random damage. Hopelessly lost, I enlisted the help of a friendly centurion, who was just

Big Deal

escorting me through the Forum when he was brusquely hijacked by a very large man wanting to know the way to the VIP desk. Didn't this guy know I was a VIP myself, a professional poker player, indeed? I must have given him my best shot at a long, dark glare, for all of a sudden this menacing giant turned away from our Roman escort, looked down and said to me, very politely, 'Excuse me, sir'. The guard looked at me imploringly and said, 'That's OK, Mr Cooney'. As we proceeded on our way, I asked him, 'So who's this Cooney?'

'Oh, sir, that was *Jerry* Cooney,' said he, awestruck, 'the guy who fought Holmes and Spinks for the world title?' As we passed down the Appian Way towards Poseidon's Pool and thus approached the Sports Pavilion, I resolved to be careful with whom I tangled in there. Sure enough, the joint was heaving with giant, heavy-shouldered dudes.

Given today's continuing problem, my first port of call needed to be the men's room. As I fought my way through the throng, bumped into someone blocking my path and tried to elbow him out of the way, I realized how strangely intimate is the design of these arenas. From the baleful look this guy gave me, and the fact that he was wearing a shiny tunic and shorts, I finally grasped that he was a sweaty fighter leaving the ring. He had evidently just lost. What's more, he was a Chinaman. Panic. He couldn't be *my* Chinaman?

No – phew – he wasn't. That bout was next up. As I took my terrific ringside seat, courtesy of Caesar himself, I was soon appalled by the spectacle before me, which seemed to be nearing its end. This close, you can hear the crunch when a punch really lands, the deathly gasp as it finds its mark. I felt ashamed of watching, as if I had been smuggled into a fight between two captured animals. Here at Caesar's Palace, however, it all seemed a highly appropriate part of the scenery.

Two black guys beating each other up for the delectation of a mildly interested throng, busier betting on the outcome than watching for it: this must be the nearest the modern world can get to a re-creation of gladiatorial combat in Ancient Rome. If Diana Ross was currently playing, as indeed she was, in the Circus Maximus, this place should be renamed the Colosseum.

The audience itself was predominantly black, dressed to kill, exuding crisp new money – most of them oblivious to the fight, chatting away to each other as fellow blacks fought for their lives. Soon, mercifully, it was all over. Now I became just another bloodthirsty spectator, rooting for the Chinaman to win me back my grand.

Breland entered to the deafening – and menacing – strains of Michael Jackson's 'Bad'. Over the hill he might be, but he looked much bigger than my guy, who now arrived to Peter Gabriel's 'Sledgehammer'. According to the programme Breland stood 6'3" to the Chinaman's 5'10", with a reach of 77" against 69". The first round was beginning as I searched for some reassuring statistics in my guy's favour; I had failed to find any in the fifty-four seconds of the first round which it took him to get knocked out.

So much for hot tips from strangers in the Caesar's Sports Book, and so much for my $250. I had just made $200 last over five hours playing poker, and this guy had lost it in fifty-four seconds. Now I was even deeper in the mire: $1,450 down on the day, and no immediate prospect of recouping it.

As the Honeyghan fight loomed, mobs of British lager louts were making their presence noisily felt all over the hall, baying for blood like the English football supporters whose shirts they were wearing. The sight filled me with loathing of my homeland, and renewed affection for my adopted home town of Las Vegas. Intuitively, I sprinted back into the Sports Book and bet $500 at 2:1 on Starling to beat Honeyghan. Not very patriotic, but a betting man's gotta do what he's gotta do, even if he knows in his heart he is wrong.

Back in the hall, the VIPs were being introduced. Big names like Spinks and Sugar Ray Leonard were here, all around me – even Mike Tyson, at the height of his marital troubles, three weeks before his title fight with Britain's Frank Bruno. Amarillo Slim, too, was introduced to the crowd, but for once there was little response; tonight poker got strictly second billing to the lust for blood you can *see*. The 'Star-Spangled Banner' was sung flat, but few noticed amid the crude, drunken chants of the British hooligans. Now they were even roaring, 'Malvinas Inglaterra'. Maggie, I thought, these are your children; and wished I had doubled that bet.

Seething with conflicting emotions, I recalled Honeyghan's soft-spoken pleasantness when I had recently sat next to him on a breakfast television sofa; now the prospect of filthy lucre had reduced me to abandoning him in his hour of greatest need. His opponent arrived (to 'Bad' again), and the champ to music too loud to be decipherable. As the fight got under way I was happy not to watch, savouring instead the sight of the British yobboes being none too gently removed by the Las Vegas police, chanting racist slogans as they went.

Poor old Honeyghan. He deserved better than that. He was in trouble as early as the fourth round, and lost his world title when the ref finally stopped the massacre in the ninth.

Never have I felt gloomier about winning $1,000.

The next day marked the arrival of the Moll, whom I met at the airport in the longest limo Caesar's could muster, complete with white flowers and an iced bottle of champagne. Tired out by carrying all that jewellery, she went straight to sleep in our heart-shaped bed – and awoke to find me gone.

Around 3 a.m., having enjoyed a full night's rest, she came down to find me deeply embroiled in a $150 satellite for the next day's tournament – Caesar's Super Challenge, a $1,500-entry No Limit Hold 'em event, offering prize money in the region of $250,000. For the winner, there was an added perk which already had me drooling. Parked in the middle of the Sports Book, *en route* to the tournament area, was a customized 1989 Chevrolet Astro Tiara roadster, its interior fitted out with every comfort known to the motor trade, ready for the winner of Caesar's Super Challenge to drive away.

First, I had to win my entry into the tournament. As the Moll caught up with me, I was all-in for $300 with 6-7 in the hole. Showing touching confidence in something – it can't have been the hand or the player – she settled herself down comfortably in a seat at my shoulder, as if this thing weren't over yet. The familiar waft of *Fracas* signalled another upturn in my fortunes as the flop promptly brought 5-9-J . . . Q . . . 8. From that moment on, it was only a matter of time before I won. My opponent in the head-to-head was so patently inexperienced that this time I was offering no deals.

Another $1,350 saved in entry fees. As elated as I was, the Moll chose this moment to swell her own bank-roll – a task all too easy to accomplish in Vegas. All around the casino walls are a growing army of cash-card machines, which can whistle up your credit limit at the punch of a personal identification number. In her enthusiasm, alas, the Moll had stuck her card in the wrong machine, which she was now unable to provide with the PIN number for which it politely enquired. After we had punched every button in sight, the machine unilaterally decided she was up to no good and swallowed her only visible means of support.

This was not good for morale. The Moll is no sponger. A faithful believer in American efficiency, she made light of the hour, now approaching 5 a.m., by telephoning the emergency service crew who spend their entire lives roaming Vegas to deal with the tantrums of these overworked, long-suffering life-support systems. When a world-weary engineer finally arrived, he was not in the mood for explanations. He'd heard them all before, and then some. When he opened up the machine, out onto the floor tumbled a vignette of raw Vegas. In the previous twenty-four hours this one machine – one of scores in Caesar's Palace alone, hundreds on the Strip, thousands in the entire town – had swallowed the credit cards of no fewer than one hundred and seventy-three punters mounting vain attempts to exceed their credit limits. It was astonishing, I reflected, that Caesar's Olympic-sized pool was not awash with corpses.

How did these people pay their bills? Were there unseen innumerable hordes even now slaving their way through the imperial washing-up? Was that passing phalanx of centurions comprised of former guests working off unpaid accounts? How many gamblers who checked in as millionaires checked out as bell boys? Forget Gibbon. When it came to declines and falls, this place put Ancient Rome in the shade.

Seven hours of fitful sleep later, I began the Caesar's Super Challenge at Table Five, Seat Two, next to the genial 'Cowboy' Wolford, a former rodeo rider who wears exotic denim dungarees bejewelled with his name and various winning hands from his career as a poker pro. Ancient Rome still seemed to be the dominant theme as we watched some poor guy at our table bust out on the first hand with a pair of aces. Arty Cobb, one of the more colourful professionals, famous for wearing outrageously ornamental baseball hats, had called him all-in with the K-8 of hearts. The flop brought 6-7-10, then Q-9. Cobb, already out of his seat before the river, drew astonished looks when he rolled over the eight of hearts which had made his flukey straight. 'It's my lucky card,' he explained without apology. 'I always play it.'

Still dazed, perhaps, I messed up the first hand in which I got involved, by check-raising my A-7 of clubs into a potential straight which duly came up. Bad position was no excuse for such a lapse, which cost me half my $1,500. On the verge of going out in the first hour, I now found myself in a showdown with the two players I feared most at the table, Cowboy and Cobb. Dealt the A-K of diamonds, I raised the maximum before the flop, only to find them both calling me. When the board showed K-10-J, and I was first to speak, I considered for a minute whether either of them could be holding A-Q; decided against; and figured I might as well make them pay to find out if I had it. So I went all-in, to the tune of $500.

They both folded. Whew. Back to quits. It was only 1.40 p.m. – we'd been going just twenty minutes, and already I was exhausted. Nerves all over the room, mine included, were being stretched to extremes by the public address system, which was open-endedly replaying a rowdy country-and-western number entitled, 'D'you dare make a bet with Amarillo Slim?' The punchline adjudged: 'Hell, the *devil* don't bet with Amarillo Slim.' The man himself wandered around expansively, savouring the instant immortality the song conferred. When it restarted for the umpteenth time, however, howls of derision finally drowned it into silence.

2.35 p.m.: Big blind (Cowboy) against small blind (me) and he's set me all-in for $900. The flop of K-Q-x scares me because I have A-Q. Two more rags come. Cowboy shows a pair of tens, and concedes gracefully. Back up to $1,800, I make a vow to play fewer hands than yesterday.

2.55 p.m.: Twenty minutes – a whole round – has passed before I find myself caught in action on my small blind again, against the same opposition in the shape of Cowboy's big blind and a call from Cobb. Again I find myself forced to go all-in, this time with A-9 of spades after a flop of A-4-4. Cowboy folds, but Arty Cobb calls, saying that an ace will win it. He had me rattled there, but has jacked me up to $2,350.

3.55 p.m.: Dealt A-K, I bet $500. Everyone folds, probably because it's the first bet I've made for an hour. Self-discipline can be so boring at times. It would be more fun watching grass grow or paint dry. I have $2,650. We've been going two and a half hours, and there are only sixty-one players left out of 150 starters.

4.15 p.m.: Now there are six tables left, meaning some fifty players (one-third of the field) with $225,000 between them. The maths, for once, are easy. Needing around $4,500 to be keeping up with the field, I have $3,050. It seemed a lot a minute ago, but now I've got to start trying to build again.

4.20 p.m.: I get my chance, and bust someone out with A-K of clubs – which takes me up to $5,500, ahead of the game. Then, like an idiot, I walk smack into Chip Reece, regarded by his fellow pros as perhaps the best all-round player in the world. How can I have played so carefully for so long, only to risk throwing it away – well, most of it – on a crazy hunch? Both of us, it is clear, have aces to pair the one on the board.

But who has the better kicker? It costs me $3,000 to find out that it is, of course, him – with a king to my queen. I have slumped way back down to a little over $1,000 again.

That was an unbelievably expensive mistake; just when I was advancing satisfactorily, I have very little realistic chance of getting back into this thing. Moodily, I play A-5 and climb back a bit, to $1,735. Never say die.

4.35 p.m.: Forty-five players left. My cards have gone dead again, just when I need some action.

5.10 p.m.: Forty players left, and I'm down to $1,000 or so. The antes are $25 per player, the blinds $100-$200. I have barely enough to last two rounds. I've gotta go for it.

5.20 p.m.: I go for it. Exit London Tony in thirty-seventh place. No need to worry about a transatlantic export licence for the Chevy Astro Tiara.

The poor old Moll. She had a hangdog poker pro to cheer up that night, and an even more miserable one the next day. But *that* was entirely her fault.

Eleven o'clock the next morning, a curiously early time for me to be awake, let alone vertical, found us walking hand in hand past Caesar's ornamental fountains, across the road and into the Dunes, to slam down our entry fees for a $25 buy-in Limit Hold 'em tournament, with an hour of $20 rebuys. Out of the twenty starters there would be three money winners, with (as it turned out, after the rebuys) $600 for first place.

After cautious starts at separate tables, and no rebuys by either of us, we were delighted to be reunited at the final table, where the last nine players settled down to fight it out. Only when a pair of kings beat my A-J, and she gave me a sympathetic smile as I found myself on the verge of extinction in seventh place, did I suddenly realize how bad it was going to be for my morale to see the Moll finish higher. She was still going, with or without my support, long after I was out, and the hour was approaching for the media tournament back at Caesar's. By then she was one of four players fighting to get into the money.

I told her I didn't want to make her nervous, and beat a hasty retreat, booking us both seats for Slim's media knees-up – which turned out, to my chagrin, to be seven-card stud rather than Hold 'em. Stud, you see, is the Moll's game. The dealers were just shuffling up when she charged in to claim her seat, exultantly clutching an envelope which contained the third-place Dunes prize of $190.

There were sixty-five starters in Amarillo Slim's media tournament, seven of whom would receive cash prizes. Though stud is not my forte, I found myself doing OK. So did the Moll. After a couple of hours eating the press rookies for breakfast, we again met up at the final table.

This time, I managed to improve on my showing at the Dunes. I was knocked out in ninth place, only *two* behind the Moll, who picked up the seventh-place prize of $50 and had her name written up on the wall.

By the time she found me, slumped in the bar of Cleopatra's Barge, I was all set to sail home. What point was there in trying to prove myself as a seasoned professional if she was going to breeze into town and start out-performing me? Didn't she realize how thoughtless she had been? With the World

Series only three months away, didn't she care about the effect on what was once called my self-confidence?

There are times when the Moll disappears into some mental telephone kiosk, turns into Supermoll, and moves effortlessly into self-effacing overdrive. This, she could see, was going to have to be one of them. The first thing she did was to spend half her winnings buying me the best dinner Caesar's can offer – a doubly magnanimous gesture when we could have eaten for free in the Palladium, the poker player's nightly buffet. The second was to remind me that these were mere 'rinky-dink' tournaments compared to the major league events in which I was putting up consistently strong showings. My satellite wins alone, she said, were much more impressive achievements than the lucky little results she had enjoyed that day. Then she said that if I wrote a book about all this one day, and somehow failed to mention the fact that she had won money in back-to-back Las Vegas poker tournaments, she would kill me.

That night, as the Moll dropped into a contented sleep long before midnight, a self-satisfied smile still adorning her once angelic features, I felt a need to punish myself. The toughest sentence I could think of was to enter myself for the Marina's 'Graveyard Shift' tournament.

The only contest in town which begins at 3 a.m., this one is for the *really* desperate. Most of the participants are dealers from other casinos fresh off the night shift. Themselves hotshot poker players, desperate for action after watching others win and lose all day, these are the only people alert enough to spark their ignition at this time of night. To wake myself up, inflict an extra degree of indignity, and remember how long it was since I had won any money, I forced myself to walk there rather than spend any of my $35 entry fee on a taxi.

There are only two sorts of people walking the streets of Las Vegas at 2 a.m. on a winter's night: muggers, and broken souls not worth mugging. As I picked my way through the bag-people, wondering if the $35 entry fee in my hip pocket was really worth dying for, it began to snow. Now it was a cold night – that much, without a coat, I had noticed – but *snow*! My self-inflicted sufferings had grown cruel and unusual, especially now I realized that three blocks on a map of Las Vegas constitute a rather longer walk than I had bargained for. An hour later, when I finally made it to the Marina – intact, apart from frostbite – I was told that this was the first snowfall in February in Las Vegas for seventeen years. As the casino stragglers discussed what odds that constituted, I reflected that to choose this particular night for my first long walk in a decade of coming here showed just how my luck was running.

But my mood grew all the more determined. By 3.30 a.m. there were twenty-five lost souls ready to sit down and contest the Graveyard Shift tournament, two-thirds of them dealers from the Palace Station and points west. They were in merry, de-mob mood, which made mine even grimmer. The lone stranger with the English accent kept his own counsel in Seat Five of Table Two, conspicuously unamused by the banter of this jolly throng. He continued to maintain a joke-proof, anti-social silence, playing as tight as the lid of a child-proof pill-box, when he made it to the final table. Roseate dawn was fingering the flops before he finally got busted in the first hand of the head-to-head, and wearily pocketed the second-place envelope containing $250.

If I hadn't finished in the money, would I have made myself walk back? We will never know. At least I read the cab driver right. I knew he was going to say he couldn't change the $50 bill, but I let him keep it anyway. Now, just as she was waking, I could face the Moll again.

The daylight hours of our last full day in Vegas I spent asleep, she kibitzing around the Big Boys. Having missed the satellites for the Main Event, the Superbowl itself, I was in no position to squander the $5,000 entry fee. I was $1,500 down on the week, again despite a notional $3,000 profit from satellite entries into two big tournaments, which had the global bank-roll still wondering if it would make it to the world championships. It had stood at $5,000 down when I left home, and would not thank me for returning minus all $9,999. On present tournament form, another four-figure entry fee would be so much more money ploughed into a poker economy already doing just fine out of me.

By the time I headed downstairs, refreshed and ready for action, most of the heavy mob were out of the big tournament and deep into some even bigger side-games. It was the last night of this particular get-together, and the action was fast and furious. When I found the Moll, she said she was more than happy watching the heavy mob beating each other up. Imagine her surprise, after some 'retail therapy' down the Appian Way, to find that her man had decided to go for broke and join them.

Clutching a feeble $1,500 in chips and cash, the most I dared risk losing, I had sat down with Perry Green and a few of his pals in a $5–$10–$25 game of Pot Limit Hold 'em. On the second hand, under the gun, I was dealt K-2 suited, and brashly made it $50 to come in. Four of them did. So there was $250 in the pot, including $50 of mine, as I watched the dealer roll K-K-2. Could I have been living right? It's so hard to tell.

This time I was going to exploit my early position and make it tough for them. I bet the maximum, $250. There were three folds before the final player, a youngish stranger in a cap and pony tail, saw my bet and raised it $500. Obviously he was holding the case king with a much better kicker. But my full house was already made, and the odds were on my side. I called his $500 and re-raised him $700, thus parting with my entire $1,500. Without much hesitation he called, and turned over an A-K. With two cards to go, only an ace stood between me and a pot of $3,200 – $1,700 of it profit. The dealer burnt a card and rolled a three, burnt another and rolled a ten. As I raked in the readies, I permitted myself a smile in the Moll's direction, at which she permitted herself to order a large vodka.

There were too many calculations going on in my head, which was now above water for the week, but still blowing bubbles over the year. From a low point of $13,000, I had now worked my original $20,000 back to around $16,000 – give or take a few hundred, which are merely tips hereabouts. Could this game actually put me ahead for the first time all year? To hell with tournaments. They may be good experience, but they are no way for a freshman pro to expect to win money. Cash games were my true element; for an upwardly mobile poker pro they were, in the end, the only way to travel. Take it easy now, I kept telling myself, and your entire personal landscape could alter. Stay as calm as you're attempting to look, hang in there for the right moment, and this trip could at last be the making of you.

Sure enough, after a couple of cautious hours holding my own, along came the decisive hand I'd been expecting – the one which would either earn me my entry fee for the World Series in May, or send me home a broken reed.

With Q-Q in the hole, and $3,500 in front of me, I raised

$50 before the flop and got all of four callers. The dealer turned Qc-5c-4d. First to speak, I tried a trap check, and it worked. When Pony Tail, to my right, bet $250, I raised him $500. To my astonishment, he was one of three people to call. What *could* they have? Could 2-3 or 6-7 have called that raise before the flop? Everyone was playing a canny game here. Only one of them could have queens up. The other two might have trip fives or trip fours, but two pairs seemed more likely, straight and flush draws even more so. This was going to be some hand – and, so far, I was winning it.

So the pot totalled $3,375 – *real* dollars, for once, not tournament funny money – as the turn produced another five, giving me an electric shock to go with my full house.

Could Pony Tail have four fives? This was not the moment for a check-raise. I gave him a sly look, only to find him gazing at me with agonized uncertainty clouding those blue eyes. Now I knew: he was holding 4-5, and had made his full house. He was thinking back through the betting to see if I could possibly be holding two queens. How I wished for six-figure funds in front of me, and the chance to scare him to death. The paltry sum I had, however, left no room for mistakes. The only thing to do was to bet it, and hope he misread my hand. In went my remaining $2,700.

I was just thinking what a shame it was that they wouldn't be able to call, when all three of them did. What the heck could they have? All I knew was that, unlike me, they had more money left, and looked ready to bet it. The pot now stood at more than $14,000, representing a profit in excess of $10,000 soon to be heading my way. It would be the biggest single hand I had ever won in Vegas. It would put the bank-roll into profit for the first time all year. If I managed to check out of the hotel without blowing it on some passing temptation, I'd be heading home a substantial winner. Would I ever be able to sit down in the $20–$40 game again? This was my true blooding as a professional.

I was miles away as the river brought another five, Pony Tail bet his remaining $2,000 on the side, and the others folded muttering. It still took me a minute, as he rolled his 4-5, to see that some malevolent deity had torn up the odds sheet and handed him four miraculous, unbeatable fives – depriving me not merely of my $10,000 profit, and my blooding as a professional, but of every penny I had about my person.

I got up and left without even bothering to show my hand. Murmurs of sympathy – unlikely, anyway – would have been quite drowned out by the hammering of the blacksmith's forge newly installed in my head, the churning of the jacuzzi in the pit of my stomach. Even the Moll knew to follow at a discreet distance as I staggered in a daze towards a legion of centurions doing their nightly rounds. Poker pro? I might as well apply for a job as a gladiator.

It was hours before I could talk about anything else. I'd left $5,000 at home, come here with twice that much, and was now facing the long journey back with a depleted stack I had lost the will to risk. The road to the World Series was more than half travelled; my original twenty grand was now down to twelve, leaving me a laughable $2,000 to play with if I wanted to be sure of that critical $10,000 entry fee. How could that guy *think* about coming all that way with the low trips, even calling a raise with the two low pairs he had started with? The question dogged us all the way to Los Angeles airport, where a mere $200 worth of white stretched limo, white flowers and white wine – ordered and paid for a week before – suddenly seemed like ridiculous value for money. By the time we had got Boston on the carphone, to tell the Moll's mother that I was treating her daughter in the style to which she deserved to become accustomed, the pain was beginning to seep from my back into the white leather seats, from the soles of my feet into the deep-pile white carpet, and out through the top of my head into the wine-stained, smoke-filled upper ether.

I checked The Watch and then the bank-roll. I still had the best part of eight thousand – all right, then, nearer seven – in my pocket. We would hit the town, sure, splash out on a star-spotting meal in Beverly Hills, take in the disco she had so long been denied . . . Then maybe we could, just for a while, mosey down to the Bicycle Club and check out the action? There were bound to be some tourists, and my luck was surely due for a change? In that hand, after all, the odds *had* been on my side. *Anybody* would say I'd played it right. In fact, it seemed to me I'd played it rather well. That raise of mine, when you came to think about it . . .

The Moll smiled sweetly, stretched out on the white leather and closed her eyes.

9

An Ear Full Of Cider

♥ ♣ ♦ ♠

In 'The Idyll of Miss Sarah Brown', the short story which inspired the musical *Guys and Dolls*, Damon Runyon first blessed the world with the character of Obadiah Masterson, popularly known as Sky. 'The reason he is called the Sky is because he goes so high when it comes to betting on any proposition whatsoever. He will bet all he has, and nobody can bet more than this.'

In Runyon's story, Obadiah is a less than favourite son of a little town in southern Colorado, where his old man is 'a very well-known citizen, and something of a sport himself'. Young Obadiah has learnt to shoot craps, and play cards, and one thing and another, to the point where he finally 'cleans up all the loose scratch around his home town and decides he needs more room'. His old man, who thoroughly approves of the decision, offers Obadiah a little farewell advice.

'Son,' the old guy says, 'you are now going out into the wide, wide world to make your own way, and it is a very good thing to do, as there are no more opportunities for you in this burg. I am only sorry that I am not able to bank-roll you to a very large start, but not having any potatoes to give you, I am now going to stake you to some very valuable advice, which I personally collect in my years of experience around and about, and I hope and trust you will always bear this advice in mind.

> *'Son, no matter how far you travel, or how smart you get, always remember this: Some day, somewhere, a guy is going to come to you and show you a nice brand-new deck of cards on which the seal is never broken, and this guy is going to offer to bet you that the jack of spades will jump out of this deck and squirt cider in your ear. But, son, do not bet him, for as sure as you do you are going to get an ear full of cider.'*

This immortal advice subsequently stands young Obadiah in good stead. He makes only one mistake, and that directly after leaving his home town for the first time in his life and arriving in St Louis, Missouri. Here he readily bets some local guy that St Louis is the biggest town in the world, thus losing all his potatoes and being forced to start again from scratch. His mistakes thereafter are few.

Aficionados of the movie version of *Guys and Dolls* will remember Marlon Brando's Sky Masterson quoting his old man's advice while refusing a rigged bet from Frank Sinatra's Nathan Detroit about the respective amounts of cheesecake and strudel consumed each day at Mindy's, their favourite New York watering-hole. Within minutes, however, Sky has accepted an alternative challenge: that he will not be able to persuade any girl of Nathan's choice to accompany him to dinner that same evening in Havana, Cuba. When the Salvation Army band marches by the window, and Nathan points to the prim young lady at its head, Sister Sarah Brown, Sky duly rolls his eyes to the heavens and observes: 'Daddy, I just got an ear full of cider.'

Though Brando has hijacked the role in the public psyche, Runyon modelled the character of 'Sky' Masterson on the greatest proposition player the world has known, equally unparalleled as gambler, poker player, hustler and con man:

Alvin Clarence Thomas, known to posterity as the unsinkable 'Titanic' Thompson.

Unlike Sky Masterson, 'Ty' Thompson had no father to give him death-bed advice. His old man was out gambling the night he was born in Rogers, Arkansas, in 1892, and within six months had vanished altogether. But something lurked in the blood. Ty was just six when he pulled off his first big coup, at the fishing hole near his childhood home in the Arkansas backwoods. Though adept with his own wooden pole, the boy coveted the smart casting-rods of the city folk who came there at weekends. One of them, in turn, admired the boy's spaniel, Carlo, and one day offered to buy it.

Ty demurred, saying that he could never part with Carlo for money. But the dog, he went on, was even smarter than the stranger knew. Why, he could dive to the bottom of that twenty-feet-deep pond and retrieve the very stone you threw for him. When the stranger expressed disbelief, Ty stood his ground. He was willing to bet the dog against the stranger's rod that it was true.

The stranger instantly accepted the bet, and chose a rock about the size of a rubber ball. The boy marked it with an X, and let the man throw it into the deepest part of the pond. Carlo duly bounded after it, disappeared underwater for some thirty seconds, then reappeared with a rock in its mouth. When the dog panted back to them, the stranger was astonished to see an X on the rock it dropped at their feet.

The man, of course, said he had 'just been foolin'', and the six-year-old needed to whip out his .22 to collect his winnings. But the story really ends with Ty's subsequent explanation: 'That dog of mine was good at that trick. He was very good. But I ain't one for taking chances. A few days before, I'd covered the bottom of that hole with dozens of rocks marked with an X. That slicker never had a prayer.'

Ty's subsequent life was a history of such pre-calculated chances – propositions which now ring through gambling history. There was the summer day in 1917, in Hot Springs, Arkansas, when he sat on the porch of the Arlington Hotel eating a bag of Danish walnuts. When a couple of locals joined him, they were grateful enough to share Ty's walnuts, but did not believe his boast that he could throw a walnut over the hotel across the street. Each had put up a bet of a hundred dollars, and had given Ty odds of 3:1, before he let them choose a nut, sauntered off the porch, and lofted it high over the five-storey building. After they had paid up in astonishment, Thompson disappeared round the back of the hotel to retrieve the lead-filled Danish walnut he had palmed from his pocket.

There was the night Ty dug up the Missouri signpost saying, JOPLIN – 20 MILES, and moved it five miles nearer town. Next day, driving past the spot with some local gamblers, he bet them the sign was wrong: 'Can't be more than fifteen miles to Joplin from here.' That was good for another five hundred apiece, as was the episode of the passing wagonload of water melons. In the countryside near Evansville, Indiana, Ty stopped a passing wagon and bought its entire load of melons, on condition that the driver counted them for him, then drove the wagon at a pre-appointed hour through the centre of Evansville, past the old McCurdy Hotel, a favourite haunt of gamblers. Sitting nonchalantly on the porch when the wagon hove into sight, Ty got odds from every man in the place that he couldn't guess the size of the load to the nearest melon.

He played poker straight, and golf with refinements. In town after town Ty would play a round well within his abilities, let the victors crow in the bar afterwards, then mop up next day with subsequent, bigger bets. One winter his bar-room boast was that he could drive a golf ball five hundred yards; after taking thousands in bets, he teed up on a hilltop overlooking a frozen lake, and the ball was still bouncing while he collected. But his most frequent scam was to pick out the local millionaire, let him win, then offer to play him again for double the stakes – left-handed. Johnny Moss witnessed one such contest in Ruidoso, New Mexico. 'After losing by four strokes, the millionaire wrote out a cheque in real anguish, mumbling, "I just don't understand it." Then a caddy told him: "You would, sir, if you knew that Titanic was a natural-born left-hander who taught himself to play right-handed almost as well."'

The beginning and end of Ty's heyday on the road were marked by two momentous poker games. He did not really become a free, independent spirit until the age of sixteen, when he exorcized a ghost in a marathon game in Old City, a boom town on the Texas–Louisiana border. After a long search Ty had finally found the opponent he had been seeking – the father who had walked out when he was six months old. Throughout a fifteen-hour head-to-head contest the teenager concealed his identity – until, around dawn, the grouchy old-timer lost a hand which put him $5,000 down. Rising from the table, he said: 'You're a winner, boy. That's all I care to lose today.'

Ty pushed the chips back across the table: 'I'm giving you your money back. You never had a chance to beat me.' Only then did he reveal who he was. Father and son spent the next few weeks together before Ty got bored – 'We didn't have much in common' – and moved on. They never met again.

Two decades later, in 1928, Ty was one of the winners in

the celebrated New York poker game which led to the murder of Arnold Rothstein, the wealthiest and most notorious gambler of his day. The man who had fixed the 1919 World Series, famous for winning $500,000 on the 1921 Dempsey–Tunney fight, Rothstein was Scott Fitzgerald's model for Wolfsheim, the gambler in *The Great Gatsby*. He lost a total of $475,000 that night; six weeks later, after failing to pay up, he was found dead in his Central Park hotel room. The bookmaker who had organized the game, George McManus, was subsequently charged with Rothstein's murder, but acquitted for lack of evidence. For Ty, who appeared as a witness, the trial was a watershed. It was the first time his picture had appeared in the newspapers, and he did not like it. He did not like it at all. Hustling his way around the country, offering propositions to wealthy innocents, thereafter became much more difficult.

Titanic Thompson got caught up in many a fight, killing several men in defence of his bank-roll, but he finally died of natural causes in Fort Worth, Texas, in 1974, at the age of eighty-two, flat broke. Today there are lamentably few proposition players left in this increasingly colourless world – people who will bet on anything, any time, anywhere. But soft, I think I can hear one of them right now, boasting about the time he outran a racehorse – for a wager, of course. 'This was no hunch,' I can hear him saying. 'I don't bet on hunches because I don't believe in hunches. Hunches are for dogs making love.'

That voice, that accent: it can be only one man. Last time we saw Amarillo 'Slim' Preston, he was hosting his own Superbowl at Caesar's Palace, Las Vegas. Now he has joined us for lunch beside a ritzy Moroccan swimming-pool and is waxing nostalgic. There was the time he beat Minnesota Fats at pool, playing with a broom handle . . . the time he beat Willie Nelson at golf, playing with a bow and arrow . . .

'Another time a few years back, I was playing golf with some gambling buddies out there in Amarillo. Among them was Big Jim, who'll bet on anything. Big Jim knows about me and that racehorse, and he says to me, "Slim, d'you think you can outrun anybody that's here on this golf course right now?" I tell him, "You're goddam right I think I can, buddy."

'Well, I'm a fairly fleet-of-foot cat. But I notice that Big Jim's caddy is a long-legged, loose-jointed kid who floats on his feet and looks like he can outrun a gazelle. So I begin to limp a little, and I say, "Dammit, Jim, I hurt my heel some-how on that last hole. I don't think I can run a race. But I tell you what: I'll bet you I can long jump further than anyone on the links right now. You name him!"

'Jim hitches up his pants and gets a cat-that-ate-the-bird kind of a grin on his face. Now it don't take a Nobel Prize scientist to figure that his entry will be this caddy of his. So when Jim draws a jumping line on the grass, I say, "Hold on a minute, pardner. Since this is a golf course, let's jump from behind a golf club." And I lay down an iron.

'Then I make a stipulation – without which, I tell him, I ain't gonna make no bet. If either jumper even *touches* this golf club, he's disqualified and loses the money. Big Jim looks a mite suspicious, but he finally agrees, and starts huddling with buddies, pooling all their money to make that pot higher than a rich junkie.

'While they're busy doing that I pretend to tie my shoe-laces, and I have a quiet word with this caddy of his, who looks like he could jump further than a goosed frog. "Son," I tell him, "let me give you some friendly advice. Big Jim and those friends of his are tough babies, and if you make a mistake and lose them a bundle of money, why, they're liable to kick your ass all the way down to the creek and back. Of course if you lose because I outjump you, that's a horse of a different colour. But, son, don't you accidentally touch that golf club!"

'The kid's eyes grow as big as basketballs. I go first, give it all I've got, and make a pretty good distance, which we mark with a stick. Then the kid's running like hell out of the blue yonder – seems like the length of a whole city block – and I'm very glad I'm not racing him. Suddenly he takes off, and he's a good two yards behind that golf club! Even then it looks to me he's going into orbit. When he finally comes down, even after that two-yard safety margin, he's barely a few inches behind my jump.

'I collect the money, but I tell you, neighbour, I'd never have won that bet without a little psychology.'

The Moll and I gasp appropriately, and Slim's off on a roll. 'But, hell, that's nothing. In my time I've bet big money that I could pick any thirty people at random and two of them would have the same birthday. I've bet a champion checker player that he could never trap my one king with his two kings, no matter how many moves he made. And one time, in a smart club, I bet that a stray cat that wandered in could carry an empty Coke bottle across the room and set it on the cash register . . . And I won every one of these bets.'

Of course he did, because each of them required applied psychology – or, more likely, advance information. The birthday trick is an old one, which stands up to sound mathematical proof, but the cat and the Coke bottle take a lot of explaining. Slim shares Ty Thompson's penchant for conjuring bets out of nowhere; but he's also learnt Ty's trick of charting nowhere first, and fixing himself an edge.

Well, we all know the devil don't bet with Amarillo Slim, but did Slim ever take a bet with Titanic Thompson? 'Hell, yes. Too many. Even for me, too many . . .

'One time on the road I met up with Ty. He was fleecing people by pretending he couldn't shoot skeet, then picking them all out of a clear blue sky. But I knew I could shoot even better than him, so I let Ty set up a challenge.

'First time, I shoot at a dozen and down just eleven. Ah could swear I hit that twelfth little fella, but he just flies on regardless. Ty suggests a second bet, and the same thing happens. Then again, and again. Now I'm losing a bundle.

'Well, I knew what I could smell cooking warn't on the fire. I send Ty off in the opposite direction, then go down and check on the skeet they'd been putting up for us. They all look OK. It isn't until I kick 'em all, hard, that this twelfth little fella jars my foot good and proper.

'He was made o' metal.'

So how did he get his revenge? 'I switched skeet on him, naturally, raised the stakes, and got all my money back. Ty never could figure how I downed that metal bird o' his.'

I could listen to this stuff all afternoon, but now, alas, a liveried flunkey arrives to tell us that our presence is required within, where they are drawing seats for the Morocco Open Poker Championships. Without Slim and me, the field would barely fill the final table.

The Ayatollah Khomeini was the last person I expected to have much influence on my year as a poker pro, but February saw the shadow of his long arm hovering over the green baize of Muslim North Africa. Only a few days before Khomeini had pronounced his notorious *fatwa* on Salman Rushdie, author of *The Satanic Verses*. In the ensuing furore, when merely to board a flight out of London seemed tantamount to suicide, scores of players had pulled out of the Moroccan shindig, latest in a long line of exotic one-off events laid on by a British promoter, Colin Roberts.

I did not discover quite how many had chickened out until it was too late, and I had arrived. Only a handful of Americans, Slim and Eric Drache among them, had made the long journey here, and even fewer Britons. Personally, as I had jetted my way via Casablanca to Marrakesh, courtesy of Royal Air Maroc, I would have bet even Ty Thompson that it was somewhat less safe on the ground than aboard a Muslim flight with a Muslim airline to a Muslim country.

Johnny Chan had been one of the first to arrive, equally immune to world events – and without a clue as to Morocco's whereabouts until, somewhere over the mid-Atlantic, he finally found the place on his in-flight map. But it was not the trifling rewards of the Golden Oasis Poker Tournament which had lured the reigning world champion all this way. It was the prospect of a French millionaire with more money than card sense – the kind of person who will fly in the world champ at his own expense, so that he can waste enormous amounts of money in a vain attempt to be able to say he once beat him. This kind of *folie de grandeur*, according to the growing ranks of former world champions, is perhaps the single biggest perk of winning the title. Everywhere they go, idiots want to try and beat them. Rich idiots even pay their executioner's expenses. Chan's two years as world champion are said to have given him the chance to score several million bucks this way.

Not this time, however. For three days Johnny sat in the lobby of the Mamounia Hotel, waiting fairly patiently, before a curious message arrived from Paris. At the weekend the French millionaire had apparently been entertaining some English house-guests, whom he felt obliged to take sightseeing, and thus to the top of the Eiffel Tower. Here an unfortunate accident had occurred, involving a wind-blown pane of glass and the tip of the finger of the English house-guests' daughter. Naturally, the French millionaire felt unable to leave Paris until his friends' daughter had made a full recovery.

I had heard some tall tales this year, many too tall even to bear repetition in these pages, but this one seemed to me to cap the lot. It sounded so unlikely that it was probably true. Either way, Chan wasn't going to hang around to find out. Nor would he bother, now he had come all this way, to see if he could add the Moroccan title to his growing list of laurels. With a buy-in of a mere $2,500, it wasn't worth kicking his heels around the pool for another week, savouring the luxury treatment which had recently brought the likes of Mick Jagger, Adnan Khashoggi and the honeymooning Joan Collins to this hotel. No: as I was checking in, Chan was checking out, unsure whether to head west for some poker or east for some Pai Gau action. He would probably see what flight would take him in which direction faster.

Well, that was a relief. Now there was only Slim, Eric and a handful of undaunted itinerant pros between me and the Moroccan title. First, however, there was a sybaritic week of gentle action and gracious luxury to enjoy.

Local legend has it that there has always been a magical garden in the heart of Marrakesh, a garden so bewitching that its eighteenth-century owners, Sultan Sidi Mohammed and his wife, the tempestuous Lalla Fatima, handed it down to their son as a wedding present. The garden then became a famous shrine of the high life, where the most lavish entertainments of the day were laid on for wealthy and celebrated guests from all over the world. In the 1920s the Mamounia Hotel was opened in that same garden, and aspired to that same tradition. Now it was Paul Valéry and Maurice Ravel, Rita

Hayworth and Eric von Stroheim, Rothschilds and Rockefellers who came here to play – and, most famously, Winston Churchill to relax, even during the rigours of war. Here, in later life, because the light at the edge of the Sahara can be so exquisite, the great man still came regularly, to paint water-colours of the Atlas mountains. Today, even by the same exquisite light, I'd lay 6:4 that Churchill wouldn't recognize the place.

The Mamounia, like most of the rest of Morocco, is the personal property of His Majesty King Hassan II, who a few years ago decided that it needed a face-lift. Seventy million dollars later – even at full capacity, say the management, it would take a hundred years to recoup the investment – the place is a priceless Art Deco temple of hedonism. Exquisite mosaics, vast Persian rugs, Andalusian patios *à la* Alhambra and sumptuous ornaments from the School of Vienna adorn the Carrara marble interior; outside, beyond the $2,000-a-night villas frequented by La Collins and her chums, the scent of bougainvillaea and oleander escort you down olive-tree avenues carved through seven acres of parkland. The suites suggest what Caesar's Palace might be like if the world had been scoured for the highest-quality marbles, gold and silver available, all of which had been flown in with no regard for expense. All this, six bars, six restaurants, and satellite television too. 'Here,' as Jacques Brel testifies in the polyglot brochure, its English at times a little shaky, 'you find everything that the Northerner graves.'

All of which made it a great shame that, thanks to the Ayatollah, the Golden Oasis Poker Tournament was a pretty resounding flop. Those few of us who actually turned up had a terrific time, as would anyone visiting the Mamounia on the cusp of spring, when the temperatures around one of the world's most seductive pools are in the balmy eighties, rather than the ferocious summer heat of 150°F. But one Moroccan meal goes an awful long way, and we all agreed that we might have thought twice about coming if we had known how few of us were actually going to turn up.

The poker action was a joke. To take part in the side-games, you had to be an eccentric or an extremely rash millionaire. 'London' lowball – not my game at the best of times, let alone when people are risking five figures on a dodgy draw – was the only game in town. Last seen in Vegas at Christmas, it seemed to be following me around the world, filling me with a tantalizing mix of envy and relief as I watched bundles of money beyond my orbit changing hands on the wildest chances. I had managed to win the air fare to Morocco off the Tuesday boys; but when your bank-roll was as low as mine, and you dared budget only for the limited liability of tournament play, the best thing to do was admire the scenery.

At least we'd had the good sense to arrive late, for Morocco's real-life King had even managed to treat the prompter players, itching for action, to the worst possible welcome. Two days before the tournament began, Hassan had summarily emptied all the Mamounia's two hundred and twenty rooms to make way for the princes, potentates and other grandee guests arriving for the annual celebration of the anniversary of his coronation. The Mamounia was, after all, his personal guest-house – as involuntary refugees, under the impression that they were paying hotel-guests, and high-paying ones at that, found out to their cost. Professional poker players, world champions included, were not best pleased. Themselves accustomed to VIP treatment, usually *gratis*, they were certainly not used to paying *and* being bumped, especially by freeloading foreigners.

Evicted to a scruffy-looking dive downtown, some of them never came back. So by the time the Moll and I arrived, later that week, there were just twenty or so survivors to flout the dress code of the Mamounia's sumptuous built-in casino, where the leaves of the palm trees are wrought in sterling silver. Each day saw a $1,000-entry tournament, the first of which had been won by Slim, the following three all by Eric Drache. He might have won $30,000 in prize money, but he was losing it all in the side-games, said Eric, as yet again he bought everyone dinner.

To stage a poker tournament in a Muslim country, where gambling is forbidden under Islamic law, may itself seem something of a gamble. It certainly ensured that the local opposition wasn't too strong. No Muslim Moroccans were able to enter any of the tournaments, including what was billed as their national championships, nor had one Jewish or Christian Moroccan yet been sighted in the casino corner set aside for poker. Upon learning all this, Amarillo Slim began to waylay strangers, offering odds that the title of Moroccan poker champion would go to a foreigner. Colonel Gadhafi was said to be in town, but had yet to put in an appearance at the Golden Oasis – as indeed had Adnan Khashoggi, said to be a regular, and promised this week as bait for the American high rollers. As yet, in the midst of his legal difficulties, Khashoggi was proving as elusive as that accident-prone Parisian millionaire.

As was the run of luck which had yet to bless my professional career. I came close to the money in all three preliminary Omaha and Hold 'em tournaments, finishing fifth in two of them and fourth in one. With only twenty or so starters, that may not sound too impressive; but they were a mean bunch, turned all the sourer by the low turnout, and the lack of their kind of side-action in the evenings. Only Slim's presence brought the occasion to life, from the moment he arrived for the PLO tournament – whisper those initials around *here* at your peril – with camel dung on his sneakers.

'Hell, that 'ornery critter's left me his calling-card,' cried Slim when a group at the next table complained about the smell. He removed the offending shoe, summoned the cocktail girl, and handed it over, saying: 'Honey, would you get your mother to clean this up for me? Then come back with your sister and we'll all have some fun, huh?'

This counted as a pleasant interlude in the constant flow of needling backchat and sharp verbal practice Slim kept up at the table. '"Get a lot of it" was my daddy's advice, and I've spent my whole life doing just that . . . I'm sixty-five and I've been playing poker for a hundred years . . . Come on, let's build that pot till it's higher than a dawg could jump over.' Slim's favourite tactic is to home in on the quieter players, the ones who look like they can't stand up for themselves, and give them a hard time until they go on tilt.

Today – well, it had to come some time – that's me. A dismal run of cards had me looking pretty glum and playing very few hands. 'Ain't you *ever* gonna join us in one of these here pots? Come on in, the water's fine. No use waitin' for four aces at this game, you know! Hell, this fella's tighter than a nun's . . . oh, excuse me, ma'am' – this, with a huge grin, to the Moll, to whom Slim had taken rather a shine. Normally no slouch at green baize repartee, I found it very hard to quip back. Compared to Slim's broad Texan gargle, my English accent sounded so unspeakably dull that most of my ripostes seemed to peter out halfway across the table. Finally, after grinning and bearing it for a couple of hours, I managed to ambush the master in a decisive hand, the one sure way of making him turn his attention elsewhere.

The relief was almost palpable when Slim's barbs started flying the other way. 'Now *this* fella couldn't track a horse in four feet o' snow,' he chided a bull-necked East End bookie – one of a small cockney contingent, evidently unused to absorbing such taunts in silence, who soon crumpled under the pressure. First, they lost their cool, and began to hurl abuse; then, as was entirely the object of Slim's exercise, they waged a personal war against him, playing hands they should have folded, and trying to scare him into big raises. If there's one thing that sure don't scare Amarillo Slim, it's a big raise – especially if he is being bank-rolled by Caesar's Palace, for whom he is here as a roving ambassador. One look at the wizened old water-carriers by the hotel entrance, their native fez now incongruously supplanted by Caesar's imperial baseball caps, could have told the cockneys that.

Once he'd got rid of them, Slim opened the sluice-gates on Donnacha O'Dea, one of the leading Irish players, highly respected on the international circuit. A Dublin bookie, who swam for his country in the 1968 Olympics, Donnacha has in his time made it to the final table of the world championship itself. He is one of poker's gentlemen; for all his soft-spoken, courteous exterior, Donnacha is a razor-sharp player, not easily rattled. When the flop showed two hearts, and Dublin pondered a big bet from Texas, Slim tried to help him out with a cry of, 'Hey, Irish, I ain't got no heart in my hand!'

Without looking up, or even appearing to interrupt his train of thought, Donnacha muttered back: 'Slim, you ain't got a heart in your whole body.'

Eric Drache had been used to Slim's banter too long to let it bother him. His replies tended to carry a broader wisdom derived from living life as one long poker game. 'Nervous,

Eric?' jibed Slim, as they faced each other down in a big pot. 'Hell, Slim,' replied Eric, 'how can *any* hand make you nervous when you know there are fifty million more to play?'

A relaxed Eric duly proceeded to bust out Slim, then two more Americans, then me and three other Englishmen before winning this, his fourth tournament of the week. 'They'll never believe this back in Vegas,' he said, before anyone else could. For me, finishing ahead of Slim was ample consolation for the loss of yet another tournament entry fee, and the collapse of the bank-roll back to half its starting-point. All I had left was the $10,000 entry fee for the world championships.

Somehow it all depressed me less than it had in Vegas. The last time I had been in Morocco was to tag along with Hassan's 'Green March' – the 1977 invasion of Spanish Sahara which had united his loyal citizens and visiting journalists as so much cannon-fodder. For three years I had unavoidably risked life and limb as a reporter in Northern Ireland; in the Sahara, for the first time in my life, I had found myself literally looking down the barrels of malevolent enemy tanks. The resultant copy had been heroic, the gut sensations less so. The point right now, a dozen years later, was that I had scarcely had time to enjoy the night-life of Marrakesh. So that evening, in high spirits wilfully defiant of my current state of play, the Moll and I dove deep into the *souk* for an exotic Moroccan night out.

It was time to take the advice of the Mamounia's brochure, and 'discover the heart of Marrakesh as though you were peeling an orange'. Round the city's massive ochre ramparts we rode in a carriage, just like it told us to, stopping at the tanners' gate, the Bab ed Debbagh, where a labyrinth of craftsmen were indeed preparing skins 'of unbelievable softness'. On we went to meditate before the Sa'adi tombs, stroll round the lake of the El Badi palace and barter in the colourful chaos of the medina. At 'the witching hour of dusk' we reported to Jemma El Fna, to see the acrobats, clowns, storytellers and snake-charmers, before subsiding into a supposed secret of a restaurant – the best not just in town, but in the whole of Morocco – where we walked straight into a noisy transatlantic gang of poker players.

By the time we got back, the peacetime British press had arrived in the shape of John David Morley – yes, he of the Salzburg sandals – who had heard of exotic events in the desert and high-tailed it here on behalf of the *Observer* colour magazine. Put Morley together with Slim for a while, spice the mixture with Slim's travelling companion, Larry Sanders, manager of the Caesar's Palace card room, and you are sure to emerge with a proposition worthy of the memory of Titanic Thompson. Tonight was no exception.

Sanders started it, after indulging in a little childhood nostalgia. His father, he told us, worked in a logging camp, where his wife allowed him to play poker each Friday night so long as he took young Larry along with him. That's how the kid learnt the game, just by watching. One night, when his father filled his inside straight at draw, he showed it to the boy to keep him from growing restless. 'Hey, Dad, you made your hand!' cried young Larry, at which all the other players promptly folded. The story served to prove that Larry Sanders could read poker hands from the age of six.

Various tales from Slim's childhood followed, leading to yet more about his life on the road with Larry. Sanders told us about the time Slim brought his horses up from Texas for a rodeo event at the High Sierra casino in Lake Tahoe. 'You know what Slim did? He rode one of those darned horses right into the casino. For a fact he did.'

'For a bet, you mean,' interrupted Slim. 'Somebody'd put me up to it. But the High Sierra's manager didn't like me riding this beautiful beast of mine into his casino. No, sir, he didn't like it one little bit. So I backed my hoss right up to the crap table, and I said to him, "You know how these here crap tables got their name? You wan' me to show ya?"'

Somewhere between Slim, Sanders, Morley, that story and the local tipple emerged another bet, which would now pre-occupy the rest of our week. Discreet enquiries revealed that a camel had never been seen inside the Grand Casino La Mamounia. Duly challenged to set matters to rights, for a sum rumoured to be in the region of $1,000, Slim had set off by dawn next morning in search of a compliant mount.

So that afternoon's tournament started without him, until the unwonted peace was shattered by a cry of, 'Hey, it's so quiet in here you could hear a mouse pee on cotton!' Slim had evidently been bartering in the *souk*, as he was wearing an Arab robe and fez. 'Hey, how do you guys like this? Poker fez!'

'Keep it dahn, mate, we're in a hand here,' mumbled one of the cockneys, already skewered by Slim's mere arrival, let alone his scene-stealing get-up. Any such attempt to gain the high ground wound up merely offering more hostages to fortune. 'What's that word "mate"? Where ah come from, we only use it for breedin' animals . . .

'Hey, Tahoe, you sonofagun, how ya doin'?'

Slim's good humour was bolstered further that day by the arrival of two more familiar faces, a pair of American pros who travel and play as partners. David Bellucci and Howard 'Tahoe' Andrew had flown in the night before after dallying awhile in London. Bellucci, the senior partner financially, is a California realtor who has played poker all his life 'strictly for pleasure . . . To me, it's a social game. It tests your mind, keeps you alert. I can drop twenty, thirty thousand dollars at a time and it won't hurt me.' So how rich is he? 'Up, up, *up*!' was all he would say in response to guesses. In baseball cap, sweatshirt, shorts and sandals, the richest man at the table was, even by local standards, the most sloppily dressed.

Tahoe is also a California businessman, also in real estate, but not as loaded as Bellucci. When he joined Morley at the bar after being busted out of the big game, he looked blasted. How did he feel? 'Like I bought some real estate and found it all got hit by one helluva earthquake.' He was tired from other games, he said, even before he arrived in Morocco; but, like most mere mortals, he cared about the money. 'To them,' he said, with a forlorn gesture at us pros, 'money is just ammunition.'

Tahoe had been tangling with 'Zapata', a twenty-eight-year-old Sikh from England's West Midlands, who had become a buddy of mine on the road somewhere between Las Vegas and Wolverhampton. Like most British professionals, Zapata is on permanent flight from the taxman. His occasional work as an electrical engineer, which is the occupation on his passport, brings in rather less than the £40,000 per annum he reckons to earn at poker. A finely calculating player, not afraid of taking big risks, he is so quiet at the table that he can all too easily be overlooked.

This was the mistake which had seen Tahoe stake a premature place at the bar, though it was not much longer before he had the consolation of being able to buy Zapata a drink. When I, too, bust out, we were joined by my candidate for Britain's leading player, another refugee from the name and occupation on his passport, who is far too grand to play in mere tournaments.

'Why waste the money? They don't offer odds as good as careful play in a real-money game.'

'Danny', let's call him, also from the Midlands, is a quiet and pensive fellow capable of playing America's highest rollers at their own game. Why did he think the Brits were otherwise so feeble on the international poker scene? This turned out to be a pet topic of his. 'One, the class system. Two, the restrictive gambling laws in Britain. Three, which follows from one and two, the lack of decent opposition.' Three reasons why Danny, having earned his fare in the London or Midland clubs, regularly packs his bags for Vegas.

Back at the tables, this was turning out to be just another day of Moroccan mirages. A Frenchman who had been watching the tournament offered Eric Drache $20,000 to play with, for a slice of his action. Why, wailed the rest of us, did he choose Eric? 'I guess,' said the man himself, 'it's because I was the only player wearing a tie.' Whatever the reason, the Frenchman failed to keep the appointment made that evening to hand over the readies. Meanwhile, two tough-looking loners from Nevada, who had picked up the scent of the poker trail in Casablanca, materialized overnight amid a spray of dollars – 'a new way', to Morley, 'of greening the desert' – and dematerialized at dawn with empty pockets. The *Observer*'s correspondent also spotted a minister from Kuwait, a prince to boot, who 'appeared in the casino to a resounding riffle of expectant chips, turned magnificently on his heel, and disappeared with his dirhams' – or 'diddy-rams', as Slim insisted on calling them – 'intact'.

The next day was our penultimate here, and the date set for the Moroccan Open. Still no Moroccan had entered the lists, and still Slim had not been seen inside the casino aboard a camel. A certain amount of heavy irony was brought to bear on both situations, leaving Slim quite unmoved. 'Hell, ain't no Moroccan gonna take me, anyway. Just as well for them they ain't allowed to play. But I can sure as heck beat 'em at their own game. 'Ornery critturs, camels. Ain't easy to *get* up there, never mind *stay* up there. But ain't no camel gonna put one over on ol' Slim. Ah'm just waitin' for you boys to up the ante.'

There were, sensibly enough, no takers. Nobody would put anything beyond Slim, not even *playing* aboard a camel. As we took our seats for the main event, however, there was not a desert beast in sight. Slim's sense of occasion had him appear in all his western finery, complete with rattlesnake stetson, the most discernible feature beneath which was a knowing smile.

There were eighteen starters at two tables, all of them American or European, putting up $2,500 each, and so $45,000 between them. The winner would receive $22,500, the second $15,000 and the third $7,500. The worst position to finish, therefore, was fourth.

For once, I managed to do better than that. I came fifth.

Five hours after play started, there were six of us left. At the last table we had seen off Bellucci and Tahoe, locally known as the dynamic duo, and all but one of the cockneys. Donnacha O'Dea was leading the tournament, closely followed by Eric, despite the fact that he kept nodding off. Every so often there would be a snort, and a cry of, 'Where am I? How am I doing?' Slim, Zapata, the one surviving East-Ender and I were all hanging in there. Morley and the Moll roamed the room restlessly, worried about my mood at dinner that night if Slim were to bust me, then ride to victory aboard a camel. When the opposite happened, and I busted out Slim, they suddenly began to fancy my chances.

So did I, when Zapata and I squared up for a showdown

which would put one of us on terms with the leaders. Even a finish in second place would miraculously hike my bank-roll into a blushing *ingénu* profit; a win, apart from bringing me a national title, would take it into some undreamed-of stratosphere where the costs of the world championship would be secured, with the working total back where it started, and two major tournaments to go. I was just cursing myself for working all this out, wasting those precious grey cells on amateur irrelevancies, when I discovered in the hole the means to that very redemption. With only five players left, I knew that the pair of queens I thought I had seen – I checked twice to make sure they were not another mirage – were vastly increased in pre-flop value. So I raised $3,000, half my stack, before the flop. To my delight, and his apparent unease, Zapata felt obliged to call. Our respective emotions were transparently confirmed when the flop brought three low cards.

I'd got him. I knew it. First to bet, I pushed my entire stack into the middle. He didn't seem to like it much, but finally shrugged – what kind of hick tournament was this, anyway? – and also went all-in. Before the issue was decided, we agreed to reveal our hands. When he saw my two ladies – 'Four big titties!' cried Slim from the rail – Zapata turned over a pair of jacks and stood up, ready to make a gracious exit. To him, this was no great drama, much less a matter of life and death than it was to me. The turn brought a ten, and I began to readjust to finishing in the money, even becoming the Moroccan champion and relishing an open-ended future as a poker pro. The dealer burnt the final card and rolled . . . a jack, the only card in the deck which could beat me.

For the first time in my tournament experience, there were universal expressions of sympathy at my appalling luck. For all my internal agonies, professional cool prevented me from revealing, either by grimace or gesture, the scale of the disaster that freak knave had wrought. Sure, we'd had fun, and I'd covered our expenses at blackjack; but that 22:1 reversal had taken the bank-roll to its lowest point yet, below $7,500. Forty-four cards would have won the pot for me; just two could for him, and one of them had appeared. I was reminded of poor old Doug Sanders, one of my childhood golfing heroes, missing that three-feet putt to win the British Open at St Andrews in 1970. That stylish fellow is now remembered primarily for that moment. Maybe the same would happen to me. Sanders' miss had cost him who knows how many dollars in prize money and endorsements. Well, I wasn't expecting anyone to market 'Golden Holden' playing cards. But the swing in my fortunes, had I wound up winning this crazy tournament, amounted to $22,500 which I needed rather badly – more than the entire personal fortune I had devoted to this odyssey, which had started out as a glorious adventure, and now seemed like a slow death by numbers.

As I sat there mesmerized, no-one at the table could know the full personal impact of the kind of blow they had all suffered far more often than me. As the unusual chorus of commiseration continued, my pain was eased only by the sheer humour of the whole event. That, as its end approached, was the kind of week it had been. The absurdity of a national tournament with only a handful of starters, none of them indigenous, had bonded us all into a happy little group on vacation from the Big Time; and now it was time for me to rejoin the *bonhomie*. Zapata himself patted me on the back, apologized, and shook my hand as he took my money. Eric mumbled, 'Now that *was* a bad beat, Tony!' – a phrase he does not use lightly – and Donnacha smiled at me ruefully. Even Slim was on my team: 'Hell, I'd have bet one o' them oil wells out there that you was gonna win that pot. You had that feller in about the same spot as the Texas coyote that got caught in a trap, chewed off three of his legs and still was in it . . .

'Tony, you're one unlucky s-o-b. Ah'm sure glad it ain't you gonna lose that grand when ah rides my camel in here . . .'

When Donnacha, through no fault of his own, finally lost the Moroccan title to an anonymous Englishman no-one had noticed before, who described himself as 'a businessman', confessed to living 'somewhere in Hertfordshire', and seemed extremely reluctant to see his name in print, it was as if the realms of the surreal had finally surrendered to Dada – who, as the Moll reminded me, Freud says it's all about, anyway.

Back home, I found even less than usual to communicate to friends about the nether world in which I was living, moving and having my being. How to tell even the Tuesday Night boys how sick I felt about being ranked fifth in Morocco, which they all seemed to find rather impressive? How to capture the absurd glee with which Slim, next morning, duly bestrode the steps of the Grand Casino El Mamounia like a desert colossus, demanding entry aboard a recalcitrant dromedary which proceeded to topple the silver palm-fronds and leave its calling-cards all over the deep-pile?

That life had become stranger than fiction was subsequently confirmed by the *Observer* magazine, which managed to print Morley's story about Slim, the bet and the camel *without* a picture of Slim aboard the camel – in my day, a sure-fire cover photo – presumably on the premiss that such things were best left to its readers' imagination. By then, I had anyway begun to wonder if I had dreamt the entire episode. My shaky sense of self was not helped by Morley's description of me as 'one of poker's rising stars, Anthony Holden Ltd' – a phrase with which I could have done with some help from the *Observer*'s sub-editors – or his suggestion that my quest for stardom in the poker world 'may take longer than a year'. Short odds were being quoted, apparently, that I would 'disappear inside it altogether'.

Sustaining his metaphor, Morley summarized the world of the poker pro as 'a singularity in the universe, a black hole with an infinite capacity for absorbing time, money and any residual sense of place'. To people like me, life itself was 'a precarious form of liquidity, anyway, which in the long run can neither be won nor lost, and is accordingly made more enjoyable by just keeping the chips in circulation'.

He was beginning to sound uncomfortably like the Shrink, with whom life was growing a mite tense. In his view I was now managing to turn our sessions into yet another kind of game. He was here to offer ideas, not to compete with me. If I stopped to think *why* I was quite so intent on justifying my current existence, I would see that I was pushing my argument much too far. A sceptical cast of mind, perhaps my natural state, was healthy enough; but to interpret life's vicissitudes *entirely* in terms of a game was to slump into a diseased degree of cynicism. It presupposed a deep mistrust of one's fellow man, as unseemly as it was unhealthy, bordering at times on terminal misanthropy. As one so intent on self-knowledge, and so scornful of others in this department, I was in serious danger of overplaying my hand.

So I didn't dare tell my clinical guru that my new way of life seemed to be infecting my children. In his school's annual singing competition – studded with treble trillings of 'Pie Jesu', 'Silent Night' and 'O for the wings of a dove' – nine-year-old Ben Holden carried off first prize with a dynamic rendition of Sky Masterson's 'Luck be a Lady, tonight!' His father's pride was only heightened by the appalled glances other parents gave The Watch, notably a titled lady of my acquaintance who shrieked, 'Where on *earth* did you get that *ghastly* timepiece?' But what had I done? Little did the poor fellow know that his school fees were now in jeopardy. A distinct sense of unreality, sharpened by the grim, grey banality of the London skyline – had I ever been away? – was no help in deciding whether to spend Easter in Dublin, where Terry Rogers was hosting a seasonal shindig, or head back west on another journey into the unknown.

All year, from Malta to Las Vegas, California to Morocco, I had been told that the one absolute 'must' on the poker circuit was the Cajun Cup, held each Easter weekend in a small town two hours west of New Orleans. The food was apparently great, the scenery stunning, and the action terrific – the more so because it was illegal.

But other such events, for that very reason, had recently foundered. Twice in the previous twelve months, tournaments at Myrtle Beach, South Carolina, and Mobile, Alabama, had been wound up before they even got under way. Poker players had now become reluctant to risk travelling to these shindigs – universally known, thanks to the omnipotence of Nevadans in these matters, as 'out-of-state' tournaments – for fear of wasting their time and money. These worries were redoubled at Easter, which I would really have preferred, like the rest of those few poker pros with soft hearts, to spend with my children. In my case, they were uniquely quadrupled by the fact that I would be travelling all the way from England.

A personal letter from the tournament organizers squarely addressed these problems, and seemed enough to staunch my doubts. One of them, after all, was Louisiana's own Eldon Elias, the very man who had driven off that Chevrolet roadster I had so coveted after winning Slim's $225,000 Superbowl at Caesar's Palace. The other was another familiar name on the circuit, Kenny Pyle. Both penned their signatures to a letter concluding: 'We would like to reassure everyone that the 4th Annual Cajun Cup of Poker will be held in spite of recent unfortunate circumstances which have occurred, causing tournaments in several other states to be cancelled.' Characteristically, they added their personal telephone numbers, should anyone seek further reassurance.

I thought of New Orleans, one of my favourite American cities, of Cajun food, and above all of the pigeons prophesied in such numbers by my Christmas dinner companion at the Horseshoe, Billy Mac. Pigeons might be my only chance ever to get the bank-roll back in shape. I rang around a bit, to discover that most of the circuit regulars would be there. I would have to miss the first week, but could make it in time for $500 Limit and Pot Limit Hold 'em and Omaha tournaments, not to mention the main event, a $1,500 No Limit Hold 'em freeze-out, dedicated to the memory of Jack Straus.

I had only $7,500 left to take with me, too little now to worry about those American immigration checks. And this would be a double-barrelled trip: in my original masterplan, the Cajun Cup was a mere preliminary to a poker cruise peopled with patsies. But morale was at rock bottom, self-confidence shot. If I wanted to play in the world championships again, and improve on my increasingly laughable world ranking, it was beginning to look like I would have to sell my car, or increase the mortgage on a house I had yet to find, let alone buy, just to raise an entry fee I would surely lose.

As the Moll bravely counselled perseverance, I didn't dare consult either Shrink or Crony. A hustler, I struggled to remind myself, is a hustler. A pro is a pro is a pro, or he is nothing worth. If I were ever to claim to have been either, there was no way I could give up now.

Louisiana, here I came.

10

Run Out Of Town

♥ ♣ ♦ ♠

In December 1829, while on tour in the United States, the English actor Joseph Cowell watched a shady-looking group of men playing cards aboard one of the greatest Mississippi paddle steamers, *en route* from Louisville to New Orleans. The description Cowell later published in his memoirs remains the first recorded account we have of a game of poker.

It proved sensible of the actor to watch rather than play, as this particular game – surprise, surprise – was rigged. In a thick fog the boat apparently ran aground with a bump. As all the other passengers rushed to the windows to see what was happening, only one of the players – a dead giveaway in green spectacles and a diamond stickpin – remained at the table impassively shuffling and cutting the cards. He was about to stage one of the favourite con-tricks of the original riverboat card-sharps: dealing remarkably good hands to all the other players, good enough for them to bet everything they had, and an even better one to himself.

The reader is as delighted as Cowell, however, when amid the confusion old 'Green Spectacles' manages to misdeal. After distributing the hands, Cowell tells us, 'he did not lift his cards, but sat quietly watching the countenances of the others. The man on his left had bet ten dollars: a young lawyer (son to the then mayor of Pittsburgh, who little dreamed of what his boy was about), who had hardly recovered from his shock, bet ten more.' The next player called the ten and raised five hundred.

"'I must see that," said Green Spectacles, who now took up his hand with, "I am sure to win," trembling at his fingers' ends: for you could not see his eyes through his glasses. He paused a moment in disappointed astonishment, sighed, "I pass," and threw his cards upon the table. The left-hand man bet: "That five hundred dollars and one thousand dollars better!"

'The young lawyer had had time to calculate the power of his hand – four kings with an ace – it could not be beat! But still he hesitated at the impossibility, as if he thought it could – looked at the money staked and then at his hand again, and, lingeringly, put his wallet on the table and called. The left-hand man had four queens, with an ace; and the next, the four jacks and an ace.

"'Did you ever see the like on't?" said he, good-humouredly, as he pushed the money towards the lawyer, who very agreeably astonished, pocketed his two thousand and twenty-three dollars clear!'

Green Specs, it appears, had dealt himself the four tens with an ace which he had intended for the lucky young lawyer. We do not know whether he showed his hand before folding it; but it seems highly unlikely, for even these greenhorns might have wondered how he could possibly fold the fourth-best hand in the deck – straight flushes had yet to be invented – and would surely have smelt a rat. As Cowell wryly observed: 'In that pursuit, as in all others, even among the players, some black-sheep and black-legs will creep in.'

This particular Englishman, however, belied his country's traditional sense of fair play, and revealed himself to be very much a spirit of those times, by sympathizing with the frustrated con-man. His victims may complain about being 'taken' by the black-leg, Cowell went on, but they nevertheless played against him regularly, and would in turn have cheated him out of 'every dollar he had, if they knew how'. Cheating, at the time, was so widespread as to be an accepted, almost endemic part of any game of poker, especially for anyone rash enough to sit down with strangers.

This otherwise unremembered British thespian concludes with a coda worthy of de Tocqueville, in which he divines the role poker would come to play, via the pioneer spirit of the old frontier, in the birth of the American dream. 'A trip down the river,' he noted, invariably meant 'an uncontrolled yearly opportunity for the young merchants and their clerks to go at it with a perfect looseness, mixed up indiscriminately with vagabonds of all nations, who then made New Orleans their jumping-off place. All moral and social restraint was placed in the shade – there Jack was as good as his master – and never was Republicanism more practically republicanized.'

The game of poker had been born in New Orleans a few years before, in the early 1820s, when French sailors imported their own version of a game called *as*, which they had picked up in Persia. A direct descendant of the ancient Persian game *as nas*, which dates back to the fourteenth century, the French game of *poque* was played with a pack of twenty cards: four aces, kings, queens, jacks and tens. Five cards each were dealt to four players. The notion of drawing fresh cards had yet to be conceived; straights and flushes would not be introduced for another fifty years. The players would simply bet their hands until they reached a showdown; the element of bluff, therefore, was evidently the game's primary skill and attraction.

Poker historians also refer to a German game called *Pochspiel*, a variant of brag, in which players bid with a cry of 'Ich poche'. But it is generally held that the derivation of the word 'poker' can be heard in the attempts of early Americans of the deep south to say the French word, *poque*. Southerners were never too keen on leaving any final 'e' silent.

In retrospect, it seems inevitable that games of chance should have played so large a role in the development of the American character. By the time of the American War of Independence, financed in large part by lotteries, public auctions had been a routine alternative to taxation since Queen Elizabeth I sanctioned England's first raffle in 1566, to finance harbour improvements. In the early seventeenth century it was a lottery which funded the first permanent English settlement in North America, at Jamestown, North Virginia. By the early nineteenth century, however, national characteristics were beginning to develop and diverge in ways which have since become emblematic. Whereas gambling in England was still the preserve of the elegant upper classes, among the pioneer Americans it was an activity which transcended class distinctions, reflecting the open, dispersed, crock-of-gold society they were developing in contrast to England's rigid hierarchism.

Nowhere was this emergent American spirit more evident than amid the frontier society of the lower Mississippi River Valley, where Spanish, French and other itinerant European influences combined with the transience of life along the river to forge a rich and colourful new culture. Risk-taking, by definition, is a fundamental aspect of any pioneer or frontier ethic. By the 1820s casino games were already flourishing in river towns between St Louis and New Orleans, whence they were naturally taken aboard the growing fleet of steamboats – where a new breed of American entrepreneur, the riverboat gambler, was soon playing his wily trade.

It was because of the hazardous, impermanent nature of life

along the river that gambling in the south was at first conducted more openly than anywhere else in the Western world – certainly more so than in the starchier townships of the American East. The gamblers living beneath the bluffs of the new southern settlements became as much a part of the community as their riverboat brethren, and were at first accepted as an essential part of its economic structure. But gamblers were also associated with a generally undesirable recklessness, and even less desirably loose morals. What's more, as the *Natchez Courier* proclaimed in an early manifestation of true American values, their presence drove down property prices. By the mid-1830s, as each settlement grew self-confident and prosperous enough to wish to become a permanent township, the gamblers were the first to go. Throughout the south there developed a pattern of giving them twenty-four hours to move on, with lynch mobs only too ready to round up the stragglers.

The most celebrated blow for southern respectability was struck at Vicksburg, Mississippi, in July 1835, when vigilante settlers publicly strung up five gamblers and declared martial law. Located high on a bluff overlooking the junction of the Mississippi and the Yazoo, Vicksburg was then in a state of transition typical of such towns as its main commercial rivals, Memphis and Natchez. Law and order yielded priority to the making of money; 'business men' of all descriptions, including gamblers, walked the streets armed with pistols and knives; juries were generally too frightened to bring in convictions; and women were only too happy for their place to be in the home, behind firmly battened doors. Vicksburg, reported one passing Alabaman, was a town 'run mad with speculation. They do business in a kind of phrenzy. Money is scarce, but credit is plenty.'

The boom had arrived with the railroad connecting Vicksburg and its cotton fields with Clinton, Mississippi. In poured speculators aplenty, prime targets for the local gamblers, so that by 1835 Vicksburg was known as 'the liveliest gambling place in the whole South-West'. Black-legs, or crooked card-sharps, now had the commercial clout to emerge from beneath their bluffs and practise their trade openly, numbering among their clientele anyone from prominent local gentry to black slaves. An English geologist by the name of G. W. Featherstonehaugh, travelling down the Mississippi in 1835, noted with distaste the social mix who boarded his boat at Vicksburg: 'Gentlemen, some of whom were planters of great respectability' spent the entire voyage to New Orleans 'wagering, drinking and carousing with an unsavoury collection of black-legs.'

It was not the gambling itself to which the city fathers objected so much as its social consequences. While the church elders held professional gamblers responsible for the breakdown of law and order, the aristocratic planter élite saw them as an obstacle to the civic refinement required to emulate the prosperous civilization of their eastern fellow-countrymen. If Vicksburg were to have a thriving commercial future as a cotton railhead, eastern standards of civility were essential to the process of economic growth, and the gamblers would have to go.

In the words of the *Vicksburg Register*, they had 'poisoned the springs of morality, and interrupted the relations of society'. The spur for action came in 1835 with a rumour – ironically, as it transpired, a false one – that crooked gamblers were behind an imminent slave revolt. When they inevitably ignored an order giving them a week to get out of town, the only option open to otherwise law-abiding citizens was to root them out in whatever way they could. A random shot from a cornered group of gamblers killed one of the vigilantes, and what had begun as a routine tarring-and-feathering turned into a wholesale hanging party.

The late 1830s saw this pattern repeated, with varying degrees of violence, all along the Mississippi Basin and beyond. In the Kentucky towns of Lexington and Covington, in Natchez and Memphis, New Orleans and Mobile, St Louis and Cincinnati, gamblers were given their marching orders and summary justice if they ignored them. Though they could not be banished from the wandering riverboats, where card-sharps continued to thrive until the 1860s, it was the beginning of the end of the river frontier. Although the gamblers had helped lay the economic foundations of the American south, their expulsion begat the God-fearing, Bible-bashing belt still with us today.

My seventeen-hour Easter journey from 1835 Vicksburg, Mississippi, to 1989 Lafayette, Louisiana, was to prove that nothing much has changed in America's deep south in the last 150 years.

This was to be the fourth successive year in which some local black magic would manage to side-step Louisiana's state ordinance against gambling, and see poker players converge from all over the United States on this depressed post-industrial town on the banks of the Vermilion River, in the commercial shadow of Baton Rouge. Beyond the fact that the rundown local economy benefited enormously – over the weekend the high rollers tended to unload at least a million bucks in local shops, hotels and restaurants – explanations for the organizers' apparent immunity from prosecution were hard to find in advance. The local cops, it seemed, were 'looked after' – well enough, in fact, to act as the security men for the tournament, which was openly held in the Hilton Hotel. A handsome dona-tion was also, apparently, enough to ensure that the local church elders – spiritual descendants, no doubt, of the vigi-lantes of Vicksburg – turned a blind eye to the proceedings.

This, after all, is one of America's most fiercely independ-ent regions. The twenty-two parishes which comprise the Cajun country of southern Louisiana also like to be known as Acadiana, and even fly their own Acadian flag, so proud are they of their descent from religious and political exiles trans-ported here from Nova Scotia in the mid-eighteenth century. But this, more to the point, is the late twentieth century. If the forefathers of this weekend's visitors were driven out 150 years ago, a brief revival of the old frontier spirit seemed to me long overdue, in keeping with the American penchant for charm-ing period nostalgia.

There had just been time to catch Ben's reprise of 'Luck be a Lady' in the end-of-term revue before reporting to Gatwick for what used to be the British Caledonian flight to Houston, recently swallowed up by a newly privatized British Airways. BA's computer had magnificently malfunctioned – or so it seemed – when comparing first-class fares to Lafayette, with onward connection to New York, via Dallas, Houston and New Orleans. At first we were talking well over £4,000 – an utter impossibility, given the state of my bank-roll. But on learning that this time I intended to move on to the East rather than the West Coast (an assumption which it could by now be forgiven for making), BA's computer suddenly came up with a deep South routing which fell something below £2,000.

It was a quarter of my entire remaining bank-roll, but I was so sick of long-haul flights that the thought of sitting in the rear of the cattle-truck all that way had me back on the verge of quitting. Desperation now combined with wishful thinking to convert me to Micawber economics: I would get hold of some funds *somehow*, something was bound to turn up. Eric Drache always flew first-class; so why, for once, shouldn't I? Wasn't that, for professionals, the only way to travel? Besides, I was 'in blood stepp'd in so far . . .'. Macbeth, like me, must have felt permanently jet-lagged. To give him his due, he never moaned about money; but unlike him I could, for now, divert the cost on to a credit card, and hope that my luck would turn before the day of reckoning. Some cute combination of all these self-deceits had me snapping up BA's offer without, for once, even asking about the economy fare.

Still I was choosing to overlook the obvious truth that all *dedicated* gamblers scour the special offers for the cheapest flights they can get anywhere, saving every penny they can for use at the tables. I'd been hanging around Eric Drache so much that I thought *all* long-service pros lived in his kind of style, taking the high life as their due. I couldn't have been more wrong.

At the time, this was ignorance of the blissful variety. Even in first class, another eleven-hour flight took some enduring. Presented with yet another questionnaire, I found myself complaining about the hardness of the seats, which were probably softer than swan's down. Then there were three tired and tedious hours to kill at Houston before catching – with mounting excitement overcoming my nerves – a hop of a flight to Lafayette in one of those little commuter aircraft which appear to be held together by rubber bands. This time the suitcase had made it, but Lafayette airport proved too tiny to boast the waiting line of taxis I had come to take for granted in the United States. This, I was learning fast, was Cajun country. Borrowing nickels and dimes to summon a cab by telephone proved fruitless. The Hilton freephone was permanently engaged. Spirits were sinking fast – and visibly enough, apparently, for a friendly stranger to offer me a ride into town.

Seventeen hours after leaving home I finally struggled through the door of the Lafayette Hilton, which was held open for me by a local cop, evidently one of the tournament security guards I had heard about. That much was promising. But what was that curious smirk on his face?

The lobby was a scene of utter desolation. Poker players were milling about moodily, gathering in noisily argumentative groups, giving the staff at reception a hard time. Why weren't they playing poker? As if in response to my unspoken question, one very fat man took off his Cajun Cup T-shirt and ceremonially tore it to pieces, right there in the middle of the lobby. Something was seriously amiss.

Amid the throng I picked out the friendly face of Seymour Liebowitz, veteran of any tournament anywhere, and asked him what the heck was going on. It transpired that the local authorities had been just fine, but things did not seem to have been squared away at state level. An hour or so ago, right in the middle of the seven-card high tournament, the district attorney had walked into the Hilton, seized the microphone and called a halt to the proceedings. The Cajun Cup had been busted. Closed down.

So if there had been a cab at the airport, I reflected, I'd have sat down just in time to be stood up again. Seymour began to laugh. So, at his side, did T. J. Cloutier, the former pro football player. Word quickly passed around the lobby that this guy from England had just checked in – well, he hadn't even checked in yet. This guy from England – you know, that Tony from London – had flown seventeen hours and just come through the front door at the same moment as the law. The laughter spread right round the lobby, until all I could do was join in. I was the biggest joke in Louisiana.

The joke began to fade when, like our nineteenth-century forerunners in Vicksburg, we were given twenty-four hours to get out of town. Had the tournament continued, said district attorney Nathan Stansbury, all players would be liable to arrest, and all property – cards, chips, gambling equipment, even the Hilton itself – in danger of seizure. The problem was not so much the tournament itself: that was no more illegal, said the DA, 'than a golf scramble in which the winner takes the pot'. No, the problem was the size of the 'rake' – the table money charged by the organizers, per player per hour, for side-games. 'The organizers,' declared Stansbury, 'were taking in more money than it costs to hold the event . . . The money had got so big that there was obviously going to be some left over.' It had been costing $10 an hour to play even at the smaller limits. Clearly, in the eyes of the law, someone was making a hefty profit out of this event – and that, technically, was the legal stumbling-block. An anonymous letter had been circulating, suggesting that the organizers had made a profit of $80,000 the previous year.

The poker players were unfazed by these revelations. Eldon and Kenny, the consensus went, deserved to make some money out of it. The relevant figure was the $450,000 pocketed so far by tournament winners, and the $100,000 first prize looming in the big weekend event. One hundred and fifty more players were due in from Vegas for the Easter weekend. That meant terrific side-action. It was time to speak up. 'Hey,' someone inevitably asked the DA, 'd'ya wanna make a federal case out of this?'

The answer, for once, was yes. Step forward assistant US attorney, Gerald Bertinot, to explain that federal jurisdiction becomes possible in gambling cases if state laws are violated. He advised all concerned to 'fold their tent and leave town'. But who had lodged any complaints? The only protest received by the local DA, he said, came *after* he had stepped in to close the joint down. A local trader had telephoned 'to gripe about the loss to the economy'.

Now the finger began to point towards the church. 'I don't want to alienate the district attorney,' said one Lafayette player, Mike Barry, 'but I think he succumbed to church pressure.' It was recalled that a local clergyman, the Reverend Perry Sanders, had complained about the tournament the previous year. And sure enough, on hearing today's news, Reverend Sanders declared himself 'thrilled . . . I tried to get Nathan to do that three or four years ago'. It seemed fruitless now to ask the organizers about their supposed donations to church funds. We were living in a flashback to 1835. Nothing much had changed hereabouts since the Vicksburg lynchings – except that lynching, luckily, was also illegal these days.

Collapsed into the tranquillity of my room, my whole frame still buzzing as if on a permanent aircraft, a state of incipient despair fast descending, I was forced to review my situation. Which did not, to be frank, look too good.

Six blank days, including the Easter weekend, stretched ahead of me before I was due in New York. What were the alternatives? My first thought was to head straight back home, and over to Terry Rogers's Easter tournament in Dublin. Maybe I could even get a direct flight to Dublin? It would be ruinously expensive, and the transatlantic slog would be worsened by a sense of utterly wasted time and money, but it was worth investigating. Preliminary enquiries about flights to Ireland revealed only that this was Easter weekend and there weren't any flights to be had to anywhere. Lafayette was a small town, sir. The only flights out were to Dallas and Houston, and they were fully booked. Indeed they were now overbooked, because one of the two small aircraft was experiencing technical difficulties, and there was a long waiting-list at the airport since a group at the Hilton had suddenly decided to leave *en masse*. No, sir, there was no other route out of Lafayette, and there was certainly no need to take that attitude. Click.

It was all very well to give us twenty-four hours to get out of town, but I had not, alas, brought my pack-mule along on this trip. One friendly pro called my room with excited thoughts of a fun weekend in New Orleans. But I hadn't come all this way to socialize with poker players marooned in southern Louisiana – or even, now that the possibility crossed my mind, to invite myself to spend Easter with friends in Long Island or Malibu. I had crossed the Atlantic to play poker. Once that particular purpose is settled in your head, there is room for no other.

What would a seasoned poker pro do in these circumstances? What were two hundred of them doing, come to that, at this very minute? Some were heading home to their families – or trying to, given that they had arrived on fixed-term discount tickets good for return travel only on the Tuesday after Easter. The rest – even the ones who lived there – were hustling their way to Las Vegas.

Of course. It was by now early evening, although it felt like the day after tomorrow. A quick trip to the airport, on the mistaken premiss that personal contact might work better than a disembodied voice on the telephone, revealed only scores of angry poker players fighting to get onto one rubber-band aeroplane, and even more angrily paying several hundred dollars over the price of their useless discount ticket for the privilege. There were fifty dealers and other staff under the twenty-four-hour guillotine, quite apart from the two hundred players. Much better, I decided, to take advantage of my failing body clock; sleep now; wake early, and get to the airport while they were all stuck in the overnight poker games which would surely materialize once they realized there was no way out of this burg.

Back in my hotel room I was just out of the shower and ready to fall asleep to the HBO movie when the phone rang. It was Fred, a professional gambler from Yorkshire, who had a booking at the best Cajun restaurant in the neighbourhood. His brother was over from England. They had heard about my mistimed arrival and wanted to try to cheer me up. How could I refuse?

A few more hours and an argument about Thatcher's Britain later – did I, I asked myself, come all this way to argue with Englishmen about bloody Thatcher? – I finally crawled into bed around midnight, leaving Fred and his brother to hit the town without me. Some chance of making it to the airport at six the following morning.

At such moments, however, body can triumph over mind. Dawn saw me heading back out to Lafayette airport – and, sure enough, seizing an abandoned no-show stand-by seat for the flight to Dallas which might or might not materialize in the next few hours. It was with a surreal sense of triumph that I waited for an aircraft which might never come – until I realized my next problem. It was the day before Good Friday and Easter weekend. Vegas would be overflowing. My only chance was a collect call – sorry, Henri – to Henri Bollinger, who could telephone around for me from LA. Obliging as always, Henri not only accepted the call but promised to do what he could.

One group of poker players had spent the entire night at the airport and were now desperate enough to be willing to fly out in a twin-engined plane with one defunct engine, pausing only to figure the odds against survival. The rubber-band plane with *two* functioning engines eventually took off – with me aboard, after an unseemly scramble across the tarmac – but then decided to make several unscheduled stops *en route* to Dallas because its sibling was still out of commission. The only reason I made my connection in Dallas-Fort Worth was that some drunk had thrown up on the incoming flight, and the mopping-up operation had delayed its departure just long enough for this panting, dishevelled British punter to scramble aboard with seconds to spare. Twelve hours and another $500 after leaving Lafayette, I was in Vegas – a guest of Jack Binion's at the Horseshoe, shamelessly 'comped' again.

My three-day journey had been a fast-forward re-enactment of the history of poker. Run out of Louisiana, I had followed the frontier spirits west, pausing briefly in California before heading back across Death Valley to Las Vegas. Never had the place seemed more like home. I all but embraced Pierre, my perennial Horseshoe bellboy, and was in seventh heaven to discover that I had again been allotted a suite, with a view across Fremont Street and the Nugget to the spectacular mountains beyond, where the DC-10s circling over McCarran now looked to me like some twentieth-century wagon train. This time, I didn't even bother with the unpacking-and-savouring routine. I had already spent the best part of three days merely travelling. There was not a moment to be lost.

But reluctant decisions had been made *en route*. Due to my acute shortage of funds, this trip would have to see me quelling my male ego, and working Vegas from the bottom up. The schedule in *Card Player* magazine (to which I was then one of a dozen London subscribers) mentioned a small-time tournament at the Sahara: a $25 Hold 'em freeze-out with $20 rebuys. That would have to be my starting-point. The cab ride from the Horseshoe was itself the equivalent of a buy-in, but then times were hard. I arrived to find Dame Fortune herself, who had reduced me to these straits, in merrier mood than me tonight: out of some 200 players, their positions allotted strictly at random, she managed to sit me next to an old friend from both London and Vegas, whom I hadn't seen all year. Don was gratifyingly pleased to see me. He was living in Vegas, eking out his daily bread in the $2–$5 games, while writing the Great American Novel. There would be time, he predicted, to have meals together.

Sure, but first there was a tournament to win. The action began slowly and solemnly enough, with my first rebuy coming in a matter of minutes. At these stakes, I couldn't muster the patience to play properly. I should have been using the opportunity to sharpen up my self-discipline; but Don's high spirits were contagious, and we soon found ourselves the centre of more table talk than other players will usually tolerate. At one point, still thinking of the view of the mountains from my Horseshoe window, I asked what that particular range was called. But Vegas is surrounded by mountains, came the response. You know, I said, the ones behind the Palace Station as you look from the Four Queens.

'Oh, that's the Sierra Nevada, isn't it?'

Nobody seemed sure, and the table went silent for a hand or two. As is the way with table talk, the topic resurfaced a few hands later, as if it had never gone away. While brooding on his cards, Don had also been musing on mountains.

'Well, I'm Humphrey Bogart tonight,' he said. 'I'm going to find the treasure of the Sierra Nevada.'

'In that case,' I replied, 'you're in the wrong game. You should be looking in the Sierra Madre.'

It was a master-stroke. Don was psyched for the next few hands, and I watched my stack grow gratifyingly until he was forced to rebuy.

Much long-term good did it do me. Five minutes after the rebuys ended, I busted out on some remote chance or other, and left Don and his pals to it. With my entry fee and four rebuys, that little waste of time had cost me $105. Annoyed with myself, I decided to win it back at a stroke, at the black-jack tables blocking my path to the exit. One $100 pop, a Q-Q, a busted dealer, and three hours of poker agony had been wiped out in thirty seconds. Could I stop at that? Of course not. Through some special dispensation from Olympus, Dame Fortune again came along for the ride: within minutes I had converted my $100 stake into $1,000, and even had the good sense to cash in. In my usual first-day-in-Vegas-state – bone-weary, and slightly the worse for drink – I hailed a cab down-town. Time for bed.

At the junction of Fremont Street and Casino Center Boulevard, some sort of drama was in progress. There is noth-ing too unusual about that; a paramedic ambulance hovers on permanent stand-by at that junction, so high is the index of heart attacks in the casinos and fist fights outside. Tonight, however, it meant that my driver was forced to unload me across the street from the Horseshoe, at the side-entrance to the Golden Nugget – inside of which, it now occurred to me, lurked my lucky blackjack tables.

I parlayed the $1,000 up to $2,000, broke my golden rule, and played on. At this stage, the amounts involved lose all their normal proportions. Dissatisfied with converting $100 into $2,000, I was even more annoyed to drop a paltry $300.

That, for tonight, was the moment I decided to quit. As I did so, the elegant female floorperson supervising the room sidled up and whispered, 'Would you like to have dinner with me tonight?'

Unused to being propositioned in Vegas, and unsure of what day it was, let alone what time, I hesitated, my tired wits trying to formulate a polite refusal. She smiled. 'No, I didn't mean what you're thinking. Relax. I'm trying to offer you a meal here at the Nugget, with the compliments of the management.' Now we both laughed, and I accepted gratefully. I was being treated like a medium high roller. She booked me into Lily Langtry's Chinese restaurant for the following evening, where everything I could eat and drink would cost Steve Wynn less than one of my madcap blackjack units.

With $1,700 in my pocket, I stumbled across Fremont and found myself threading my way to bed through the Horseshoe's blackjack tables. Now wait a minute. Maybe I could beat my Horseshoe blackjack jinx, and work that $1,700 back up to $2,000? Five minutes and five hundred dollars later, I was in the elevator with just $1,200 in my pocket. Although it represented a profit of $995 on the evening, minus two $20 cab fares, I was by now in full Dostoevsky mode. It could have been $2,000 – it *had* been $2,000 – was the irritated theme to which I finally fell asleep.

Good Friday sunshine woke me around noon, just in time for a coffee-shop lunch with Henri Bollinger and Jack Binion. As I strolled along the Food Promenade, I thought I was seeing things. Had I been dreaming? Overnight – literally, unless I was much mistaken – there had appeared a Burger King stall where yesterday people had queued for Haagen-Dazs ice-cream. Jack Binion, I happened to know, was particularly fond of ice-cream. 'You're right, Tony,' he said. 'Too fond. Every time I walked past Haagen-Dazs I couldn't stop myself having one. Got to putting on too much weight. Had to cancel their franchise.'

The hotelier in Jack was fascinated by my tales of King Hassan and the Mamounia, especially the night the king threw out the poker players. 'Some guys,' mused Jack, chewing on his toothpick, 'treat hotels like doll houses. I like to think of mine as a bank.'

Since he took charge of the business his father had started, Jack Binion's mission in life has been to minimize overheads and maximize profits. That year the Horseshoe had just shown a net profit of $45 million on a turnover of $108 million, way above the Vegas casino average of 15 per cent return on investment. 'It's so simple,' he said, 'that I'm amazed our competitors can't see it. We just give the folks better value for their gambling.'

That was true at the casino tables, which are all 'looser' at the Horseshoe than at any other joint in town. The food at Binion's Horseshoe is cheap and wholesome, the rooms spare, the décor minimalist. I told Jack that there had been just one sheet of paper on the notepad by my telephone when I had checked in; I had since used it, but the pad had not been replaced. As his guest, 'comped' up to the eyeballs, and even now eating a meal for which he would inevitably sign, I did not wish to appear ungrateful. But was I wrong to regard this, with some admiration, as typical of his management style? Like, while we were at it, the fact that the slivers of free soap in my bathroom were still stamped 'Mint' rather than 'Horseshoe'? 'All I know,' said he with a huge grin, 'is that you writer fellas never carry no paper around with you. Almost as mean as me.'

I was left with the distinct impression that the chambermaid on my floor would, for her commendable economy, receive a bonus far larger than the cost of a new notepad; and that it would not be replaced until I actually asked for a new one. This still held true two days later, when I crossed the street to pay homage at Benny's equestrian statue, only to find my path blocked by three juggernaut lorry-loads of turkeys. 'Christmas is coming!' I quipped imaginatively to the poor soul unloading them into Binion's warehouse. 'Yeah,' he replied, 'and these are just the ones the Binions give to their staff.'

As only a truly successful businessman can be, Jack Binion is an infuriating combination of meanness and generosity. He is said to have married his wife Phyllis, a former cocktail girl at the Horseshoe, because she was the most efficient waitress in his employ. The lady in question has far too many charms for this to be anything but a gentle tease against Jack and his little ways; but she has been known to complain that Jack won't stump up enough cash to fix their bathroom at home, while spending ten times as much helicoptering friends in and out of a skiing weekend in the hills.

Jack's only weakness, apart from ice-cream, is cough drops. As he strolls the floor of the Horseshoe, maintaining his watch on both staff and customers, he is usually to be found sucking one – and rarely for medicinal reasons. The ultimate Jack Binion story tells of the day he wandered past a poker game, sucking thoughtfully, when Jack Straus yelled after him: 'Hey, Jack, gimme a cough drop!'

The multi-millionaire President of Binion's Horseshoe paused briefly, looked Straus square in the eye and said: 'Jack, lemme hear ya cough.'

It took me just ninety minutes at the Horseshoe's $20–$40 game to fulfil a little promise I had made myself, and work last night's $1,200 back up to $2,000, where it belonged. I even managed to add another $700 before, to general irritation around the table, standing up and cashing in. Though I seemed to be on a roll, I was only too happy to quit while ahead. It was time to head up to the Dunes, where I had promised to meet Don for another of these small-stakes marathons, a $25 entry Hold 'em tourney with $20 rebuys. This time I rebought only once, and busted out nice and early, only $45 to the bad. My heart had never been in it. What I really wanted to do was call in on the card room manager, an old friend by the name of Bob Thompson, and ask him what size of bankroll I would need for my next assignment – a poker cruise to the Caribbean, due out of Miami the following weekend, on which Bob would be in charge of the action.

His trademark stetson could be seen a mile off. Bob was as liberal as ever with his advice, then gestured towards an empty seat in the highest-stakes game in his card room – a $2–$5–$10 Pot Limit Hold 'em table, all of its players appearing to have at least $5,000 in front of them. One of them was Seymour Liebowitz.

'No, thanks, Bob, I must get to bed,' I said feebly. 'I'll just say hi to Seymour. We both got stuck in Lafayette.'

All day, veterans of the Lafayette disaster had been arriving back in Vegas with travellers' tales enough to keep the *National Geographic* going for a while. We were all getting plenty of mileage out of it, not to mention the kudos, and people loved my self-deprecating British humour about being the biggest joke in town. Seymour, it transpired, had managed to get out of Lafayette the evening the tournament closed, but had made it no further than Dallas. 'Missed every connection. Had to bed down for the night . . . Good to be back, huh? Why don't you join us?'

Why, after all, didn't I? I had the best part of $3,000 in my pocket, which had been a mere $200 twenty-four hours ago. It was time I risked a bigger game like this, especially with other people's money. As I pulled out my bank-roll and sat down, Bob Thompson was at my shoulder with a knowing grin. 'Bedtime, huh, Tony? Can I get you some chips, sir?'

At the table were Seymour, a chatty old boy called Charlie, a wizened face I knew as Harry, a stranger known to them but not to me, and a young local pro called Ron Stanley, whom Bob had already pointed out to me as Best All-Round Player on the last poker cruise. I felt reasonably good about my information, less good about the fact that Harry, Charlie, Seymour and the Stranger were adding a straddle – a second big blind of $20 – before each deal, making it $40 to come in. That way, even without raises, the first bet after the flop would be at least $200. This was bigger stuff than I was used to. 'God, I'm tired,' I said, stretching, to show them in advance that I had good reason to play slow and tight. '*You're* tired!' said Charlie. 'I just got two hours' sleep, and that's three more than I've had all week.'

Rather than wait for the blinds to come round, I paid my $40, with no raising privileges, to be in the first hand blind. It seemed a good way of appearing confident. My suspicions were proved right when I was dealt K-4 suited: a decent enough hand, but one I might well have cautiously folded, had I had the option, to watch the game for a while before getting involved. Ron folded before the flop, but nobody else raised, and I was able to watch with astonishment as the dealer revealed Ks-4c-3c. I had two pairs, kings up – second only to trips as the boss hand, but vulnerable to straight and flush draws.

I bet the pot, $200. Seymour folded, Harry folded, the

Stranger folded. As Charlie pondered, I didn't know whether I wanted him in or not. He was unlikely to have three kings or three fours, as I had one of each. But three threes? Entirely possible, because in early position he could not risk an exploratory raise before the flop. It looked like I was riding for a fall. What if he had limped in with A-2 or 5-6, which would now give him two shots at a straight, one of them open-ended? Or a flush draw? Even a straight flush draw? Charlie interrupted my reverie by raising the maximum, my $200 and another $600. I called without hesitation.

The turn brought another king. I had a full house. It was tempting to get smart and try a check-raise. But I was not feeling settled enough, and did not want to be revealed as a smart ass. So I simply bet the pot again, now $1,800 – which looked confident enough, as it was almost everything I had left in front of me. I could only hope that they thought I had more in my pocket. Seeing that I had only $300 left, Charlie naturally called my bet and set me in for the rest, counting enough $100 bills into the middle to scare me rigid. Now I figured he *must* have that pair of threes – a full house, but a smaller one than mine. The last card was the five of clubs. Oh hell, could he have a straight flush? If so, I was walking back to the Horseshoe.

I had no money left – so, praise be, there was no more betting. I showed my K-4, which I had suavely refrained from doing when he set me in. He looked at his cards long and hard, and a terrific thrill shot through me. I knew I had won – but not by much. Charlie didn't have to, but he generously showed me his hand. Sure enough, it was that unlucky pair of threes. He must have put me on three kings, and thought he had it won. I would have.

'Good hand,' he muttered, as good losers do, and gave me

a little pat on the shoulder as I scooped in a $6,000 pot, of which $3,060 was profit – the biggest single hand I had ever won in Vegas. I tried to look nonchalant as I stacked the $100 bills, while also trying *not* to look as if I was counting them. A few hands later, still numb from so sudden an advance, I took the chance to count them publicly while pretending to think about a major raise. Yes, my $200 of last night was now more than $6,000.

A couple of hours later, at about three in the morning, it was up to more than $7,000. I was $4,000-plus ahead on the evening, and trying to hang on to it, when I felt compelled to play A-5 suited and watched the flop bring A-5-10. This time it was the Stranger who had me sweating. On the turn, which brought a useless-looking deuce, we just checked along, which gave me hope. I figured he had a lone ace, without my second pair. But there were all sorts of other possibilities. He could be slow-playing an ace-ten, or even trip tens, though that seemed unlikely. Or he could be trying to draw to the top straight (in which case I should have bet). At least there were no flush possibilities to worry about. When he checked again on the river, a king, I instinctively felt I ought to look more confident, and bet the pot.

As soon as I had thrown my money in, I realized I had made a mistake. I could have won the hand then and there – if, indeed, I had won it – without risking more money. As the Stranger thought about it, or appeared to think about it, I realized I would be hard-pressed to call if he raised me back. Could he have pulled that top straight, after all? I had probably played straight into his hands.

To my astonishment, he merely called, and surrendered when I revealed my two pairs. As he spun his cards towards the muck, he showed me one ace, again proving my first thoughts correct, and watched my face very closely as I took it in. What on earth did he think *I* had, to call me at the end with just a pair of aces? But that, I could only suppose, was the advantage of being an unknown face, none too adept at hiding my nerves. 'Played like a pro,' said the Stranger genially, as I scooped in another decent pot. Did he really mean it? Or, more likely, was he trying to flatter me into going on tilt? I couldn't tell any more, but I felt my confidence begin to surrender to my nerves.

Over the next half-hour I gave a loose $700 back before stretching and yawning my way through a few hands, then declaring myself unable to keep my eyes open, mentioning Lafayette once again to remind everyone what a long day I had had – and standing up to cash in, just over $6,000 to the good.

'Nice playin' with ya,' said Charlie as I took my leave. 'Maybe see ya tomorrow night,' I responded, in the hope of eliciting some tell-tale reaction. But answer came there none. I hailed a cab to the Horseshoe feeling like a million dollars, and spent the ride discreetly recounting the $9,000 in my pocket. But I still didn't know whether I'd played like a pro.

Of course I had, I reflected next morning, awakening just in time for Binion's world-beating hash brunch. There is nothing like waking up in Las Vegas, groping around in your mind for what happened the night before, and registering the memory of a major win. Morale was soaring – perhaps a mite too high – as I put my name on the list for the $20–$40 Limit Hold 'em game. I was only halfway through my long weekend here; there was time enough to decide whether or not to risk tangling with the pot-limit boys again. I was feeling in good psychological shape – good enough to avoid the traditional poker trap set by the omnipotent male ego.

The Shrink and I had talked this one through. It is the moment the ego comes up against the Peter Principle, which famously decrees that everyone rises to the level of their own incompetence. How does it apply in poker? Once you've held your own in a pot-limit game, and been seen to do so, sheer vanity has you reluctant to be seen back at a lower level. A player who can win steadily at the $10–$20 table will naturally graduate to the $20–$40; but when he begins to lose there, he finds it extraordinarily hard to lose face by returning, tail between legs, to the $10–$20.

Not me. Take pride in your wonderfully open relationship with your own ego, I told myself over a Benny Binion Early Bird Special. Recognize that you were out of your depth last night. You were, let's face it, lucky. Swallow your pride – and your greed – and put in some hard graft at the $20–$40 rockface.

I toiled there, in the end, all day – never once dipping into the red. Clearly, I was on some sort of a roll. People came and went – most of them fairly po-faced, silent types, waiting for their moment to come, usually in vain. I found myself playing a rather loose game, partly through boredom, partly through the tourist's fatal sense of limited time; and for once it worked. The relatively small limits enabled me to stay in on pulling hands, in contented defiance of the odds, for this was one of those wonderful days when I just *knew* that the poker gods were with me. Playing that way, and winning, so annoys the other players that they tend to go on tilt. By their standards I was not playing well, and sooner or later must begin to haemorrhage the pyramid of chips I was nursing. But I suffered few reverses. And any loose calls which went nowhere were anyway other people's money.

By 2 a.m., and the arrival of a noisily bad loser I mentally nicknamed 'Asshole', I had been playing nearly twelve hours and was $1,200 up – a handsome amount at $20–$40 Limit. A hundred dollars an hour may not seem a high rate of pay; but poker at this level was proving therapeutic – relaxing, even – after the previous night's thrills and spills. It was also a cheap way of getting deeper and deeper into the mysteries of Texas Hold 'em. If I got paid for my lessons, so much the better.

All thoughts of the pot-limit game at the Dunes had long since evaporated. I might as well keep on trucking here, I thought, until I fall asleep. Asshole's antics, however, grew so obnoxious that he began to drive other players away. He made it clear that he regarded me, from the way I was playing, as some sort of pigeon. I could tell from his eyes that he was on drugs, even if he hadn't been unable to stay still, squirming around in his chair and leaping about behind it, shouting comments on the rest of us to his friends across the room, generally spoiling the atmosphere at what had been a very happy little group, hitherto savouring a long-drawn-out battle of wits. Now, thanks to him, I wasn't enjoying myself so much either, which was presumably what he intended. So my first decision was not to lose any of my money to *him*. Then I decided to beat him out of one big pot, and irritate the hell out of him by immediately standing up and cashing in. Which, at 3.06 a.m., is precisely what I did, heading up to bed $1,800 to the good, Asshole's jeers ringing in my ears all the way to the elevator.

Next morning's noon saw me savouring Benny's brunch in my room to the soothing inanities of a midday television soap. Today being my last full day in town, I decided to take my current profit – all $10,800 of it – back to the Dunes for some real heavyweight poker in the pot-limit game. It was Easter Sunday, after all; the town was full of tourists; as well as the Harrys, there might well be some Toms and Dicks there who didn't know what they were doing.

Heart in mouth, therefore, I was making my way to the Fremont Street cab stand, past the $20–$40 table which now seemed like home, when I noticed something rather remarkable. The seat I had occupied all day yesterday was empty, with no pre-emptive chips in front of it, which was unusual enough in itself. Opposite it, however, where last night Asshole had been holding coke-ridden court, there now sat none other than Johnny Moss, the Grand Old Man of Poker himself. What was 'The Man' doing in the $20–$40 game? If that seat of mine really were empty, not just temporarily abandoned by someone soon to return, this was a chance to take him on.

A check at the desk revealed, to my amazement, that 'my' seat was indeed up for grabs, and there was no-one ahead of me in the queue. This I regarded as some sort of omen, for the $20–$40 list had been choked with names all weekend, and a two-to-three-hour wait for a seat was nothing unusual. 'Help yourself, Tony,' said the floorman with a grin, sensing my excitement at the prospect of playing with the great man. I was living proof of the Binions' Moss Policy – that the mere presence of The Man would attract idiots to sit down with him, like moths to a flame. And I didn't mind it one little bit.

Armed with two racks of chips – $500 in 5s and $500 in 25s – I arrived to find Mr Moss grinning at me. 'Nice to see ya, Tony,' he said to my surprise, as so few of these people ever remember the name of occasional players like myself. It caused a bit of a stir around the table, too. The other players were astonished and slightly awed by the fact that the great man knew me well enough to address me by name. This, I reflected, was both a Good and a Bad Thing. It gave me instant respect at the table. But it blew my cover as an innocent amateur playing over his head.

I found myself clicking my heels and giving Mr Moss a respectful little bow. 'Mrs Moss,' I added politely, with an equally respectful nod to acknowledge Virgie, his wife of sixty years, seated as always at his shoulder. I sat down and quietly arranged my chips into the beginnings of a pyramid, to show the other players that I had ambitions of Tutankhamun proportions.

Feeling my way through the first few hands, I soon realized that everyone at the table of course knew who they were playing with, but poker etiquette had prevented them making too much fuss about it. No-one, it seemed, had yet addressed Johnny Moss by name. They obviously felt cooler treating him like just any other player – though I also noticed that any raise from him sent them smartly scuttling out of the pot. After yesterday I felt utterly at home here, and my self-confidence was running high. Could I, I wondered, be the one to break the Moss rhythm? In my own head, I formed the dangerous fantasy that I was Nick the Greek replaying that marathon – but this time I was going to win.

My first chance came when I was dealt A-K, and the flop brought another ace with two low cards. Being the first to speak, I bet the regulation $20. All around the table they folded, on the correct assumption that I could not bet under the gun unless I was holding an ace – until it reached Moss, who gave me one of his hooded looks, and raised me another $20. I just called. The turn was irrelevant, offering no straight or flush opportunities, but no second pair for me either. I checked, and Moss bet again: $40. So we were into a battle of the aces, and the odds were that he had his kicker paired too. Blind ambition, however, drove me on; too timid to raise The Man and risk a re-raise, I merely called him. After the final card was revealed, still leaving me with my lone pair of aces, I thought I'd try a bet, just in case he thought my hand better than it really was. Moss called, and looked at me enquiringly. Slightly shame-faced, I turned over my A-K. With a broad grin he revealed A-J. We had both been playing the same game, but I'd been playing it with a little edge.

As I scooped in the pot, I felt the urge to say something. If the Shrink had been there to make me rationalize it, I would have said that I wanted to pay my respects to the Great Man, without appearing cocky, while at the same time seeking to crow over the other players. So I heard myself saying, without any forethought, 'I just wanted to be able to tell the folks back home that I beat Johnny Moss out of a pot.' Moss grinned pleasantly, as if to say there was nothing new about that, and the player on my left allowed himself a little chuckle.

The next hand brought me a pair of 7s, and a flop of Q-Q-2. Chuckler on my left opened the betting, and only Moss had called by the time it reached me. Feeling illogically confident, I decided to defy the odds and call. Clearly one of them, perhaps both, held a queen, but I had a feeling in my gut that I was going to see a seven come up out there. The turn brought a five. Chuckler bet the max, $40, and Moss immediately raised. Could he have a house? Absurdly, I called the eighty, to find Chuckler re-raising. Moss called – and so, trapped by my own ambitions, did I. They must have been wondering what the heck I was holding.

I was none too sure myself, until the dealer turned over the final card – that seven I knew was in there somewhere. Clearly, by now, the one with the queen, Chuckler led the betting again, but less confidently than before. Moss called. When I raised,

Chuckler emitted a gasp of astonishment, while Moss remained as impassive as ever. They both called, and I was forced to show my flukey full house, with a grovelling, 'Sorry, I was just playing my rush'. Moss, with a smile, flipped over a pair of fives. He had been winning on Fourth Street. Chuckler, agasp that the hand had eluded him, showed an A-Q, looked at both of us, and said: 'I just wanted to tell the folks back home that I beat the man who beat Johnny Moss out of a pot . . . Guess I'll just have to keep on trying.'

It was a biggish pot by $20–$40 standards, some $700, and everyone knew that I should never have been in it. The knowing looks around the table did nothing, however, to staunch my enjoyment as I hauled in a pile of chips so huge by local standards that I had difficulty getting them out of the way as the dealer got on with the next hand. His face as laconic as ever, Moss caught my eye as I began to stack the chips. 'Ah didn' wanna win that pot anyhow,' he drawled. 'All that stackin' . . .'

When I fluked the next hand as well, this time outdrawing an unknown party down the far end, Moss's years of experience had him vicariously enjoying my lucky streak. 'Nothin' to it, is there?' he grinned, as I hauled in another pile before I had managed to stack the last one. And so it continued until 5 p.m., when I had agreed to meet Don for a meal before heading up to the regular Sunday-night tournament at the Hilton.

The prospect of this appointment had been causing me some grief until Moss himself abruptly stood up at 4.45 p.m., and said goodbye with another kindly smile. So I was not going to miss any more Moss stories for the folks back home, and I could feel good about quitting while still handsomely ahead. My roll, it seemed, was working in all areas of life. I was

$1,600 ahead on the day, a little over $12,000 on the weekend. The bank-roll, which had started this trip at a mere $7,500, was now just $300 short of its original $20,000 self. If I could keep on building like this, I might even be able to leave the $10,000 entry fee for the World Series on deposit here when I moved on. With that in mind, I kept $2,000-plus to see me through the evening, and decided to put the rest out of harm's way. At the cage, the teller raised a rather hurtful eyebrow as she watched me place $10,000 worth of $100 bills in my safe deposit box. 'I'm not,' I told her, 'as rich as I look.'

By 5.01 p.m., there was a huge scrum outside Binion's premier restaurant, Spaghetti Red's, which is supposed to open at five. We hungry people were on the point of beating down the door when an inconspicuously small figure in a large stetson hat appeared at the back of the line, and seemed ready to stand there patiently. It was Benny Binion himself. Such was Benny's stage presence in these parts that I, up front, felt an urge to try and warn the hapless Italians inside just whom they were keeping waiting. Apparently reading my body-language, and wishing to spare his paying customers any more of a wait, Binion himself was ambling politely towards the front when the doors miraculously opened from the inside. As I passed through behind the boss, I quietly congratulated the visibly terrified *maître d'* on the clearest case of 'Open Sesame' I have ever seen.

By the time I looked again, Johnny and Virgie Moss had joined Benny at his secluded corner table. I was just thinking of the Great Game with the Greek all those years ago, and of how much subsequent poker history was now sat in that there corner, when Moss gestured me over to join them. 'What you doin' here, son? You shoulda stuck to your run down there.' Without listening to whatever explanation I muttered, he went on: 'Have a drink. We're celebrating. D'you know what we're celebrating?' All I knew, and said so, was that his birthday fell in May, near mine, around the beginning of the World Series. 'No, no,' he said, 'and it sure ain't Easter, either.' He looked over at Binion, who cracked a grin. 'Benny and I are celebrating seventy-five years of friendship.'

Benny Binion was to die nine months later; but at the time he seemed immortal. I raised my glass in an awestruck toast, listened to a few of their childhood tales, and then felt I should leave them to it. I know when I am out of my league. Besides, Don and I had agreed to play my rush in the mega-tournament held every Sunday night at the Las Vegas Hilton, where countless rebuys build a few score $30 entry fees into hugely disproportionate rewards. After some energy-building pasta, we rushed uptown to find the Hilton odds – as always – the most rewarding, if daunting, in town. At the two-hour break, eighty starters had indulged in one hundred and twenty rebuys, swelling the prize pot to more than $6,000, a 200:1 return on investment. There were only seventy-nine others to beat it.

Poor old Don's generosity of spirit was now facing its sternest test. OK, so he'd had a couple of free meals out of my sustained good fortune. But all week he had slaved away to modest avail in the $3–$6 game while I had effortlessly mopped up across the room with the $20–$40 boys. Now he got busted out soon after the end of the rebuys, only to hang around and see me make it all the way into the money. This really was my week. By midnight I was proudly seated at the final table, where I got caught up in a showdown with Bill Smith, one of the few former world champs who play in these rinkydink events. Their play, however, is far from rinkydink. Bill's pair stood up against my optimistic flush draw, and I capitulated in eighth place. It had taken me five hours to beat seventy-two other starters – one hundred and ninety-two if you factor in the rebuys – and it had won me a prize of $75. Plus a Hilton card-room baseball cap.

Wow. It seemed a somewhat hollow victory. This was my last night in Vegas, and I could have been playing this rush to rather more effect in my new $20–$40 home at Binion's, or even more ambitiously elsewhere. How much would I have won *there*, let alone in the pot-limit, if I had played with such sustained success? The only way to find out was to return for a final stand.

Uncannily, my afternoon seat was again empty, as if it were waiting for me. Apart from this evening's break at the Hilton, I had been playing in it for going on forty-eight hours. My romance with the $20–$40 table was taking on overtones of the open-ended games of old. A few other faces had been there all day, though none had survived since I sat down here yesterday morning. Only I knew that I had to leave for the airport in seven hours.

The minute I settled back – a veteran at this table, though half the players weren't to know it – I got involved in a row. It probably showed how tired I was, though I was pleased to see that my chief antagonist put it down to my being an amateur. I thought I knew all the etiquette by now, but there was a loud complaint from 'Moustache', an edgy young night-time scavenger, when I pulled what looked like a fast one. Aspiring to raise his $40 bet, I extended a hand clutching an arbitrary number of chips, which turned out to total $75. When I reached back for the missing five, he cried foul – or, to be precise, 'string bet'. The other players slumped back in their chairs, ready for a long row – par for the course in Vegas, even though they are settled there much more swiftly and amicably than in London, thanks to the greater expertise of the dealers. Rather than argue back, as expected, I quietly pleaded innocence. After a brief chiding I was marked down as a tourist, just in off the street, and allowed to finish my raise.

It was the end of Moustache, and the beginning of another, last-gasp rush for me. By 2 a.m. I was $1,100 ahead and still in the driving seat. But I was breaking up the game. It was Easter Sunday-going-on-Monday, and folks clearly weren't in the mood to go to bed broke. Unlike me, they had to gamble their way through tomorrow as well. By 2.30 a.m. there were only three of us left. For the first time all night we actually talked to each other, to discuss whether it was worth playing on. Give it half an hour, I suggested, mindful of my imminent departure for Los Angeles, and the need for a little sleep before presenting myself at a glitzy Oscar luncheon. This seemed to go down OK, and we killed half an hour toying with each other. At 3 a.m., by common consent, the game broke up.

On cashing in, I found I was $1,487 ahead. Add that to my hard-won $45 profit at the Hilton, and I was ending the weekend with a three-day profit of $13,732. With the cruise still to come, the bank-roll had swollen from $7,500 to more than $21,000. For the first time all year, I was showing a profit.

It was, I decided, enough. Yes, I could permit myself to savour the moment towards which I had been working all year, and leave $10,000 on deposit here at the Horseshoe – to await my return, barely six weeks from now, for the World Series of Poker.

The entry fee was won!

11

Cruising For A Bruising

♥ ♣ ♦ ♠

If you've got it, flaunt it.

A major poker win can be absurdly exhilarating, much more so than a windfall earned by more conventional means. With five clear days before my next stop on the pro tour, the Caribbean poker cruise out of Miami, I decided to take Slim's advice and live life 'high on the hog'.

When I was a child, I paid as a child, with plastic; now I was a man, I put away childish things like credit cards and let the $100 bills flow. The immediate result, just like the Book says, was that I saw through a glass darkly – the smog of LA being rendered yet denser by the tinted windows of my VIP stretch limo, licence plate CELEB 1.

Even the Horseshoe had seemed rather shocked to be paid in cash. Making $13,732 in three days cost me $230 in phone calls and room service, the tab for the rest being Jack Binion's continuing courtesy to a now fully-fledged pro. But the airline had never seen anything like it. For the flight to Burbank, they wanted precisely $101. US Air's lugubrious clerk was already instinctively reaching for the credit card form as I waved two greenbacks under his nose. 'Airlines,' he said, 'aren't used to dealing in cash, sir.' The computer liked it even less, taking all of ten minutes to spit out my ticket resentfully.

En route to the gate, I passed a desk labelled HELP MAKE SICK KIDS SMILE. Far from soliciting passers-by – perhaps she had realized by now that more losers than winners fly out of Las Vegas – the woman behind it had her nose buried in *People* magazine. As much for this reason as a sudden rush of guilt, heavily tinged with superstition, I ambled over and held out a hundred-dollar bill, momentarily distracting her attention from the latest news on Jackie O. 'I'm sorry, sir,' she said, 'we can't give change.' Knowing, for once, how it must feel to be a Rockefeller, I simply smiled, pushed the bill into her collecting box, waved away the pink lapel sticker she offered, and walked on towards the gate, feeling her eyes following me in bafflement.

It was the nearest I came all year to paying any dues to any poker deities. Who was I trying to bribe? The law of averages or my own conscience? In the end, I suspect, I was taking out a rather grubby insurance against the end of my rush. When the check-in desk promptly offered me a free upgrade to Business Class, I tried to resist any theories of cause and effect. All I knew was that I was still on a roll.

On and on I kept rolling through forty-eight Oscar-time hours in Beverly Hills, limo-hopping from luncheon to reception to dinner party, my good humour immune even to the disappointed groans when my limo failed to disgorge Tom Cruise or Kim Basinger. The unknown figure before the gawping throngs wasn't even expensively enough dressed to be some off-camera power-broker. But I gave them a cheery wave, nonetheless, and stood still for the cameras.

Taking the limo down to the Bike was the master-stroke. At the $15–$30 Hold 'em table – for all my new-found wealth, I still knew my limitations – there was much ironic speculation about the uniformed driver sitting patiently, his peaked cap on his lap, awaiting his master's next caprice. Who was this guy in Seat Three? Some kind of rich English eccentric?

I could see them figuring out that the minimum limo rate must be twice the buy-in. Some inscrutable British raising soon had all but the most fossilized rocks on tilt.

If indifference to money is one of the keys to good poker playing, I managed to muster even more indifference than I had money. It took only three hours to win $1,200, enough to cover both hotel and limo, before checking out of the Bike, the hotel, the limo and California. It was time to head East, to hustle up some legitimate finance and boost the bank-roll for the cruise. My run of good luck now had me filled with premonitions of doom.

Barely an hour out of LA, flying over Vegas, I was ambushed by nostalgia. Three days away seemed like three days wasted. From up here, as I pictured the action teeming within it, the place looked uncannily still; but beneath those monolithic concrete slabs lay the giant, eternal poker game of my dreams. To have been in this part of the world, and played truant in Hollywood's fast lane, now seemed like criminal neglect. The thought of all those card rooms buzzing in my absence, of all those pots I could have been attacking, was like that familiar rage about the prospect of death: that the world will have the nerve to carry on without me, and I will never know who won and who lost.

Even from 35,000 feet I could make out Jack Binion's golden horseshoe atop the tower which was now my home-from-home. To the west, up on the Strip, the skeletal hulk of Steve Wynn's emergent Mirage was already making its next-door neighbour, Caesar's Palace, look almost demure. Donald Trump, then in and out of Vegas almost as much as me, was rumoured to be manœuvring to buy Caesar's. From this height it seemed shrewd of him to wait to assess the impact of the Mirage. All property tycoons, it struck me, would be well advised to take this God's eye view of potential investments: after mine, that day, I would have settled for the franchise on the Mirage car-park, which looked about the size of Wales.

I broke the journey in Cincinnati, Ohio, keeping a long-standing, mildly superstitious promise to myself to visit the headquarters of the US Playing Card Company, whose name I had so often seen (though not, of course, as often as I would have liked) inscribed upon the ace of spades in each deck of its famous Bicycle cards. I suppose I believed that a visit to the shrine might bring more aces my way.

To see sheet after sheet of playing cards pouring from the presses, to watch heedless machines cut, trim and stack them into decks of fifty-two, is to marvel at the scale of human misery their little red and black markings can cause. Human happiness, too, of course, but for some reason it was the thought of the houses lost, the families broken up, the businesses busted, even the brains blown out which clouded my sense of awe at the remorseless mass production of anything so small and simple, so innocent and yet so potent.

I picked up an uncut sheet of cards hot from the press, bemused by the sight of these too familiar patterns in one ordered, unfamiliar whole – the kings, queens and jacks really looking like a contented nuclear family, and the all-important aces so puny, mere dots in a desert of white. Whose fortunes in what part of the world would ride on this particular sheet of heavy-duty cardboard? Would it catch up with *me* some-where – pay off my mortgage, perhaps, win me the world championships of poker, or see me turn to crime? The sheet in my hands exuded such a sense of danger, so out of tune with its bland, two-dimensional beauty, that I felt an absurd sense of protectiveness towards its potential victims, myself included, and rolled it up to take home and frame before it could cause any damage.

The particular card which had drawn me here possesses its own unique dimension of menace. Throughout the Far East the ace of spades is known as the 'Card of Death'. In 1966 this plant produced several million for use as a secret weapon by American troops in Vietnam. At the request of the US government, acting on the suggestion of two lieutenants of 'C' company, second battalion, 35th regiment, 25th Infantry Division, whole decks of aces of spades, packed in plain white boxes, were flown out to the front, where they are said to have spread terror among the Vietcong. The aces from the Bicycle deck were especially requested because they carry in their centre a picture of a woman, modelled on the statue of 'Freedom' designed by Thomas Crawford in 1865 for the dome of the US Capitol building. To the Vietcong, apparently, a woman is also a symbol of evil.

In the Second World War, the company supplied the military with special sets of cards aiding aircraft and naval ship recognition, and 'survival cards' indicating poisonous plants, insects and reptiles. The OSS was also provided with decks of especially ingenious Bicycle cards, inside which were sewn laminated maps of Germany to assist prisoners of war in their attempts to escape.

Subsequent special requests have included flame-proof sets for use by Apollo 14 astronauts in the 100 per cent oxygen atmosphere of the Skylab orbital space workshops. In the company's private archives I was shown copies of decks specially designed for poker playing VIPs from President Eisenhower to Howard Hughes. The most valuable, and the most coveted, is the limited edition produced for Hugh Hefner, which would surely have spread even more terror amid the

Vietcong. Each is embellished with a different Playboy 'play-mate' in a pose suggesting she has recently lost a showdown at strip poker.

The playing cards manufactured here in the Cincinnati suburb of Norwood since 1867 – notably the Bicycle and its upmarket in-house rival, the Bee – are now used in 90 per cent of the world's casinos. Even a century ago, in 1889, some 630 employees on this site were producing as many as 30,000 decks a day. The Bicycle card itself dates from 1885, when the newly invented bicycle was the peak of hi-tech sophistication, on which Americans were spending $20 million a year at a time when eggs were a cent each. In its first hundred years of life, the familiar red or blue back showing Cupid astride a bike has gone through eighty-four different designs, keeping up with such advances as the demise of the penny-farthing and the birth of the motor-bike. On the whole, however, the US Playing Card Company has stumbled on to an industrialist's dream product: as sales continue to climb steadily, the consumer is positively resistant to change. Poker players and bridge players (who favour Cincinnati's Congress brand) are at one, for once, in *hating* fancy decks.

Again the ace of spades plays a central role, identifying the manufacturer and the serial number of the design. For years poker players of my acquaintance have suspected that the number 808 on the USPCC's ace of spades must carry some magic significance; now I would be able to tell them that it is merely the serial number assigned to the Bicycle brand.

Because they are known to have invented paper, the Chinese are credited by default with the invention of playing cards; but their division into the suits and symbols familiar today dates from fifteenth-century Europe. Even before the invention of printing, the Italians were producing hand-painted decks of seventy-eight Tarot cards, whose court cards included king, queen, mounted knight and page. The Germans were the first to mass-produce playing cards, changing the Italian suits of swords, batons, cups and coins to leaves, acorns, bells and hearts. Then the French discarded the Tarot's twenty-two trumps, rationalizing the deck to fifty-two cards, combining the knight and the page into a jack, and introducing the suits of hearts, diamonds, clubs and spades.

In the Middle Ages these suits reflected the structure of medieval society. Hearts (cups or chalices) symbolized the Church; spades (or swords) the military; diamonds (coins) the merchant class; and clubs (batons) agriculture, or the peasantry.

The French were also the first to identify court cards, overprinting the relevant name on each one. The four kings, for instance, represented the four civilizations which begat western culture: the Hebrews, the Holy Roman Empire, the Romans and the Greeks. The images chosen in the Middle Ages to represent these four worlds still hold good on all standard playing cards to this day. The king of spades is the Biblical King David; he carries the sword belonging to his most celebrated victim, Goliath, (and on French cards a harp, as the author of the Psalms). The king of hearts, who brandishes a sword above his head, is Charlemagne. The king of diamonds, wielding a battleaxe, is Julius Caesar, who appears in profile because the only surviving contemporary images of him were profiles on coins. The king of clubs is Alexander the Great, who holds an orb, symbol of the world he conquered.

The queen of spades, the only armed queen, is Pallas Athene, Greek goddess of wisdom and war. The queen of hearts is Judith of Bavaria, daughter-in-law of Charlemagne, wife of his son Pepin. The queen of diamonds is Rachel, wife of Jacob, father of the twelve sons who founded the tribes of Israel. The queen of clubs is Argine, believed to be a Roman anagram for the word 'regina', or Queen.

The jack of spades, shown in profile carrying a marriott (or beribboned pike) is Hogier, a Danish knight of Charlemagne. The jack of hearts, who carries a battleaxe surrounded by 'faces' (a symbol of authority like the Latin *fasces*, from which we derive the word 'fascist') is 'La Hire', whose real name was Stephen de Vignoles, a knight in the court of Charles VII. The jack of clubs is Lancelot, chief knight of King Arthur's Round Table. The jack of diamonds, who carries a weapon commonly identified as a 'Welsh hook', is traditionally assumed to be Hector, the Trojan hero, though later sources identify him as Roland.

First developed in an age of bold knights and crude printing presses, these wood-block images carried a strong, dynamic look, proud to proclaim popular heroes, which is still the distinctive hallmark of our court cards today. Originally imported into England in Tudor times, by soldiers returning from duty in France, the English court cards also took on the styles and fashions of the Wars of the Roses. The kings we play with today are still dressed in the style of Henry VIII, and the queens in that of his mother, Elizabeth of York. The bi-coloured roses held by the queens symbolize the end of the war between the white and the red roses, or the Houses of York and Lancaster. The jacks are dressed as the Squire in Chaucer's *Canterbury Tales*.

Next door to the Cincinnati plant stands the US Playing Card Company's museum, where a permanent display relives the history of playing cards over more than six hundred years. Here are cards dating from all periods of history, recalling their use as propaganda weapons at times of various disputes and controversies. One English set, for instance, shows the leading characters in the Popish Plot of 1678, another the protagonists of the Monmouth Rebellion of 1685. Others show the attempts made over the years by sundry republican and revolutionary movements to eliminate the 'royal' dimension of playing cards; not even those dating from the French and American revolutions, however, found popular acceptance.

The beginning of the modern era is marked by the goat-skin cards made by the late Apache Indians, their crude markings indicating the same structure of suits and values as in a contemporary deck. Finally, in the early nineteenth century, we see the arrival of the first 'double-ended' cards, showing the same image at top and bottom. Then come the first experiments in 'index' cards; miniature cards in the corners, with numbers and suits running round the borders, which provoked great controversy in their day, before finally giving way to the numerical indexing now taken for granted.

The museum also boasts the world's only library of poker, where the visitor can browse through an extraordinary range of nineteenth- and twentieth-century manuals from both sides of the Atlantic. Especially prized is an original of the first book to codify the rules of poker, compiled in 1871 by Robert C. Schenk, then American ambassador to England – supposedly at the request of Queen Victoria, whom he had introduced to the game. By contrast, there is a first edition of a late nineteenth-century volume entitled *What I Know About Poker* by one Richard Carle, which ran to twelve pages, all of them blank. I also liked the epigraph page of an 1887 volume entitled *Poker: How to Play It, by One of Its Victims*, which capped all my efforts to drag the Bard to the green baize with a pained parody of Hamlet's famous dilemma:

To draw or not to draw, that is the question.
Whether 'tis safer in the player to take
The awful risk of skinning for a straight,
Or, standing pat, to raise 'em all the limit,
And thus, by bluffing, get it. To draw – to skin
No more – and by that skin to get a full
Or two pair, the fattest bouncin' kings
That luck is heir to – 'tis a consummation
Devoutly to be wished. To draw, to skin:
To skin! perchance to bust – aye, there's the rub!
For what in that draw of three cards may come,
When we have shuffled off this uncertain pack,
Must give us pause. There's the respect
Which makes a calamity of a bobtailed flush;
For who would bear the overwhelming blind,
The reckless straddle, the wait on the edge,
The insolence of pat hands, and the lifts
That the patient of the bluffer takes,
When he himself might be much better off
By simply passing? Who would trays uphold,
And go out on a small progressive raise,
But that the dread of something after call,
The undiscovered ace-full, to whose strength
Such hands must bow, puzzles the will
And makes us rather keep the chips we have
Than be curious about hands we know not of!
Thus bluffing doth make cowards of us all,
And thus the native hue of a four-heart flush
Is sickled o'er with some dark and cussed club,
And speculators in a jack-pot's wealth,
With this regard, their interests turn awry,
And lose the right to open.

New York was worse than ever. Long gone, for me, are the days when the thrill of the place exuded from its very paving stones; now it is a hell's kitchen of hassle, discomfort and incivility. For years I mustered any pretext I could to come here; now I just want to do my business, see my friends and get out again as fast as possible.

On this occasion, that meant thirty-six hours to clock a couple of lunches and dinners, hook up with the Moll, and boost the bank-roll. Having left $10,000 on deposit at the Horseshoe, and spent a little over $1,000 getting myself here, I had only $9,500 in my pocket for the cruise, which didn't feel anything like enough. I was, after all, a five-figure man these days. So for the first time since turning poker pro I was reduced to moonlighting at my old profession.

The editor-in-chief of the *Condé Nast Traveler* magazine, that same Harold Evans who had been my editor at *The Times* of London, proved cautiously receptive to the idea of an article on the poker cruise. Over a stylish dinner *à deux*, served in my suite at the Grand Bay Hotel, I further whetted his appetite with the prospect of men overboard before we had even left American waters. Sure, but how much was it all going to cost? Well, the stateroom I had already booked came to $3,500 including air fares to and from Miami, which made his offer of $4,500 – $2,500 in expenses, plus a fee of $2,000 for the article – seem eminently reasonable. Just one thing, though: could I possibly have the lot up front? In cash? Tomorrow morning?

No sweat, said he with an indulgent smile, turning a blind eye to my unprofessional *chutzpah* in demanding the fee in advance. Only the vagaries of the American banking system stood between me and my crock of gold as I presented myself at the *Traveler*'s office on Madison Avenue next morning, waving a cash-advance authorization signed by the boss himself. *Ah, les Anglais*, muttered the managing editor, Ms Leslie Smith, whose job it would be to deliver on Harry's promise. What on earth made me think they kept that kind of money around the place in cash? This was a magazine office, not a *bureau de change*.

However dashed his spirits, no hustler worth the name gives up without a prolonged struggle. My flight to Miami left that afternoon, so it was no use her telling me to come back tomorrow. I'd be way past Cuba by then. It took an hour of shameless pleading, dignified only by a treacle-thick veneer of English charm, to have Ms Smith writing out a cheque for the full amount on her personal account, with written instructions to her bank to pay me cash on the nail. Pausing only to dub her the patron saint of all managing editors, I was out the door and down the street to Manufacturers' Hanover Trust, who were not so easily persuaded. It took another hour of referral from desk to desk, plus a couple of phone calls to Ms Smith to establish that she was in her right mind, before I could trouser the forty-five big ones, awake the Moll from her jet-lagged slumbers and drag her off to La Guardia to get back on the road again.

A Wagnerian lightning-storm escorted our flight all the way south, giving the Atlantic skies the look of a giant video game – a dramatically beautiful rite of passage from the Land of Push-and-Shove to the geriatric calm of cruising. But we had scarcely checked into our overnight harbour hotel before we were back in the surreal realms uniquely inhabited by gamblers. A New Jersey stud-player had decided, that night, to marry the girl he was bringing on the cruise. The ceremony was going on right now, up in their hotel room, with the champagne being served by room service, who were also providing the witnesses. The president of Poker Cruises International, Robin Powell, was acting as best man, with the card room manager, Bob Thompson of the Dunes, giving away the bride. The honeymoon was to be spent playing poker.

Twenty-four hours later, as the *SS Norway* pulled out of Miami Sound, it was clear that this was going to be no ordinary cruise. Before the ship had even weighed anchor, the Checkers Cabaret Lounge had been converted into a garish Las Vegas-style card room, staffed by dealers and floormen from West Coast casinos, with whom high rollers were already leaving hefty deposits. The ship's safe deposit boxes had all been snapped up before the purser's staff knew what hit them. Now the Welcome Aboard cocktail party was reluctantly metamorphosing into a compulsory Lifeboat Drill.

As first-class passengers dutifully assembled, looking like beached whales in their bulky yellow life-jackets, beguiling young maidens were moving among them with flysheets. On close inspection they were not the Emergency Evacuation Procedures, but a beginner's guide to the Rules of Poker. These unsuspecting, vacationing innocents were the bait which had lured the high rollers aboard. Already there were slips of paper beneath all the high-rent cabin doors offering FREE POKER LESSONS in the Checkers Cabaret Lounge. 'Don't be shy,' they suggested. 'Come on in and try your hand . . .'

Of the 2,000 passengers aboard the *Norway* – formerly the *France*, and still the biggest cruise liner afloat – well over a hundred were card-carrying poker players from California to New Jersey, Nevada to Florida. After a wasted twenty-four hours travelling to get here, that evening saw them all seated and waiting, ready to ante up, even before their baggage had found its way to their staterooms. Within the statutory half-hour of leaving port, six tables swung into action, offering anything from $1–$2–$5 stud to $50–$100 Hold 'em.

If not quite Nathan Detroit's floating craps game, it was the next best thing. The clack of chips, the cries of 'Raise', 'Fold' and 'Pair the board' vied with the throb of the engines as darkness fell and the *Norway* passed imperceptibly out to sea. Second honeymooners, religious package groups, black-tied swells and steerage students gaped on with awe as high rollers casually contested pots twice the size of a first-class fare. The riverboat gamblers of old would have had a field day.

Pros and amateurs alike were soon so thoroughly at home, so absorbed in the run of the cards, that this solitary Londoner was repeatedly asked, 'Are you from here?' The question persisted even when we were somewhere out in the Bermuda Triangle. For all the notice they took of their surroundings, these card-sharps might as well have been cruising towards Staten Island as St Maarten.

When we broke up for dinner that first evening, already with some reluctance, the Moll and I were surprised to find ourselves seated at the Poker Cruises top table – with Robin Powell and his wife Janis, Eric Drache, some comely card room staff and a couple of friendly millionaires and their wives. Tonight, the drinks were on our host.

A thirty-six-year-old Englishman born in Rhodesia, Powell has served the most peripatetic possible gaming apprenticeship, having worked in casinos from Africa to Australia, London to Monte Carlo, Spain to the Bahamas. Now he was a floorman at the Golden Nugget, Las Vegas, looking after the high flying baccarat tables.

It was his friend Bob Thompson of the Dunes who had first suggested the idea of poker cruises, and Powell and his wife who had embarked on the gamble of their lives by taking him seriously. This was the third they had organized, and looked like being the first to make a profit. Future plans already included cruises out of California, north and south to Alaska and Mexico, *en route* to Powell's ultimate goal: to buy his own ship. Meanwhile, his maritime catchline became: 'Oh good, I think it's going to rain. Excuse me while I organize some more tables.'

The *Norway*'s mass-produced food was barely edible, but the Dom Pérignon flowed in all the abundance of the moonlit ocean around us. By midnight, and my return to the action, I had managed by some osmosis to recreate my usual state of arrival in Vegas: weary, well-wined and raring to go. Back in the Checkers Cabaret Lounge the pros were playing alternate rounds of stud and Hold 'em for stratospheric amounts of money; already the on-board chips were unable to cope, and they were dealing in mental IOUs, to be settled back ashore. It was something of a jump to the next biggest game available – $10–$20 Hold 'em, small beer by my recent standards, but better than nothing. My new millionaire friends, cheerful about their amateur status, seemed to be throwing their money around freely enough, so I eagerly snapped up the last seat available.

Three hours later, having had a terrific run of cards at just the right moment, I was an astonishing $1,700 ahead. The millionaires had gone to bed blotto, and I was left playing head-to-head with one of the world's leading women players, Barbara Enright. It takes no excess of feminist zeal to hold the greatest respect for Barbara's abilities; but my run was continuing, and I kept getting the better of her. As she pulled bill after bill from her handbag, Barbara played on with a gracious and knowing smile, in unspoken, mutual acknowledgement that surely this couldn't last. I was not so much defying the odds as letting them bend in my favour. Ten $100 bills, however, proved enough to convince her that lately I must have been living right. My first-night profit was $2,700 when I headed bedwards at 6 a.m., a comfortable eight hours before the start of my first seaborne poker tournament.

But first, there was a major mathematical moment to savour. Calculations of this order required fresh air, so I took one turn around the darkened, deserted deck as I ran the figures through my tired brain just one more time. I had left $10,000 at the Horseshoe; I had arrived in New York with $9,500 in my pocket, then made a notional thousand profit on the *Condé Nast* deal (if I wrote the article, as it were, for free). Subtract $700 in cash for the New York hotel, and tonight's $2,700 profit took the running total to $22,500. Forget the $2,000 or so I owed British Airways; for the purposes of this moment, thanks to the wonders of plastic, that could stay on hold. The real point was just as I suspected. All expenses paid up to date, and the bank-roll was still showing a profit.

There followed the sweetest sleep I had known all year – so sweet that I missed breakfast, despite having paid for it. So this is how the rich live, I flattered myself next morn, before discovering that I was not the only poker cruiser to have failed that particular feast. Everyone had. As dawn rose over the Checkers Cabaret Lounge, where all-nighters were still tucking into cardboard trays of fried chicken, it soon became apparent that Norwegian Cruise Lines weren't used to all this. With all meals included in the pre-paid fare, it was apparently unprecedented for a ten-seater table to remain completely empty throughout both breakfast sittings. The information sheets which flowed beneath our cabin door, exhorting us to HAVE FUN!!! – a close call between the Amateur Talent Contest, the Olympic Swimming Trials, or the Trivia Quiz on

Dolphin Deck – filled the waste-bin twice over before we had surfaced for the day. Lunch, too, was a threadbare affair at the heart of the Leeward Dining Room, most of us opting for an outdoor brunch at the Lido Bar.

It was said to be the first time in the history of ocean-going room service that sandwiches and fried chicken were delivered to the Checkers Cabaret Lounge at all hours of night and day. *Norway*'s waiters were equally unused to being tipped $50 for a glass of mineral water. Word quickly spread around the crew that the poker room was the place to be. The captain himself looked in from time to time, evidently unable to believe the reports reaching the bridge. It was only after a shout of, 'Hey, skip, shall we deal you in?' that his visits became less frequent.

Regular passengers had earned themselves a hearty lunch next day, with a morning of clay pigeon shooting and deck quoits, before twenty-nine bleary-eyed low rollers paid $350 each to enter Bob Thompson's seven-card stud tournament. After the management's rake of $50 per player, that made a pool of $8,700 in prize money – not enough to interest the heavy mob, over at their $50–$100 table, where they were playing for more than that per hand. Most of them, by the look of it, had been in action since the rest of us went to bed. Weary dealers slumped in the corner bore witness to the stamina of the all-night brigade.

'OK, ante up and deal!' Half the tournament field were wealthy, high-class amateurs, the other half beady-eyed, calculating pros, who knew that they ought to beat out these tyro holiday-makers. But today the Poker God – himself, no doubt, in holiday mood – chose to smile upon some part-timers. It took me four whole hours to exit in thirteenth place, ahead of the Moll for once, but proving yet again that stud just ain't my game. The final table was still playing after midnight, when the first prize of $3,915 finally went to a Florida hypnotherapist and the third to a pro bowl player. Between them in second place, and up all night for the second consecutive night of his honeymoon, was the New Jersey newly-wed.

His bride seemed unsurprised to have become a poker widow within twenty-four hours. Most non-playing wives and girlfriends, come to that, seemed to count themselves lucky to be along for the ride. But even they sure knew how to hustle. Hanging around the table, carefully interrupting at all the wrong moments, and raising the dread possibility that they might be watching when some huge pot went awry, was a sure way to have their man palm a big chip and pass it over, his eyes never leaving the action in front of him, with a murmur of, 'Here, honey, go buy yourself something nice'. It would suit both parties just fine not to meet up again until dinner time.

I was just wondering about lunch when I looked up to see people wandering about in evening dress. Today's remorseless flow of instructions beneath our cabin door decreed formal dress code in the evening, but no-one in the poker room was getting too excited about the Captain's Party. As black-tied swells and their overdressed wives milled past us, queueing thirty minutes to shake the captain's hand, life in the Checkers Cabaret Lounge proceeded as normal, only the winners occasionally quitting on the pretext that they must go dress for dinner. To the losers, stuck there in their T-shirts and jeans, eating was a luxury they could ill afford.

Not possessing a dinner jacket, anyway, I spent the evening on tilt. There weren't enough takers for $20–$40 Hold 'em, the game at which I was currently endowed with such magical powers. Superstitious dread overwhelmed me: could this be the end of my roll? No way was I going to accept the blandishments of the big boys, Eric Drache and Phil Hellmuth among them, and risk losing my entire bank-roll in one of their gargantuan hands. The only group playing at my financial level insisted on alternate rounds of Hold 'em and stud, thus tempting me to spend half the time playing my best game, half the time my worst. It cost me six hundred gracelessly begrudged dollars before I thought I might as well try something else, even a game I had never played in my life before. The poker pro's Holy Grail, after all, is versatility.

At the next table a black-tied throng were starting a $10–$20 version of tomorrow's tournament game – 'Eight or better', or high-low stud, in which the low hand must comprise five different cards no higher than an eight (straights and flushes disallowed). I was reasonably familiar with the odds from similar Tuesday Night eccentricities, but it was strictly beginner's luck which saw me recoup half my lost $600 before finally surrendering to the need for sleep. The last of the big spenders, I had magnanimously promised to bank-roll the Moll as well as myself through the $350 tournaments, so my total deficit for the day was a highly irritating thou.

It was, given the state of my bank-roll, a modest enough loss; but this had been my first losing day of the entire trip, the first since setting out for Lafayette what seemed like a year ago, and it hurt like hell. Night had already turned into day – only the third, but I was beginning to lose count – as I took a lonely, windswept walk on deck, contemplating the awful truth that my roll was finally over.

Or was it? I arose at noon in determined mood, hell-bent on proving otherwise. The eight-or-better stud tournament mustered twenty-six starters, offering a total of $7,800 in prize money. So aggressively did I begin – last night's practice was sure going to come in handy – that I was the first to be busted out, after barely five minutes. Mooning around by the pool, I found myself in the midst of a large born-again contingent, conspicuous all over the ship by their evangelical T-shirts. 'Honey,' said one to her Bible-reading spouse, 'have you seen the amounts of money on the table in that card room? One of those pots is more than we raise for the Church all year!'

The Moll was not long in joining me for an alfresco cocktail. But by the time the first prize of $3,510 went to Glen 'Snow White' Abney, the reigning world gin champion, and portly proprietor of a gin club in Hollywood, California, I was deep into a $20–$40 Hold 'em game for which I had fought long and hard with the authorities.

This had involved me in several hours of in-your-face lobbying of busted tournament players, to raise a quorum of four or five, without which the floorman would not allocate us a dealer. It was slightly shaming – reminiscent of the Salzburg shoes episode – to see with what fervour I chased up to lost souls reeling from their tournament reverses, dispensed with commiserations, and proceeded to press-gang them into a game of Hold 'em for stakes somewhat higher than they would have liked. But it worked, and my luck returned. Back in my true element, I was $1,350 ahead when the tournament ended and we were joined by the two runners-up, both known to me as expert Hold 'em players: 'Chicago' Sam Petrillo (who had recently ruined his nickname by moving to Long Beach, California) and John Sutton – manager, no less, of the Bicycle Club, Los Angeles.

Though he seems to wear a permanent smile, John told me *sotto voce* that evening that he would be even happier to reach the following night intact. Some ten years ago he owned the casino franchise on a cruise liner which had better remain

nameless. One day his assistant, Tom Bowling, now manager
of the poker room at the Las Vegas Hilton, called him ship-
to-shore to say: 'The good news is that we're all safe. The
bad news is we need air tickets home.' During a fire subsequently declared suspicious, the liner had sunk to the bottom
of St Maarten harbour, the very one we were about to enter.
Everything, but everything – safe deposit boxes and all – was
consigned to Davy Jones's locker.

A firm believer that history repeats itself only as farce, I
agreed with John that we might as well get on with the game
while there still was one. Others at the table included Barbara
Enright; another former world women's champion, Linda
Ryke; Ron Stanley (from last week's pot-limit game at the
Dunes); a friendly Vegas face belonging to John Stephanian;
and a hotshot doctor who had just come fourth in the tournament. Doc appeared to be celebrating by throwing around his
money as if there were no tomorrow. I sniffed a curious air
of desperation, indeed, about everybody's play, which I
managed to turn to my advantage to the tune of over $3,000,
before realizing myself that it was precisely because there *was*
no tomorrow – at which point I, too, became infected and
handed back a loose five hundred. The problem was our imminent landfall. To normal cruisers, already soundly asleep after
a day of healthy outdoor exercises and good clean evening
fun, this meant the delights of exploring exotic St Maarten.
To poker players, it meant the unthinkable: temporary closure
of the card room.

You can't *mean* it? Poor old Robin Powell had a tough time
shutting down games, clearing the room and covering the
tables as dawn revealed the Caribbean skyline through the star-
board windows. But this was the catch for those cunning poker
husbands who had surreptitiously turned their annual vacation

into yet another open-ended card game. Every so often the ship would call ashore, as ships tend to, and the card room and casino would be declared closed until half an hour after setting sail again. To the cruise line, this was a way of ensuring that money was spent where they wanted it to be spent. To the players, dragged reluctantly ashore to swim, sunbathe, drink rum punches, bask in Caribbean luxury and sample the maritime air for the first time since coming aboard, it offered the dread prospect of having to *speak* to each other all day.

For some, sleep was a far more interesting, not to say important alternative. Phil Hellmuth regarded the shore calls as a chance to steal a march on his high-stakes opponents by sleeping soundly while they haemorrhaged grey cells and money ashore. To Robin Powell, Hellmuth's single-mindedness was reminiscent of Tom McEvoy and Yosh Nakano, on a previous cruise, when he had chartered a plane to fly the poker group over Venezuela's Angel Falls. As they circled high above one of South America's most dramatic sights, the two pros never once looked up from their backgammon board.

Aliens like me were obliged to report to the Club Internationale for immigration procedures at the unbelievable hour of 7 a.m. Stumbling through the deserted card room *en route*, after lying in fitful sleep for barely an hour, I was among the first to hear news of the fight, subsequently known as The Fight, which had broken out at closing time between two short-fused high rollers. Mr X, a professional slots player trying his hand at high-stakes poker, had offered one gibe too many to Yosh Nakano – who happens, as his name might suggest, to be something of an expert in the martial arts. Though the shorter man by several inches, it was a matter of merely seconds before Yosh had covered his assailant in bruises from head to toe. Twice they had been pulled apart by other players;

twice they had broken free and renewed hostilities. Now there was talk of lawsuits. Robin Powell was commuting between one cabin and the other, suddenly a seaborne Henry Kissinger, desperate to prevent news of the incident reaching the captain.

It was the talk of Day Four, spent ashore in St Maarten. While the poker throng headed for a nudist beach, where they were threatening to play stud all day in masks and snorkels, the Moll and I formed an *haute cuisine* splinter group with Eric Drache and a couple of casino staff. What started as a day on the beach turned into a *grande bouffe* when Eric, who had apparently shown enormous sang-froid in calming last night's combatants, took us all for a gargantuan oceanside lunch which lasted all afternoon. For me, truth to tell, it lasted all night as well, as the next thing I knew it was lunchtime the following day. I had slept through St John, and was now required to stumble ashore in St Thomas.

Over another alfresco meal with the Moll, I gradually began to recall one highlight of my twelve comatose hours. I had dreamt that for some reason I had agreed to give a sermon at Eton College. When the dread moment came, I had of course no clue what to say, and advanced down the aisle with an empty, panicking head. Suddenly I vaulted fully fifty yards, over the heads of the entire congregation, pulled off a neat mid-air twist, and landed on my feet in the pulpit, facing the audience in pious, hands-clasped-on-chest mode. Much to the annoyance of the staff, the pupils gave me a standing ovation. I then proceeded to deliver a remarkably eloquent sermon about poker, with particular reference to its great levelling powers. I told them how a rich man could sit down to play with a beggar, a poor man with a king; all would start the game equal, and the rest was up to the pagan gods of the green baize. My coda was inspirational: that for this of all audiences, the most privileged young men in the supposedly civilized world, there were many sound lessons to be learnt from the indiscriminate fall of the cards.

Where on earth did all that come from? There was no time for reflection, as the following dawn suddenly brought Day Six out of seven. Thirteenth out of thirty-one in the Hold 'em tournament, I was out another $700 in entry fees before getting down to the serious business of the evening. With almost $13,000 to play with, but only thirty-six hours left, it was time to step up a gear and sit down with the biggish boys in a $30–$60 Hold 'em game. I was a thousand to the good against a California pro and former world champ Jack Keller, my sparring partner from Malta onwards, when we were joined by that same vacationing doctor, who had just come fourth in his third consecutive tournament. This was enough to secure him the title of Best All-Round Player for the cruise, commemorated by a handsome cut-glass trophy, which he proudly set on the table in front of him. Doc then ordered a large drink, pulled out a doorstep of $100 bills, chomped on his cigar and said: 'OK, I'm a-comin' to git ya.'

Flushed with his success, the doc was soon on tilt – calling every hand, and losing most of them. When he had to disappear to the men's room, he even let the young lady at his shoulder play his cards for him, though it seemed apparent that she had never played poker in her life. Keller and the Californian shot each other looks of delight, and hunkered down for a long session. The pots grew huge, and I found myself struggling to keep up. At 4 a.m., they asked the doc if he would like to lift the stakes to $50–$100. 'Sure,' he said, 'whatever you boys say.' They couldn't believe it when I said no. It was a tough position for me to take, and I didn't at all enjoy the way they rolled their eyes at each other over my idiocy. But I was playing *them* as well as the nose-diving doctor, and still had my ego under careful control. I bore no illusions about our respective skills. Pots of at least $500–$600 each were quite enough for me.

Besides, it was rather fun to annoy them. Was it down to me, I wondered, that 'Gentleman' Jack Keller was now, for once, in a particularly sour mood, trashing the cruise and all its works? 'I don't like being told where and when to eat my meals,' he grumbled. 'I was no good at that sort of thing in the services, and I'm no good at it now.' A polite enquiry from me, just to needle him some more, established that his wife, Gloria, was hating it too. 'Sure, these islands are nice. But if I want to see them I can get on a plane.' Poker players, by definition, may be free spirits, resistant to the notorious regimentation of shipboard life, but I thought I saw 'Gentleman' Jack leaning a shade tiltwards.

However casuistic this notion, presumably to prop up my self-respect since the $50–$100 incident, it seemed to begin working. For the next ninety minutes, I reckon I was the only one at the table in full command of his *amour propre*. That's the kind of command that pays. Sixteen hundred bucks, to be precise, on top of the thou I was winning before the doc came along, which added up to enough for me to leave them to it. I wanted to get to bed before the Moll was up for breakfast.

Too late. She came into the room just as I was leaving it, so I joined her for coffee with the girls from the graveyard shift as our final poker-pooper hove into sight. Jack Keller may reckon he'd rather fly to these islands, but no airline can take even a former world champion to the Norwegian Cruise Line's private island in the Bahamas, our last port of call before returning to Miami. The day was spent sunbathing and water-pedalling round in circles – looking and feeling utterly absurd, but in truth avoiding the heavy mob's high-stakes basketball game -- before scrambling back aboard for one final night of action.

Before dinner, as he threw a lavish farewell party for staff and players in his Royal Suite, Eric Drache's bar bill for the week finally climbed through the $3,000 mark. Half of it seemed to be winding up on the rug. My first glass of Dom Pérignon went as one pro's wife kicked me in the shins, to demonstrate what she had done to a ship's officer who had 'goosed' her at a staff party she had gatecrashed. The second went as a Californian tried to squeeze by with yet more refills for a group of wives. 'Excuse me,' he said to a fellow pro, 'you're in my way.'

'Fella,' came the reply, 'I'm *always* gonna be in *your* way.'

During dinner, apparently as a gesture towards global peace, the *Norway*'s many different nationalities of dining-room staff assembled on the stairs to serenade us with, 'We are the world, we are its people'. As we sipped champagne and nibbled our caviare, the Moll pointed out that this was the anthem of Bob Geldof's Feed The Hungry movement. After nine months on the pro poker circuit, my sense of the surreal was in danger of blowing a fuse.

After dinner, the poker room was overflowing with punters desperate for what was left of the action. All week Bob Thompson had been wooing innocent passers-by, offering potential ruin to second honeymooners with gentle cries of, 'Free poker lessons! Don't be shy, come on in!' One or two little groups of amateurs had indeed gathered in corners, to the delight of the pros, who would eye the new arrivals, then each other knowingly: 'Hey, come on over, Buddy, we've a seat open here . . .'

But the pigeons had proved sensibly reluctant to fly out of

their natural orbit, and managed to make a nervous twenty dollars last several hours in super-cautious $1–$2 stud and Hold 'em games. Gradually there had emerged an all-female table, occasionally graced by the presence of the Moll, where the rules of the game appeared to have been inverted. Every time a pot was won, there were shrieks of, 'Good hand, honey!' and 'Well played, Wilma!', even, 'I was hoping you were going to win one at last!' There was much laughter at this table, even among the losers. They actually seemed to be enjoying them-selves, leaving the random fall of the cards to dictate who won and who lost. Pros who thought they had seen everything looked at each other in utter bafflement.

Deep in a heavy-duty $30–$60 Hold 'em session, I had to ask the shift boss – ever so politely, herself being female – to get the ladies to hold it down a bit. Things were growing a bit steamy around here. The prospect of their games breaking up before the night was through had everyone, at whatever level, playing as if their lives depended on it. Some of the heavy mob were running up debts which could only be settled back in California. Phil Hellmuth, though heavily down, was playing as bumptiously as ever: 'Come on, baby, let's take it all the way. Let's see you call *this* little sucker!' A number of lesser pros had already retired broke. After a wild few hours, demob caution then began to set in among the winners, myself included, hoarding the sandwich of $100 bills in my pocket with May and the World Series in mind. Across the room the amateurs were still having fun, celebrating the last few hours of the least healthy, most invigorating cruise they would ever take.

Around 3 a.m., our table finally began to break up, with much reluctant mumbling about such unknowns as 'bed' and 'sleep'. Grimly, the real world was returning even to poker players' horizons. With regular jobs to return to, the amateurs were feeling a tad guilty about a week so gloriously misspent. For the pros it was time to get back in shape for business.

With a mere flight to London to sleep through, I had no such problems. Nor, it seemed, did Sam Petrillo, with whom I played on till Robin Powell and his team started closing up the joint around us. The only way they could find to stop us, as the *Norway* re-entered Miami Sound, was to unscrew the legs from our table.

On the flight back to London, despite the extra we had paid to fly Upper Class, the Virgin cabin staff had managed to fill the smoking section with non-smokers, most of them children, whom they none too politely refused to move. Hell hath no fury like a smoker in a long-haul no smoking zone, especially if he is a non-mathematician trying to do some life-or-death calculations. Seventeen hundred bucks profit on that final evening brought the wedge of bills in my pocket to $16,900. The Moll, too, had come good in the girls' game, and proudly paid me back the $1,000 I had spent on her tournament entries. Pride made me make one attempt to refuse it, but one only; when she fell asleep, I quietly entered her contribution in the profit margin. She had made the fatal mistake of offering money to a gambler trying to maximize his assets. Like Ebenezer Scrooge with a pocket calculator, I soon bored her back awake with further fussy facts and figures. I wanted to get it exactly right. Allow for this; subtract that; add interest on the other; factor in the ten grand on deposit at the Horseshoe; run over the figures one more time, and we formally agreed that, even accounting for bed and breakfast, I was entering the home straight $7,900 to the good.

We arrived home tired and edgy, me still trying to fiddle the figures, to discover that the house had been comprehensively burgled. I had won over $8,000 on the cruise, bringing my profit for the three-week trip to a wonderful few hundred over $20,000. This felt pretty good compared with the $5,000 I had budgeted to lose in Louisiana tournament fees, which would have shrivelled the bank-roll to the verge of extinction, but lousy beside the £28,000 worth of our belongings with which the thieves had made off. As we entered a protracted wrangle with the insurance company (who took six months, in the end, to pay up half what we had lost), it was back with a bump to real money values.

With a month to go to Armageddon, I decided to take April easy. In any other sport, I would now enter a phase of intensive training; in my chosen profession, I was not sure quite what this involved. There was an Omaha tournament at the Barracuda, where my stint on the American tour seemed to pay off; for the first time in England I finished in the money, with a fourth-place pay-off of a measly eight hundred quid. Still, that helped the profit column of the bank-roll climb comfortably over the $9,000 mark, which I painlessly managed to double in three 'cameo appearances', as the boys billed them, at the Tuesday Night Game.

With our *real* money, meanwhile, the Moll and I had at last managed to buy a place big enough to house all five of our children. The waiting would finally be over in the first week of May – which also happened to be the week the kids went back to school, and the World Series of Poker entered its main phase. Too much was happening in my real life for my *alter ego* to cope with. How could we defect back to Dreamland the same week as moving house?

The Moll's solution was simple and selfless. I must take

this last trip alone. She would go all domestic for a while, take charge of the house move, and begin setting up a *vita nuova* for me to return to. Perhaps, she argued, I would even fare better without her at my side this time. I had put enough pressure on myself, anyway, with this absurd aspiration to finish higher than ninetieth. If I failed, I would have no-one else to blame.

It was all very moving – doubly so when I realized that her air fare (which I had promised to pay out of my new-found wealth) amounted to a tournament entry fee. But now the real world began to seep back with a vengeance. Hedging my bets as cautiously as ever, I had placed plans for another book on hold all year. To keep this option open, should I somehow fail to win the World Series, I must also keep a long-standing appointment in New York. It was now or never.

I might be ending the year on a high, but I had spent most of it on my knees. It was not so long since I had set out for Louisiana with barely $7,000 to my name. Had that trip gone as well as all its predecessors, I would now be selling things to make ends meet. Earlier than I had hoped, before even taking a crack at those two million dollars, I was forced to face the reluctant truth that perhaps it would not make sense to spend the rest of my life playing poker for a living. To bypass New York would be to forfeit a smooth return to my former occupation, should I need it again. It was a risk, for once, that I knew I could not take.

If I was going to go out, however, I was going to do so in style. There was a way, I reckoned, to combine *some* show of domestic decency on my part with some extravagance – or a final self-indulgent fling at the expense of others. Had I won all this money merely to lose it again to the sharks on top form at their annual convention? What was more valuable for money to buy than time? The way for me to juggle all these balls at once was to stay in London a few extra days, be around to help with the house move, see the kids back to school, and then head west at twice the speed of sound.

12

The End Of The Road

♥ ♣ ♦ ♠

As I went into training for my world title bid – largely a matter of intensive riffling practice – life with the Shrink was getting a bit heavy.

In our last pre-Vegas session, he had finally pinned down the watershed he'd been after. Beyond a Hamlet-like mission to avenge my father, there were no obvious childhood traumas behind my passion for poker – in itself, he stressed, perfectly healthy. But the turning-point which had changed me from an occasional, dilettante player into a committed, determined, at times obsessive one could apparently be traced to the Ides of March 1982.

It's a long, involved story concerning private and public disagreements with Rupert Murdoch, owner of *The Times* of London, of which I was then an assistant editor. Too many forests have already been felled in pursuit of the truth of this matter, the details of which I can spare you. Suffice it to say that March 1982 saw my abrupt resignation from Murdoch's employ – and, in retrospect, the end of my newspaper career. In twenty-four turbulent hours my status had transformed from well-paid rising star to unemployed, flat broke and anxious father-of-three.

As time passed I was pleased to make the transition from journalist to author, and had long thought I owed Murdoch an ironic vote of thanks. The Shrink, his eyebrows calling for greater candour, wasn't so sure. A healthy scepticism, about both journalism and life, seemed subsequently to have soured into cynicism. Poker had become a surrogate for bigger, more important games, with higher stakes.

The clincher, on a more practical level, was to find myself working from home for the first time in my life. After years pumping adrenalin in newspaper offices, where competitiveness is a necessary condition of survival, I had since come to relish a rather solitary existence. On Tuesday nights, my competitive instincts now demanded a whole week's worth of exercise.

Where the Tuesday Game had once represented an enjoyable interlude from the real world, it had now taken on a crazy importance in my weekly routine – perhaps even *become* my real world. Like other indolent, self-employed Tuesday Nighters, I would construct my calendar around that sacred evening, anticipation mounting as it too slowly approached. Now I began to see why the other Tuesday Night boys spent so much of the rest of the week on the phone to each other. Suddenly I, too, was conducting lengthy postmortems as early as Wednesday morning – which gradually metamorphosed, as the week wore on, into breathless check-calls about numbers and venues for the next game. Winning became uniquely exhilarating; losing led to days of self-doubt and despair.

I had been a busy newspaper executive, who relished his work, when the Crony had unnerved me by telling the world that Tuesday Nights offered the only guaranteed excitement left in his life. Now I thought he might have understated his case.

The Shrink took a very dim view. What did this tell me about myself? About the respective importance of poker, my work, my loved ones? Was I really as content with my lot as

I made out? He had no wish, of course, to be judgemental; but it might be an idea to reassess my real values, before they were irretrievably hijacked by the gods of the green baize.

This was all getting a bit close to the bone, so I had called a halt by the time I reported to the Concorde Lounge at Heathrow to embark upon my last great adventure. But somehow I felt purged. The sheer *fun* of the year behind me outweighed any worries that poker was laying siege to my psyche. Quite the reverse. As I stocked up at the free cocktail bar, staring back at my dishevelled self from its interior mirror, I felt that I had at last put poker in its place. Sure, I had relied on it too much to see me through my wilderness years. Now the Shrink had earned his money, by helping me put it all in perspective.

Students of coincidence will love what happened next.

British Airways Supersonic Flight 001 to New York was already being called as I took a long telephonic farewell of the Moll. Suave frequent flyer though now I was, casually sipping my Chablis as others stood muttering in line, I was not the only one ignoring the urgent summons of the public address system. At the next telephone was a casually dressed man chatting nonchalantly to some underling, ignoring the mounting panic of his wife, exuding confidence that the aircraft would, if need be, wait for him to finish his call. When we both at last lost our cool, hung up at the same moment and inadvertently came face to face, I saw that it was, of all the people in all the airports in all the world, Rupert Murdoch.

As if the proverbial drowning man, I was immediately, involuntarily confronted by a mental picture of the last time we had met – when I had shouted at Murdoch in front of the Queen, causing a diplomatic incident still fondly remembered in certain circles. Well, how was I to know that I would bump into him on the very evening of my resignation, at a literary party graced by the royal presence? The details seem to have got lost somewhere in my subconscious, though according to one of Murdoch's biographers, Michael Leapman, I told him that he was 'a deeply misguided man', to which Murdoch 'fumed' that I would never work for him again.

'I do not choose to,' I apparently replied (rather finely, it seems to me). Leapman continues: 'Holden rushed off to tell the story of the encounter to a circle that included Prince Philip, who was enthralled at Holden's tale of derring-do. "Hmm," Philip told the assembled company inscrutably, "I used to know Murdoch's father."'

That much I do remember. When the Prince asked me about the furore, wondering if Murdoch was still in the room, I had said, 'He's over there', which came out next day in Nigel Dempster's *Daily Mail* diary as, 'The ogre's there!'

I had subsequently heard that Murdoch bore me no ill will, and with time my own rage had subsided. But I had had no direct contact with the man since that eventful day seven years before. In a long-term, arms-length poker game, I had taken some satisfaction in accepting large amounts of his money for the serial rights to two of my books, joking that it made up for the golden handshake I had waived on stalking out of his life. Murdoch, meanwhile, had hugely expanded his global empire, buying movie studios, television stations, more newspapers and magazines, even launching satellites, on seemingly bottomless credit. Now here he was, my nemesis, at Heathrow, extending what looked like a cordial hand of greeting, as also was his novelist wife Anna (whom I had last met, as I was swift to remind her, over dinner in the Reagan White House).

'What are *you* doing here?' Murdoch began, as if I had been caught trying to stow away on his private jet.

'I'm going to America,' said I, trying to sound like I'd added, 'if that's all right with you, squire.'

'What for?'

'To represent Britain in the world championships of poker.'

OK, so I exaggerated. But Murdoch's face lit up. 'Poker, huh?'

The three of us lingered, letting the queue for Flight 001 leave us behind. Feeling sure in such company that Concorde would not take off without us, I grew expansive in reply to Mrs Murdoch's characteristically savvy questions about the difference between tournament poker and real poker. 'What,' she asked, 'are the qualities of a good tournament player?'

'Ruthlessness,' I replied, 'and aggression,' then nodded towards her husband. 'In fact *he'd* be very good at it.'

Anna laughed gratifyingly while Murdoch remained distinctly unamused. She leant forward, confidingly, but still in the hearing of her husband. 'You know, the children won't play poker with him any more. Whenever he suggests a game, they say: "Oh, no, Dad, you always want to win so much that it's no fun for the rest of us."'

'Nonsense,' snapped Murdoch.

'Come on, darling,' his wife cajoled, 'you know it's true.' I seemed to have started something.

Three and a half hours later, in the baggage area of JFK, I found myself absurdly bucked when my suitcase came off the carousel before Murdoch's. My last sight of him, as I waved a complacent goodbye, was of this mega-rich international tycoon bobbing and weaving among the *hoi polloi*, fighting for a glimpse of the luggage riding by on the carousel, struggling like the rest of us mere mortals to cope with the hideousness of long-haul travel. It struck me that the pre-immigration areas of international airports, where even the most V of VIPs are bereft of their flunkies, are among the few places left on earth where all men are truly equal.

This tiny triumph seemed to put a fit symbolic end to my seven years of *angst*, to be a neat visual aid to my psychological triumph over the poker demons. Next day I shared the story and its resonances with a galactical gathering at the Manhattan dinner table of – who else? – Harold Evans, the very editor whose dismissal had sparked my original row with Murdoch, and who had recently bank-rolled me for the poker cruise. Harry and his wife Tina Brown, the hugely successful editor of *Vanity Fair*, were toasting a friend's new novel as only Manhattan socialities know how. Among those nodding sagely as I again took my triumphant leave of Murdoch were Irving 'Swifty' Lazar, super-agent to the stars, and Ahmet Ertegun, head of Atlantic Records, who had hitherto been beguiling me with gambling adventures from his impoverished youth.

'Ah yes,' sighed Ertegun, with feeling, when I reached my dénouement, 'the baggage carousel is a great leveller.'

Like his compatriot and business rival Kerry Packer, Murdoch is as keen a gambler off-duty as he is in his business dealings. Like Donald Trump, by contrast, Ertegun now says he wouldn't gamble to save his life. Successful businessmen, who have made their millions the hard way, tend to add to them the easy way; they only gamble on sure things. 'I've never gambled in my life,' says Trump in his revealingly titled autobiography, *The Art of the Deal*. 'To me, a gambler is someone who plays slot machines. I prefer to own slot machines. It's a very good business being the house.'

That last *aperçu* comes convincingly from a man who owns a large chunk of Atlantic City. But Trump can't fool me. A few pages later, for instance, in his insufferably complacent way, he's talking exactly like Doyle Brunson: 'Money was never a big motivation for me, except as a way to keep score. The real excitement is playing the game.' Trump even knows how not to be ruffled by the winning hands that got away: 'I don't spend a lot of time worrying about what I should have done differently, or what's going to happen next.' Another of his Collected Thoughts could also come from a seasoned poker pro: 'I don't do it for the money. I've got enough, much more than I'll ever need. I do it to do it . . . Deals are my art form.'

Trump's wit and wisdom barely saw me through take-off, so I spent the rest of the flight to Vegas re-reading Sklansky. Could anyone really play *that* tight? My bookmark, as if to confirm it, was a Memo to Self written six months before, on my gloomy departure from the Horseshoe at Christmas:

If you want to come higher than ninetieth in the 1989 World Series, play only A-A/A-K/K-K/A-QJT suited, and pairs if you can get in cheap in late position. Nothing else, not even A-x suited, or K-Q, unless suited and again you can get in cheap. On Fourth Street, exercise great caution. Above all DON'T lose your seat, even if it means throwing away leading hands. Remember Slim's advice: 'Anybody who can't quit the best hand can't play.'

What a state I'd been in! As the plane banked over Las Vegas, I was appalled to feel it seeping back. My usual thrill at the outrageous view beneath was dulled by a new and unwonted sensation: nervous anticipation. In no way had I expected the sense of foreboding which now overwhelmed me. Suddenly I knew what it must feel like to be an Olympic athlete, or a golf or tennis pro, arriving at the venue appointed for the year's main event, burbling about a rendezvous with destiny. The cosily familiar landscape now seemed impersonal, even hostile; the sense of security at arriving 'home' was unhinged by concern about what lay ahead. Vegas had always spelt danger; now it exuded menace.

The Horseshoe limo, of course, awaited. This time it was not as a freeloading journalist, but as a legitimate, ranking player in the world championships that Hank greeted me, wished me luck and escorted me downtown, as if to a ritual beheading. My familiar Horseshoe suite now felt like a boxer's dressing room, or the bunker from which a general conducts a doomed campaign. It was becoming clear that I had an attitude problem, and only five days to solve it.

Even a $500 satellite profit, in my usual first-night frenzy, didn't do much for morale. The Horseshoe was teeming with figures from my recent past, only heightening the dread sense of occasion. Binion's looked like a Bayeux Tapestry of my year. There was Eric Drache and Phil Hellmuth, from Malta onwards; 'Bulldog' Sykes and the gang from the Hall of Fame; Amarillo Slim and Perry Green from February at Caesar's; Dave Bellucci, Tahoe Andrew and Donnacha O'Dea from Morocco; T. J. Cloutier and Seymour Liebowitz from the lobby of the Lafayette Hilton; Johnny Moss to remind me of my glorious Easter; Sam Petrillo, Barbara Enright and sundry Californians from the cruise. They were a reincarnation of Chaucer's pilgrims, who had finally made it to another Canterbury.

Here, too, was the *Daily Telegraph*, in the shape of David Spanier, reminding me that this was where I came in. Over dinner he joked that he was now the *Telegraph*'s 'Holden correspondent'. A World Series preview assessing my chances had appeared that morning, and he would be sending home daily reports chronicling my progress. Deep down I suspected that one short despatch would suffice.

Next day, after losing back that $500 in distracted mood at the $20–$40 table, I was in bad enough shape to take myself off to a movie for the first time ever in Las Vegas. When the lights came up after *Mississippi Burning*, I saw with a shock that I was the only white in the audience, and resigned myself to the summary lynching to which the film seemed to entitle them. Though I had walked only three blocks from the Horseshoe, I later learnt that I had managed to stroll straight into the heart of Glitter Gulch's 'combat zone'. Having never walked more than a block downtown in eleven years of coming here, I had not even known it was there.

A huge effort to pull myself together won me back that pesky $500 from the $20–$40 boys. This magic figure was fast becoming some symbolic margin of error. But I was still suffering a severe crisis of confidence about the world championship. Somehow I couldn't shake off a sense of lost innocence – a feeling that I had been better off as an amateur, happily wallowing way out of his depth. Had I learnt *too much* to play well in the Big One? How on earth had I managed to come as high as ninetieth last year? My twentieth place at Christmas, relaxed enough to be playing in two tournaments at once, seemed a very distant memory. At the time I hadn't thought too much of it, blandly assuming it was part of a steady progress towards the world crown. Now it seemed likely to prove the height of my year's achievement, a moment I should have savoured more at the time.

Could I rely on the eve-of-championship media tournament to raise my spirits? I began to think so as soon as I signed in (as the representative – what the heck – of Murdoch's *The Times*). 'Hey, this man's a *pro*!' protested Bill 'Bulldog' Sykes when I drew the seat next to him. At our table was a rooky old lady who kept fluking pots and shrieking I-told-you-so slogans. 'I don't think my heart can stand much more of this,' muttered Bulldog. The old lady obliged by busting him out.

Two draining hours later I had made it to the final table, but soon suffered my own demise at the hands of this wily *tricoteuse*. Ninth out of ninety: modestly in the money, a hard-earned $150, with the bonus of a sleek, satinesque World Series jacket. Not a bad start. What's more, I had achieved revenge on Spanier for last year's humiliation. Things were looking up.

That night, after sipping even cheaper champagne than last year, I achieved another ambition so cherished for so long that I had dared whisper it to no-one. After a tense ninety-minute struggle, yes, I repeated the miracle which had started this whole thing off. I won the one and only $1,000 satellite I was permitting myself to enter.

The effect on morale was spectacular, on the bank-roll even more so. For the second year running I had won my entry into the $10,000 world title event for just one thou. Nine of the ten grand still safely on deposit at the cage had suddenly made a dramatic leap across the ledger into the profit margin.

Eighteen thousand bucks to the good before I arrived, I realized how much it would have pained me to pay half my profit for the privilege of ritual slaughter in the world title event. Add the six hundred and fifty real dollars I had struggled to win on this final trip so far, and the plus-side of my year now stood at $17,650. Barring some spectacular disaster, or a mugging, or a hijack, or a conspiracy among transatlantic burglars, I could now sit down for the Big One next morning sure of ending the year in profit. All that remained, to achieve both my goals, was to last out the first day, and finish higher than ninetieth.

It remained an artificial goal, but an obsessive one. I knew in my heart that to have any chance of winning this thing I would have to take the kind of early risks which might eliminate me. Some pros argue otherwise; that it's basically a matter of *avoiding* risks. Wait till you have an edge, play it aggressively, and build your stack steadily. No-one ever won the World Series by just hanging in there, says one school of thought; no, says another, that's the *only* way to win it. All they agree on is that nobody ever won the world crown without a bit of luck along the way.

'It ain't the cash that counts, it's the title.' Pro after pro trotted out this time-honoured sentiment for the cameras next morning, apparently unmoved by the prospect of record prize money totalling $1.78 million. When my turn came, I broke the mould by confessing that the money would come in pretty handy. It was an honour to be playing in the event at all. My immediate goal was modest enough – to improve on my performance last year.

There – I'd said it again, despite having spent a restless night trying to psyche myself out of this irrelevance. Which school of thought did I belong to? The risk-takers or the wait-and-hopers? I was in serious danger of disappearing down some hyped-up psycho-gulf between the two.

If proof were needed that I was now a true pro, it came with my blank indifference to the opening ceremonies which last year the amateur in me had so savoured. This event is the only one in the poker calendar which has the pros visibly on edge, anxious about their reputations, wondering if this could at last be their year. At Table Eight, Seat One, sat the most apprehensive of the lot – a lone, pallid Briton whose life had been building towards this moment for as long as he could remember. At this moment all his long and careful months of psychological preparation flew straight out the air-conditioning vents. He was a hopeless bundle of nerves, unsure of his tactics, confused about odds and outs, wondering what had possessed him to put himself through this ordeal.

Attitude problem? The guy was a wreck. He was on tilt before Jack Binion's ritual cry of, 'Ante up and deal!' For the first half-hour, this idiot *dreaded seeing good cards in the hole*. Risk? He wasn't up to treading on a wet step.

The very first hand brought drama at the next table, where a full house aces was beaten by a royal flush. So some poor guy was first out within a minute – but, boy, had he gone out in style. At our table, nine cautious players were circling each other like wary gunfighters, reluctant to be the first to draw.

2 p.m.: Half an hour gone, and I have won one pot. It's my big blind and I creep in with 10-8 to see the flop come 10-10-K. OK, so who's got the pair of kings? No-one round to me, it seems. My $500 bet gets one caller, and the turn brings a five. I bet an exploratory $1,000, wondering if the case ten could have a better kicker, and again he just calls. The river brings a seven. Cautiously, I check, and so does he, before revealing 10-A. $1,500 lost. To go anywhere in this tournament, these are the kinds of pot you need to get away with. Low morale and high nerves have me on the verge of throwing up.

2.10 p.m.: I fold 9-4 – not a difficult decision – to see the flop bring 9-9-9. If it's going to be one of those days, why, oh why, did it have to choose *this* one?

2.20 p.m.: My suited K-8 seems worth calling a bet of $200, doubly so when the flop is K-Q-8. Three players check; I bet

$500 and get one caller. The turn brings another K, filling my house. It wins me only $700, but that's half my deficit wiped off.

Is my luck turning? All I know is that I'm a curiosity. Las Vegas' own Elephant Man. Someone has told the photographers that I'm an English amateur masquerading as a pro, and their flashbulbs are scorching my retina. The other players are visibly wondering what all the fuss is about. I'm certainly not playing like a star.

3.30 p.m.: I've made it to the first break, with $8,650 left. I have played only about six hands. Is that sensible caution or hopeless lack of guts?

Search me, as we head into the second phase. With the increase in antes, it now costs $1,100 an hour just to fold and watch, which is what a miserable run of cards has me doing. Ninety minutes pass without my seeing a playable hand, trying to persuade myself to stay patient; but my pent-up energy makes it very hard just to sit tight and hang in there. A few modest 'steals' keep my stack from dwindling below $7,500. One more takes me back up over $8,000 as my bladder begins to remind me of the statutory task I forgot during the break. With rolling antes at $25 a hand, it now costs me $50 just to go for a pee.

How come I had gone into this thing so pessimistically, and allowed myself to feel outgunned all day? Even after a year of playing in the major league, I had to admit to a schoolboy thrill at being a competitor – and a fancied one, according to the brochure – in the world championships of *anything*. My exterior, I think, looked appropriately cool and collected; inside, I'd been a quivering blancmange of self-doubt right from the starter's pistol. All year I had prided myself on my temperament, nerve, self-discipline, even 'heart', all of which had steadied with experience. But did I, in the end, possess the indefatigable, indefinable *insight* which distinguishes poker's great champions? Had my sheer enjoyment of playing blinded me to the finer points of mind- and card-reading, odds and outs? Or was it just that I didn't have 'the right stuff'?

If I had learnt one truth all year, it was that poker's ultimate players – a dozen or so of whom were all now seated around me – are distinguished by one remarkable quality: a serene indifference to the worldly attributes of money. To most of us, money is the method of keeping score not merely in poker, but in life; which is not to say that we necessarily measure others by their financial success, or even our own happiness by the state of our bank balance. It is simply that money is the commodity of which we need sufficient amounts to keep our own show, however humble, on the road. To these guys, money is their daily bread only in the sense that it is part of their professional equipment. They subsist, most of them, very economically. They inhabit in a world where, if they go broke, hustling up enough to live on is not an immediate problem. Hustling up enough to play with – to play serious poker, that is – involves immeasurably larger amounts.

Even these high-wire financiers divide, broadly speaking, into two very different camps. Of the world champions who have netted that vast prize at least once in their lives, several have immediately secured the lives of their wives and families – poker marriages being notoriously insecure – and parlayed the rest of their money into a secure enough bank-roll. Once you've managed that, it is not difficult to be indifferent to the stuff.

But there are others who have equally quickly blown the lot. Stu 'the Kid' Ungar, for instance, will tell you almost casually of the huge amounts he has won at poker, through skill and diligence, only to throw it all away on some impulsive bet, much less calculated but even more thrilling. This kind of fatal flaw is known to other players as a 'leak'. Johnny Chan's huge poker winnings, for instance, have recently financed a *vita nuova* at the Pai Gau Poker tables, where the results are less certain but the action much faster. Jack Straus, all his life, was up and down like some giant Yo-Yo, winning at poker with unique ingenuity, then blowing it all on some fantastical sports bet. Hundreds of thousands won the hard way would be lost the easy way, and Jack's reaction would be a cheerful enough shrug of his huge shoulders.

Bob Stupak, owner of a casino called Vegas World, and himself a leading poker player, bet $1 million on the 1989 Superbowl. (He won.) For a man with a vast annual income from the management end of gambling, it was less of a risk than his campaign the same year to become the new Mayor of Las Vegas. (He lost.) The Superbowl bet raised even the highest-rolling eyebrows. But money, in Vegas, comes and goes in such unreal amounts that, for insiders, it begins to lose its more universal meaning. When Ungar needed a passport, to travel to a foreign tournament, he couldn't face filling out the form needed to accompany his $18 fee; when all the usual deadlines had elapsed, and a friend strong-armed him over to the Post Office (a few hundred yards from the Horseshoe) to make an emergency application, he reached in his pocket and pushed three $100 bills across the counter. The clerk looked up in astonishment, said, 'But sir, it's only $18', and handed him $282 in change. The friend had to pick it up; Ungar was already on his way out the door, back to his game.

For the punters, of course, the sheer smell of money in the air is the visceral appeal of Vegas; it keeps them coming back for more, seventeen million of them in 1989, year after year. Every week, somewhere around town, someone will put one dollar in a slot and win several million. Their lives will be radically altered *in perpetuo*.

To the very top layer of poker players, there wouldn't be much of a charge in this. To make the most accurate, clear-headed decisions, involving more money than many people earn in their lifetimes, you really have to consider the stuff utterly irrelevant to the verities of your life. At this level the money you have to your name is an index more of reputation and self-esteem than of worth or lifestyle; Jack Straus's main emotion on losing was, he used to say, sheer embarrassment. For guys like this it is no big deal to be, quite literally, million-aires one day and broke the next. They rise and fall, live and die by their slogan: 'Chicken today, feathers tomorrow.'

At heart, I knew, I preferred chicken. Which meant that the Shrink would be proud of me. It meant that my dependants and my bank manager could relax. But it also meant that I wasn't going to win the world championship. Not today. Not ever.

5.45 p.m.: Still alive at the second break, with $7,900, but playing very little and far from well. Still the flash-bulbs are popping, and the other players wondering if I could be minor royalty, when a Binion's bellboy pushes his way through the security guards to bring me a cable. Can someone be dying? Apart from me?

YOU'VE GOT TO KNOW WHEN TO STICK STU,
KNOW WHEN TO RAISE REECE,
KNOW WHEN TO PLAY COOL,
KNOW YOU'RE AN ACE.
YOU CAN COUNT ALL YOUR MONEY
ONCE YOU'VE SANDBAGGED JOHNNY,
THEN WE'LL HIT THE BEACH, HONEY,
AND QUIT THIS RAT RACE.

Maybe the Moll could yet become our first American Poet Laureate.

6.40 p.m.: Bobby Baldwin arrives at our table, which somehow seems appropriate, as he it was who won the world crown in 1978, the first year I came to Vegas. Now he is the President of the Golden Nugget Corporation, Steve Wynn's right-hand man, and one of the very few professionals to have used a successful poker career as the springboard for an even more successful business career. Most people do it the other way round.

Baldwin's stack is even lower than mine. In his business suit he looks as if he's just popped across the street for a brief courtesy appearance. He's very relaxed, talking to friends around the room, looking at his watch as if it were really time he got back to his desk. At 6.50 p.m., ten minutes after he got here, he solves both his problems and mine by letting me bust him out. My pair of jacks stands up against his pair of tens; I've eliminated a former world champ, and cheered my ailing ego. Baldwin's three thou shoot me back up to even, a modest ambition to realize. A little spurt now, and this whole thing could turn around.

For the next hour I am watchful as a hawk. Baldwin's thoughtful capitulation has filled me with premonitions of some sort of turning-point. I have just called for my umpteenth glass of water, and treated myself to a new toothpick, when I peek in the hole to see my first ace in a long time. Time to savour the moment, and squee-ee-ze the other card out slowly.

Another ace. This is it.

One other player, a mousey little guy with pince-nez specs, calls me all the way to $5,000 before the flop. It's everything he's got. He's gone all-in, and I know that as yet I must be winning. The dealer burns the top card, then rolls 10-9-8, all different suits. Could Pince-Nez have J-Q? Or 9-10? Of course he could, but it doesn't make any difference now, as he's all-in. I put him on a high pair, probably kings. What else would he go all-in with? So would I now have bet if he'd had any money? It is an academic point, not worth the waste of precious grey cells at this late hour. All I can do, as the dealer burns again, is pray for an ace. The turn brings a three, the river a seven. Surely chummy can't have a six? He looks at me enquiringly over those irritating eyeglasses, sinking my heart with a look which spelt a hand. Never can aces have been rolled with less pride. With a pitying glance, Pince-Nez shows me two tens to go with the one on the board.

Some turning-point. Ten minutes later, at 8.05 p.m., I reach the third break with a mere $4,000 or so left in front of me. Sixty-four of the 178 starters have been eliminated. I'm going to be lucky to improve on last year.

At 8.25 p.m., on my small blind, I am dealt the K-J of clubs. David Bellucci, the real estate dealer from California via Morocco, still in the same shorts and T-shirt he was wearing beside the Mamounia pool, bets $1,000. I call, to see the flop bring the king of hearts, the jack of spades and the four of hearts.

I have the two best pairs. This is Armageddon. Do or die.

Bellucci bets a grand, and I raise him everything I have –
all $2,800 of it. He thinks for about three weeks, sees how
small a dent I can make on the city of chips in front of him,
gives me the ghost of a smile, and calls. The turn brings a
seemingly irrelevant seven of clubs. Then the river comes up
with the one thing I don't want to see: a heart. The three of
hearts. I've read Bellucci as a flush draw, but maybe he could
have been pulling to a Q-10? I show him my two pairs and
he flips over, yes, the A-8 of hearts. Even now I no longer
need them, the odds automatically light up on some score-
board in my head to remind me that, just like last year, I've
been busted out by a four-to-one shot.

My career as a poker pro ended in that moment. I reeled away
badly winded, as if I'd been punched hard in the stomach –
a real physical pain, gradually giving way to a deep spiritual
bruise, throbbing away with a relentlessness that only hardened professionals feel. In that brief shining moment of defeat
I finally knew for sure, strangely to my surprise, that somewhere along the line I really *had* become a pro.

After I'd stumbled up to my room, however, stood gazing
out the window for half an hour, and decided this was news
even the Moll could wait for, it was very much as an amateur,
a born-again tourist, that I sloped back downstairs.

If I had finally hung up The Watch, there was at least the
consolation that I had finished the year financially ahead.
Subtract the plastic procrastinations – the Easter air fare,
Concorde and other incidentals – and my precise net profit as
a professional poker player came to $12,300, after covering
all my costs from the Shrink to the absurd exertion of crossing the Atlantic sixteen times in eight months. I had won a

further 26,000 notional dollars in satellite victories, and played in $40,000 worth of tournaments. But my world ranking had slipped twenty-one places, to 111 – known as a 'half-Nelson' to English cricketers, who traditionally believe the number to be jinxed.

I couldn't expect Americans to sympathize with that. And it was even less help for well-wishers to remind me that the number of entrants had been higher than last year, that yet more complex mental arithmetic might thus improve my result in what self-deluding politicians, economists, pollsters, even poker players – all of them, at my personal Pearly Gates, no more than cheats – have the slippery habit of calling 'real terms'. To me, the figures were absolutes. Even I could not bring myself to adjust them according to seasonal variations, allowing for fluctuations in market forces and world trends. Last year, as an amateur, I had come ninetieth. Now, after twelve months as a professional, my world ranking was 111. That degree of demotion – *any* demotion – had *not* been the object of the exercise. If pressed, I now realized, I would rather have finished the year showing a financial loss, if the price had been a better finish in the World Series.

I had played really badly, and I knew it. For that reason, I guess, the hurt inside me persisted, growing worse before it got better, refusing to let me forget as I ill-humouredly watched the final three days of the tournament. Flying home early crossed my mind, but seemed singularly graceless; I stumbled through the rest of the week with as brave a face as I could muster, breakfasting with David Spanier, lunching with Henri Bollinger, dining with Eric Drache, even taking in George Burns at Caesar's Palace, and picking up regular $500s at the $20–$40 table without much pleasure or even satisfaction.

It was there, while winning with undisguised boredom, that

I heard the news from across the floor that Johnny Chan looked like making it three in a row. The final table had been decimated much faster than usual. Strong challengers like George Hardie, the owner of the Bicycle Club, and a maverick Irish millionaire called Noel Furlong, carrying Europe's only remaining hopes, had been blown away in the build-up to the confrontation which one of its protagonists had been predicting for twelve months. The only player between the Oriental Express and an unprecedented hat-trick was the brash young college drop-out who'd been guaranteeing his own victory all year, from Malta to the Caribbean to the card rooms of California. Phil Hellmuth Jr.

It was all over before I could bring myself to head back to the arena. Chan, with the A-7 of spades in the hole, had made a hefty bet of a half-million or so. Hellmuth, holding a pair of nines, had swiftly re-raised enough to set him in. When Chan called, all $1.76 million were riding on the flop, which brought Kc-10d-Kd. Only an ace could save Chan now. The turn was the queen of spades, the river the six of spades. Phil Hellmuth was the new world champion, and at twenty-four the youngest in the tournament's history. It did not much help my mood to note that he was born the year I left school.

Arty Cobb, he of the fancy hats and the lucky eight of hearts, was commentating at the time. Over the public address system he intoned: 'Poker may be only a game, but it is not a matter of life and death. It's a lot more serious than that.'

Tell that one, I thought, to the Shrink. Now I telephoned the Moll, who for once couldn't lift my spirits. Then I called the Crony, who could and did, by the simple expedient of reminding me that I'd be home in time for Tuesday Night.

APPENDIX 1

The Ranking Of Hands

Poker hands are ranked according to their rarity (see odds tables, Chapter 4, pages 100–101). The best hand obtainable is a royal flush, A-K-Q-J-10 of the same suit, which should occur only once in 649,740 deals (or once in a lifetime, if you're lucky). Beneath it come:

> *Straight flush*
> *Four of a kind*
> *Full house*
> *Flush*
> *Straight*
> *Three of a kind*
> *Two pairs*
> *Pair*

These hands are defined in the glossary (Appendix 4, pages 374–384). If the showdown produces two hands of the same rank, the higher card or cards decide the issue. In the case of a full house, for instance, the 'trips' are decisive, viz. 'kings on twos' (K-K-K-2-2) beats 'queens on aces' (Q-Q-Q-A-A). Similarly, an A-6-5-4-3 flush beats a K-Q-J-10-8 flush, an ace-high straight beats a king-high straight, and so on. In the case of two pairs, the higher pair is the decider: viz., aces and twos beat kings and queens. In such hands, the side-card or 'kicker' is irrelevant. If, however, the hand is between two pairs of the same rank, the 'kicker' is the decisive card: viz., K-K-Q-Q-3 beats K-K-Q-Q-2. The same applies to singleton pairs, viz. A-A-7-6-5 beats A-A-6-5-4. Between hands without so much as a pair, the high card decides: viz., A-9-7-6-5 beats K-Q-J-10-8 – or even, if you wind up with a four-straight, 7-6-4-3-2 beats 7-5-4-3-2. If you're playing hands like these, however, you should probably quit now.

APPENDIX 2

Select Bibliography

The Gambler's Book Club, five minutes from downtown Las Vegas, is the British Library of received gambling wisdom. Its resident curator, Howard Schwarz, stocks several thousand volumes covering every imaginable aspect of gaming, old and new. His mail order catalogue (available from The Gambler's Book Club, 630 South 11th Street, Las Vegas, Nevada 89127) lists almost 100 current books about poker, mostly manuals of ever-increasing technical sophistication. What follows, therefore, is a far from comprehensive guide to the available literature. It is a personal choice of the books I consulted while writing this, and is based as much on entertainment value as on technical expertise. Those I found indispensable are cited in the text.

I have listed poker manuals separately, for readers intent on improving their game; but my choice still remains highly selective. David Sklansky and Mike Caro, currently poker's most prolific theorists, have published countless specialist volumes beyond those listed here. The 'General' list is for those interested in further exploring the history, psychology or folklore of poker or gambling.

Few books in either category can, alas, be recommended on stylistic or literary grounds. There are honourable exceptions, such as Alvarez and Mamet. But the absence of eloquent writers from the rarefied world of big-time poker is

otherwise as regrettable as NASA's failure to send a poet to
the moon.

GENERAL

Alvarez, A. *Poker: Bets, Bluffs and Bad Beats*, Chronicle, San
    Francisco, 2001

Alvarez, A. *The Biggest Game in Town*, Houghton Mifflin,
    Boston, 1983

Barnhart, Russell T. *Gamblers of Yesteryear*, GBC Press, Las
    Vegas, 1983

Bergler, Edmund *The Psychology of Gambling*, Hill and Wang,
    New York, 1957

Berne, Eric *Games People Play: The Psychology of Human
    Relationships*, André Deutsch, London, 1966

Blyth, Henry *Hell & Hazard: William Crockford versus the
    Gentlemen of England*, Weidenfeld & Nicolson, London,
    1969; Henry Regnery, Chicago, 1970

Bradshaw, Jon *Fast Company*, Vintage, New York, 1987

Clark, Thomas L. *The Dictionary of Gambling and Gaming*,
    Lexic, New York, 1987

Cotton, Charles *The Compleat Gamester*, first published 1674;
    facsimile edn by Cornmarket, London, 1972

DeArment, Robert K. *Knights of the Green Cloth: The Saga of
    the Frontier Gamblers*, University of Oklahoma Press, 1982

Dostoevsky, Fyodor *The Gambler*, first published 1867; trans-
    lated by Jessie Coulson, Penguin Books, London, 1966

Dunne, John Gregory *Vegas, A Memoir of a Dark Season*,
    Random House, New York, 1974

Erdman, Paul *Palace*, Doubleday, New York, 1988

Findlay, John M. *People of Chance: Gambling in American*

Society from Jamestown to Las Vegas, Oxford University Press, Oxford, 1986

Freud, Sigmund 'Dostoevsky and Parricide' (1928), *Complete Psychological Works of Sigmund Freud*, (standard edn), Vol. XXI, Hogarth Press, London, 1961

Hayano, David M. *Poker Faces: The Life and Work of Professional Card Players*, University of California Press, 1982

Jenkins, Don *Champion of Champions Johnny Moss: A portrait of the greatest poker player of our time*, JM, Odessa, Texas, 1981

Jessup, Richard *The Cincinnati Kid*, Primus, Donald I. Fine Inc., New York, 1985

Lewis, Jerry D. (ed.) *Dealer's Choice*: The World's Greatest Poker Stories, A. S. Barnes, New York, 1955

Livingston, A.D. *Dealing with Cheats: Illustrated Methods of Card-sharps, Dice Hustlers and other Gambling Swindlers*, Lippincott, New York, 1973

McCullough, Clint *Nevada*, St Martin's Press, New York, 1986

Mamet, David: 'Things I Have Learned Playing Poker on the Hill' from *Writing in Restaurants*, Viking, New York, 1986

Messick, Hank & Goldblatt, Burt *The Only Game in Town: An Illustrated History of Gambling*, Crowell, New York, 1976

Rosecrance, John *Gambling without Guilt: The Legitimization of an American Pastime*, Brooks/Cole, Pacific Grove, California, 1988

Ross, Gary *Stung: The Incredible Obsession of Brian Molony*, Stoddart, Toronto, 1987

Runyon, Damon *Damon Runyon on Broadway*, Picador, London, 1975

Runyon, Damon *From First to Last*, Picador, London, 1975

Smith, Merriman 'How Truman Played Poker' (UPI copyright, reprinted in Lewis (ed.), *Dealer's Choice*, op.cit.)

Soares, John *Loaded Dice: The True Story of a Casino Cheat*, W. H. Allen, London, 1987

Spanier, David *Easy Money: Inside the Gambler's Mind*, Seckcr & Warburg, London, 1987

Spanier, David *The Hand I Played*, Crimetime, Harpenden, Herts, 2001

Spanier, David *Total Poker*, Secker & Warburg, London, 1977; rev. edn André Deutsch, London, 1990

Stowers, Carlton *The Unsinkable Titanic Thompson*, Eakin Press, Burnet, Texas, 1982

Time-Life Books *The Gamblers*, Time-Life Books, Alexandria, Virginia, 1978

Winston, Stuart & Harris, Harriet *Nation of Gamblers: America's Billion-Dollar-A-Day Habit*, Prentice-Hall, NJ, 1984

Wise, Leonard *The Big Biazarro*, Doubleday, New York, 1977; Drum Books, New York, 1986

Wykes, Alan *The Complete Illustrated Guide to Gambling*, Doubleday, New York, 1964

MANUALS

Baldwin, Bobby *Bobby Baldwin's Winning Poker Secrets*, B&G Publishing Co., Las Vegas, Nevada, 1979

Brunson, Doyle *Super/System* (previously titled *How I Won Over $1,000,000 Playing Poker*), B&G Publishing Co., Las Vegas, Nevada, 1978, 2nd edn 1979

Brunson, Doyle *According to Doyle*, Gambling Times/Lyle Stuart, NJ, 1984

Caro, Mike *Mike Caro's Book of Tells: The Body Language of Poker*, Gambling Times/Lyle Stuart, NJ, 1984

Caro, Mike *Poker for Women: A course in destroying male*

opponents at poker . . . and beyond, Gambling Times/Lyle Stuart, NJ, 1986

Davis, Dick *The Hold 'em Poker Bible*, Commonwealth Press Inc., Radford, Virginia, 1983; 2nd edn 1987

Fox, John *Play Poker, Quit Work and Sleep Till Noon! The Complete Psychology, Mathematics and Tactics of Winning Poker*, Bacchus, Seal Beach, California, 1981

Jacoby, Oswald *Oswald Jacoby on Poker*, rev. edn, Double-day, New York, 1981

Johnson, Chip & Tayek, Ray W. *Properties of Hold 'em Hands*, Johnson & Tayek, Alhambra, California, 1986

McEvoy, Tom & West, Roy *How to Win at Poker Tournaments*, Gambling Times/Lyle Stuart, NJ, 1985

Moorehead, Albert H. *The Complete Guide to Winning at Poker*, Simon & Schuster, New York, 1967

Preston, Amarillo 'Slim', with Cox, Bill *Play Poker to Win*, Souvenir Press, London, 1973

Scarne, John *Scarne's Guide to Modern Poker*, Fireside/Simon & Schuster, New York, 1980

Sklansky, David & Malmuth, Mason *Hold 'em Poker for Advanced Players*, Sklansky and Malmuth, Las Vegas, Nevada, 1988

Sklansky, David *Winning Poker* (formerly titled *Poker Theory*), Sklansky, Las Vegas, Nevada, 1987

Wallace, Frank R. *Poker: A Guaranteed Income for Life*, Warner Books, New York, 1968; rev. edn 1980

Yardley, Herbert O. *The Education of a Poker Player*, Jonathan Cape, London, 1979

APPENDIX 3

Acknowledgements

Many of the following have won enough money off me over the years to lend considerable irony to any public expression of thanks. But it would be churlish not to single out those who generously gave of their time, expertise, hospitality or all three during my brief, heady career as a poker pro, and my subsequent attempt to offer some account of it.

I have reason to be grateful for the generous friendship of Peter Alson; the late Benny Binion; Jack Binion, president, Binion's Horseshoe; Henri Bollinger; Tina Brown, formerly editor-in-chief, *Vanity Fair*, the *New Yorker* and *Talk* magazines; Doyle Brunson; Dale Conway; Eric Drache; Bill Eadington, Director of the Institute for the Study of Gambling, University of Nevada, Reno; Harold Evans, formerly editor-in-chief, *Condé Nast Traveler*, and president and publisher, Random House Inc.; June Field, editor, *Card Player* magazine; Dr Anthony Fry; Ron Hall; Donna Harris; Mike 'London' Haywood; Roy Houghton, formerly card-room manager of the Barracuda Club, London, now of the Gala Regency Club; Van Jones, assistant curator, the US Playing Card Company museum; Jack McClelland; Len Miller, formerly editor, *Gambling Times*; John David Morley; the late Johnny Moss; Robin and Janis Powell, Poker Cruises International; Amarillo 'Slim' Preston; Larry Sanders; Howard Schwarz, the Gambler's Book Club, Las Vegas; Leslie Smith, formerly managing editor, *Condé Nast Traveler*; John

Stephanian; the late Jack Straus; John Sutton, manager, the Bicycle Club, Los Angeles; the late Bill 'Bulldog' Sykes; Bob Thompson, card-room manager, the Dunes, Las Vegas, and now tournament director of the World Series.

I can now also offer heartfelt thanks to the many fine poker players – even more heartfelt in the case of the less fine poker players – who sat alongside me all that time without realizing what I was up to.

I am further indebted, for obvious reasons, to my bank manager, Mike Porter; my accountant, James Watts; to the Tuesday Night boys (Rennie Airth, Roy Giles, Paul Haycock, Hugh Howard, Dan Meinertzhagen, John Moorehead, Rudolf Nassauer, Archie Stirling), and any others who lent me money, or gave me time to pay; and the many other professional poker players who, for their own reasons, have asked not to be named here.

My heartfelt thanks go to Ursula Mackenzie, *Big Deal*'s original publisher at Bantam Press, for keeping the faith by republishing it in this edition at Time Warner, where I am also grateful to her colleagues Alan Samson, Catherine Hill, Rosalie Macfarlane and Rebecca Gray. The book's original editors were Jim Cochrane of Bantam (UK) and Al Silverman of Viking Penguin (US). Thanks also to Ralph Steadman for coming up with a truly gonzo jacket illustration; and, as always, to my agent Gill Coleridge.

Al Alvarez and the late David Spanier were kind enough to read the book in manuscript and offer many helpful suggestions, both technical and stylistic. Themselves authors of distinguished works in the genre, they were also generous with their own material – Alvarez sharing anecdotes about Johnny Moss, Eric Drache and Jack Straus, Spanier his cunning poker readings of Watergate.

The brief history of poker in Chapter 10 owes a debt I am pleased to acknowledge to *People of Chance*, Professor John M. Findlay's absorbing academic history of gambling in the United States. Amarillo Slim's *Play Poker to Win* offered chapter and verse on sundry anecdotes he told me on location from Morocco to the Las Vegas Strip, recounted in Chapters 8 and 9. The brief and inadequate homage to Titanic Thompson in Chapter 9 draws gratefully on Carlton Stowers's biography, *The Unsinkable Titanic Thompson*, and my late friend Jon Bradshaw's marvellous anatomy of the gambling fraternity, *Fast Company*.

Finally, my thanks to the Moll for giving me the idea in the first place.

APPENDIX 4

Glossary Of Poker Terms

ACE-HIGH: a five-card hand containing an ace but no pair; beats a king-high, but loses to any pair or above

ACES UP: two pairs, one of which is aces

ADVERTISE: to make a bluff with the deliberate intention of being exposed as a 'loose' player

ALL-IN: to bet all the chips you have left

ANTE: compulsory stake before the deal

ANTE UP: dealer's request for antes to be paid

BACK TO BACK: two paired hole cards, as in 'aces back to back' or 'aces wired'

BAD BEAT: to lose a pot against the odds, a strong hand being beaten by a lucky one

BELLY HIT: to fill an *inside straight*

BET INTO: to bet before an apparently stronger hand, or a player who bet strongly on the previous round

BET THE POT: to bet the total value of the pot

BETTING INTERVAL: period during which each active player has the right to check, bet or raise; ends when the last bet or raise has been called by all players still in the hand

BICYCLE: the lowest possible hand in lowball, A-2-3-4-5.

BIG BLIND: the largest ante; in Hold 'em, usually compulsory to the player two to the dealer's left

BLACK-LEG: nineteenth-century term (now archaic) for crooked card-sharp

BLIND (1): the compulsory bet or bets to the dealer's left

BLIND (2): to check or bet before receiving, or without looking at, hole cards

BLOW BACK: to lose back most or all of one's profits

BOARD: the five communal cards revealed in the centre of a Hold 'em or Omaha game; or the 'up' cards in a game of stud

BOBTAIL: see *open-ended straight*

BOSS: the strongest hand at that stage, as in 'boss trips'

BRING IT IN: to make the first bet

BUCK: the rotating button used by a professional dealer to indicate which player is notionally dealing the hand, and should therefore receive the last card. (Hence the expression, 'The buck stops here'.)

BULLET: an ace

BUMP: to raise

BURN: to deal off the top card, face down, before dealing out the cards (to prevent cheating); or to set aside a card which has been inadvertently revealed

BUST: a worthless hand, which has failed to improve as the player hoped

BUST A PLAYER: to deprive a player of all his chips; in tournament play, to eliminate him

BUST OUT, BE BUSTED OUT: to be eliminated from a tournament by losing all your chips

BUSTED: broke, or *tapped*

BUSTED FLUSH: four-to-a-flush which failed to fill up

BUTTON: see *buck*

BUY-IN: the minimum amount of money required to sit down in a particular game

BY ME: a popular alternative to 'check' or 'fold'

CAGE: the casino's or card room's 'bank' where you exchange chips for cash or vice-versa

CALL: to match, rather than raise, the previous bet

CALLING STATION: a player who invariably calls, and is therefore hard to bluff out

CARDS SPEAK: a form of high-low poker in which there is no declaration before the showdown

CASE CARD: the last card of a denomination or suit, when the rest have been seen, as in 'the case ace'

CASH IN: to leave a game and convert one's chips to cash, either with the dealer or at the *cage*

CASH OUT: to leave a game and cash in your chips at the *cage*

CATCH: to 'pull' the card or hand you want

CHASE: to stay in against an apparently stronger hand, usually in the hope of filling a straight or flush

CHECK (1): to offer no bet, reserving the right to call or raise if another player bets; or

CHECK (2): another name for a chip

CHECK-RAISE: see *sandbag*

CINCH HAND: a hand that cannot be beaten; see also *nuts*

COFFEE HOUSING: to attempt to mislead opponents about your hand by means of devious speech or behaviour

COLD: a bad streak, as in, 'My cards have gone cold'

COLD DECK: a deck of cards 'fixed' in advance by a cheat

COME: to play an as yet worthless hand in the hope of improving it, as in playing 'on the come'

CONNECTORS: consecutive cards, such as 9-10 or J-Q which might make a straight in Hold 'em or Omaha

COWBOY: slang for king

CUT IT UP: to divide, or split, the pot after a tie

DEAD CARD: a card no longer legally playable

DEAD HAND: a hand no longer legally playable, due to some irregularity

DEALER'S CHOICE: a game in which each dealer, in turn, chooses the type of poker to be played

DECLARATION: declaring by the use of coins or chips, in high-low poker, whether one is aiming to win the high or the low end of the pot, or both

DEUCE: a two, the lowest-ranking card in high poker

DOWN CARDS: hole cards

DRAWN OUT: to win a hand on the last card or cards, after staying with an inferior hand, 'on the come'

DRAWING DEAD: drawing to a hand that cannot win

DRIVER'S SEAT (in the): said of a player who is making all the betting and thus appears to hold the strongest hand

DROP: to fold

FAMILY POT: a pot in which most of the players are still 'in' at the showdown

FIFTH STREET: in Hold 'em, the fifth communal card to be exposed, also known as 'the river'

FILL, FILL UP: to 'pull' the card you are seeking

FLOORMAN: the card room employee supervising a group of tables; he is the ultimate arbiter of disputes

FLOP: in Hold 'em, the first three communal cards to be exposed in the centre of the table

FLUSH: five cards of the same suit; ranks above a straight and below a full house

FOLD: to withdraw from, or give up, the hand

FOUR-FLUSH: four cards of the same suit, requiring a fifth to become a flush

FOUR OF A KIND: four cards of the same denomination. Beats a full house; can be beaten only by a straight flush

FOURTH STREET: in Hold 'em, the fourth communal card to be exposed, also known as 'the turn'

FREE RIDE: to stay in a hand without being forced to bet

FREEZE-OUT: a game, usually a tournament, in which all players start with the same amount, and which continues until one player has won all the chips

FULL HOUSE: a hand containing trips and a pair. Between two full houses, the higher trips win. Beats straights and flushes; loses to four of a kind

G-NOTE: a thousand-dollar bill

GRAVEYARD: the pre-dawn shift in a Las Vegas casino

GUTSHOT: the card needed to fill an *inside straight*

HEAD TO HEAD: see *heads-up*

HEADS-UP, HEAD TO HEAD: a game between just two players, often the climax of a tournament

HIGH ROLLER: one who gambles for large amounts of money

HIGH-LOW: a species of poker in which the highest and the lowest hands share the pot

HIT: to fill, or obtain the card you are seeking

HOLE, in the: concealed card, see also *pocket*

HOLE CARD: card concealed in the player's hand

HOT: said of a player on a winning streak

HOUSE: *full house*

IGNORANT END: the low end of a straight

IMPROVE: to pull a card or cards that better one's hand

IN: a player is 'in' if he has called all bets

IN THE DARK: to check or bet *blind*, without looking at your cards

INSIDE STRAIGHT: four cards requiring (an unlikely) one in the middle to fill a straight, viz. 5-6-7-9; see also *open-ended straight*

KIBITZER: a non-playing spectator, or *railbird*

KICK IT: to raise

KICKER: the subsidiary or 'side' card to a more powerful card or cards

KNAVE: a jack

KNOCK: see *rap*

LAY DOWN: to reveal one's hand in a showdown

LIMIT POKER: a game with fixed betting intervals, viz. $10–$20, $20–$40

LIMP IN: to call late (in late position) and cheap

LITTLE BLIND: see *small blind*

LIVE ONE: an inexperienced, bad or loose player; a sucker who apparently has plenty of money to lose

LOCK: a hand that cannot lose; see also *cinch* and *nuts*

LOOK: to call the final bet (before the showdown)

LOOSE: liberal play, usually in defiance of the odds

LOWBALL: a form of poker in which the lowest hand wins

MAKE (the deck): to shuffle

MARK: a sucker

MARKER: an IOU

MECHANIC: a cheat who manipulates the deck

MEET: to *call*

MOVE IN: to go *all-in*

MUCK: the discard pile, in which all cards are dead

NUT FLUSH: the best available flush

NUTS: the best, unbeatable hand at any stage of a game

OFF-SUIT: cards of different suits

ON TILT: playing badly, usually because of being *stuck*

OPEN: to make the first bet

OPEN-ENDED STRAIGHT: four consecutive cards requiring one at either end to make a straight, viz. 5-6-7-8; also known as a two-way straight, or a 'bobtail'

OUTS: the (usually optimistic) possibilities which would turn a losing hand into a winner

OVERCARDS: in Hold 'em, cards higher than the flop cards, played in hope of catching a higher pair

PAINT: any 'picture' or court card

PAIR: two cards of the same denomination

PASS: to fold; occasionally (wrongly) used for *check*

PAT HAND: a hand that is played as dealt, without changing a card in draw games; usually a straight, flush or full house

PICTURE CARD: king, queen or jack, also known as court cards or face cards

PIP: the suit symbols on a non-court card, indicating its rank

PLAY BACK (at): to re-raise

POCKET (in the): synonym for *hole*

POSITION: your seat in relation to the dealer, and thus your place in the betting order, an important tactical consideration

POT: the chips at stake in the centre of the table

POT LIMIT: a game in which the maximum bet is the total of the pot after calling

POT ODDS: calculating the percentage of the pot you are required to invest, as against your percentage chances of winning the hand, thus assessing the worth of the investment

PROPOSITION PLAYER: a *shill*, or house player, who plays with his own money (rather than the house's)

PUT DOWN: to fold

RAGS: low, bad or unplayable cards

RAILBIRD: a non-playing spectator or *kibitzer*, often used of a broke ex-player

RAISE: to call and increase the previous bet

RAKE: chips taken from the pot by the dealer on behalf of the house

RAP: to 'knock' the table, to indicate a *check*

READ: to try to figure out the cards your opponent is holding

REBUY: to start again, for an additional entry fee, in tournament play (where permitted)

REPRESENT: to bet in a way that suggests you are holding a particular (usually strong) hand

RE-RAISE: to raise a raise

RIFFLE: to shuffle, or to fidget with your chips

RIVER: in Hold 'em, the fifth and final communal card to be exposed

ROCK: an ultra-tight, conservative player

ROLL (a card): to turn a card face up

ROYAL FLUSH: A-K-Q-J-10 of the same suit. The best possible poker hand in all but wild card games

RUN (1): synonym for a straight

RUN (2): a run of good cards, see also *rush* and *streak*

RUNNING BAD: on a losing streak

RUNNING GOOD: on a winning streak

RUSH: a run of good cards, see also *run* and *streak*. A player 'on a rush' may well 'play his rush', i.e. play an indifferent hand because he's feeling lucky, and might win against the odds

SANDBAG: to check a strong hand with the intention of raising or re-raising

SATELLITE: a small-stakes tournament whose winner obtains cheap entry into a bigger tournament

SCHOOL: collective noun for the players in a regular game

SEE: to call

SET: three of a kind, or 'trips' (correctly used of a pair in the hand and one on the board)

SET YOU IN: to bet as much as your opponent has left in front of him

SHILL: a card-room employee, often an off-duty dealer, who plays with house money to make up a game

SHOWDOWN: showing hole cards, after betting has ceased, to see which of the remaining players has won the pot

SIDE CARD: an unmatched card which may decide a pot between two hands otherwise of the same strength

SIDE POT: a separate pot contested by other players when one player is *all-in*

SKIN (1): (archaic) to change (or draw) a card at draw poker

SKIN (2): to cheat, or fix the cards

SLOWPLAY: to disguise the real value of a high hand by underbetting it, to tempt players with worse hands into the pot

SMALL BLIND: the smaller of the two big antes; in Hold 'em, compulsory to the player on the dealer's left

SOFTPLAY: to play gently against a friend

SPLIT: a tie, or *stand-off*. Occasionally this can be agreed between two players before the hand is ended

SQUEEZE: to look slowly at the extremities of your hole cards, without removing them from the table, to worry your opponents and heighten the drama

STACK: the pile of chips in front of a player, as in 'short stack'

STAND PAT: to decline an opportunity to draw cards

STAND-OFF: a tie, in which the players divide the pot equally

STAY: to remain in a hand with a call rather than a raise

STEAL: a bluff in late position, attempting to 'steal' the pot from a table of apparently weak hands

STEAMING: playing badly and wildly, to go *on tilt*

STRADDLE: to make a 'blind' raise before the deal; or another name for the *big blind*

STRAIGHT: five consecutive cards, not of the same suit; beats trips, but loses to a flush and above

STRAIGHT FLUSH: five consecutive cards of the same suit.

Beats everything but a higher straight flush, viz. a *royal flush*

STREAK: a run of good (or bad) cards, see also *run* and *rush*

STRING BET: an illegal bet in which a player puts some chips in the pot, then reaches back to his stack for more. He should declare a raise verbally before calling

STUCK: slang for losing

STUD: any form of poker in which the first card or cards are dealt down, or *in the hole*, followed by several open or 'up' cards

SUITED: cards of the same suit, as in 'A-K suited'

SWEETEN (the pot): to raise

TABLE: can be used as a collective noun for all the players in a game, as well as for the green baize itself

TABLE STAKES: a poker game in which a player cannot bet more than the money he has on the table

TAP CITY: to go broke

TAP OUT: to bet all one's chips

TAPPED OUT: broke, busted

TELL: a giveaway mannerism or nervous habit which reveals the strength or otherwise of an opponent's hand

THREE-FLUSH: three cards of the same suit

THREE OF A KIND: three cards of the same denomination, with two 'side' cards; beats two pairs, but loses to a straight or above. See also *set, triplets* and *trips*

TIGHT: a conservative player who plays only strong hands

TILT: see *on tilt*

TOKE: a tip to the dealer (illegal in Britain)

TREY: a three

TRIPLETS: three of a kind, or *trips*. Beats two pairs, but loses to a straight and above

TRIPS: slang for *triplets*

TURN: the fourth communal card to be revealed at Hold 'em or Omaha, also known as *Fourth Street*

TWO PAIRS: a hand containing two pairs plus a *kicker*; beats a pair, but loses to *triplets* or above

UNDER-RAISE: to raise less than the previous bet, allowed only if a player is going all-in

UNDER THE GUN: the first to bet

UP CARD: an 'open', or exposed, card

WHEEL: the lowest hand in lowball, A-2-3-4-5, also known as a *bicycle*

WHIPSAW: to raise before, and after, a caller who gets caught in the middle

WILD CARD: a card designated as a joker, of any value

WIRED: said of two paired hole cards, as in 'aces wired' or 'aces back to back'